CROWN, ORB
& SCEPTRE

CROWN, ORB & SCEPTRE

THE TRUE STORIES OF ENGLISH CORONATIONS

DAVID HILLIAM

SUTTON PUBLISHING

This book was first published in 2001 by
Sutton Publishing Limited · Phoenix Mill
Thrupp · Stroud · Gloucestershire · GL5 2BU

This paperback edition first published in 2002 by
Sutton Publishing Limited

British Library Cataloguing in Publication Data
A catalogue record for this book is available from the British
Library.

ISBN 0 7509 3072 1

Typesetting and origination by
Sutton Publishing Limited.
Printed and bound in Great Britain by
J.H. Haynes & Co. Ltd, Sparkford.

Contents

Preface

This book covers a thousand years of English coronations. It describes the ceremonial occasions when kings and queens have been anointed, crowned, enthroned – and thereby are entitled to loyalty and obedience.

Traditionally, the accession of a new monarch is announced with stark and brutal simplicity – 'The King is dead! Long live the King!' – the essential feature about this being that everyone knows without a shred of doubt who the next monarch will be.

No need for lengthy election campaigns; no frantic jostlings for position; no power vacuums; no fuss. Seamlessly, power passes to the next in line. Accessions simply happen. Coronations follow, often after months of elaborate preparation.

Of course, there have been moments of high drama, when usurpers have seized power, or when an unexpected crisis has occurred; but whatever the circumstances, every new monarch needs to be crowned.

And every crowning is unique. With the arrival of a new monarch, there is an inevitable sense of newness, curiosity and hope. There is always an indefinable shift of mood throughout the nation as a new reign begins.

Coronations of Saxon kings took place in various holy places, but since 1066, the 'year of three kings', all English kings and queens have been crowned at Westminster Abbey. Only two kings were never crowned: Edward V who disappeared, probably murdered in the Tower of London; and Edward VIII who abdicated.

Here is an attempt to recapture something of the spirit of all those coronations – from the time when Archbishop Dunstan crowned Edgar in Bath Abbey in the year 973, to that memorable occasion nearly ten centuries years later, when millions of people witnessed the televised coronation of Elizabeth II on 2 June 1953.

Coronations Before the Conquest

THE HERMIT-WIZARD FROM GLASTONBURY AND A RUNAWAY HORSE

We owe the English coronation service to one of the most colourful characters of the early Middle Ages – the great tenth-century archbishop and adviser to Saxon kings, Saint Dunstan. He was born in AD 909, just ten years after the death of King Alfred. It is likely that Dunstan himself was a minor member of the Saxon royal family, growing up in the court of Alfred's grandson, King Athelstan, at Glastonbury. This was at a time well before London was considered to be the capital of the country, and more than a century before Westminster Abbey was even begun.

As a teenager, young Dunstan was given a good education by the monks at Glastonbury, and he seems to have had an enquiring mind and many artistic talents; in fact he gained the reputation of being something of an eccentric among his contemporaries. He loved painting, embroidery, music, and he enjoyed reading whatever books he could find on poetry, legends and all sorts of out-of-the-way subjects. Added to this, he had strange dreams and visions that he enjoyed describing in great detail.

Eventually, his rather oddball lifestyle seems to have irritated his more normal hunting-and-fighting companions so much that they conspired to get rid of him, and they complained to Athelstan that Dunstan was a wizard! His enemies became so insistent that eventually Athelstan gave way to them and banished young Dunstan from his court on the charge of practising witchcraft and unlawful arts. The story goes that as he left he was pursued by the mob, who rolled him in mud, kicked him and beat him up.

For a while, Dunstan became a hermit, quietly practising his music, reading, and specialising in metal-working. He built himself a tiny cell, only 5 ft long and 2½ ft wide, where he would pray and enjoy his heavenly visions. A famous incident is said to have happened one day, as he was working at his forge he was visited by the devil, who tried to tempt him by making lewd conversations about sexual pleasures with women. Dunstan was so horrified that he heated his pincers until they were red hot and then suddenly grabbed the devil's nose with them so that the 'evil one' ran off screaming with pain. In Christian art, Dunstan is often depicted holding those pincers, and he is still regarded as the patron saint of goldsmiths, jewellers and locksmiths.

When Athelstan died, Dunstan was brought back to court by the new king, Edmund, but soon the old rumours about witchcraft began to circulate again, so that Dunstan was banned for a second time. He was so upset by this that he decided to go abroad and live in Germany. He was just preparing to leave the country, when an incident occurred at Cheddar Gorge, in Somerset, that was to change his luck dramatically – and, more importantly, the repercussions of this incident would change the course of English history.

One day, King Edmund was hunting at the top of the cliffs at Cheddar Gorge. As anyone knows who has been there, Cheddar is famous not only for its cheese but also for its deep, dangerous, rocky chasm, with steep vertical precipices on each side of a craggy valley. Today it is a popular tourist attraction, with its stalagmite caves and picturesque rockfaces. Edmund was chasing a deer when his horse began to gallop headlong and uncontrollably towards the brink of this chasm, and horse and rider seemed certain to plunge into the gorge beneath. Desperately, the king began to pray, vowing that he would redress the wrongs done to Dunstan if only his life were to be spared, and that he would for ever after hold Dunstan in great honour. Miraculously, the horse managed to save itself and Edmund survived; and thanks to this dramatic episode Dunstan was immediately appointed to be Abbot of Glastonbury – the first rung on a ladder of success which later enabled him to become, in succession, Bishop of Worcester, Bishop of London and Archbishop of Canterbury.

Edmund reigned for only seven years before being stabbed to death by an outlawed thief. His brother, King Edred, who succeeded him, reigned for only nine years, fighting off the Danish armies of Eric Bloodaxe before his own premature death at about thirty-two. Edred was followed on the throne by a silly and incompetent fifteen-year-old, King Edwy, who was to last only about four years before he too was murdered.

It was at Edwy's crowning ceremony, which took place at Kingston upon Thames in AD 955, that Dunstan – still Abbot of Glastonbury – was involved in one of the most notoriously embarrassing incidents ever to take place at an English coronation. Young Edwy, nephew of his predecessor King Edred, obviously felt that as king he could do just as he liked, and at his coronation feast he abruptly left the royal banquet to have sex in a nearby room with a lady friend and her daughter. When the nobles and Archbishop Odo of Canterbury realised just what was happening, they were suitably scandalised, and deputed Dunstan and the Bishop of Lichfield to go and fetch the newly-crowned king back to table. A medieval chronicler describes with ill-concealed glee how, when Dunstan and the bishop entered, they found Edwy 'repeatedly wallowing between the two of them in evil fashion, as if in a vile sty.' Apparently, the royal crown, 'bound with wondrous metal, gold and silver and gems', had been carelessly thrown down on to the floor. Dunstan is said to have thrust this crown back on the lustful teenager's head and to have literally dragged him back to the coronation banquet, giving him a sound telling off as he did so. Naturally enough, King Edwy was not exactly pleased by this, and Dunstan found it necessary to retire abroad to Flanders for the rest of Edwy's reign. However, this exile in Ghent was to prove immensely important for the future history of Christianity in England, for it was here that Dunstan encountered at first hand the Benedictine monastic way of life. It seized his imagination, and he was determined to introduce it to monasteries in England if ever he were to return.

Edwy's sheer incompetence led to his downfall and probable murder in AD 959, and his more successful brother Edgar was elected to take over the kingdom. It was a turning point in English history; King Edgar brought stability and prosperity to the country – he was known as Edgar the Peaceful.

One of Edgar's first acts was to bring back Dunstan and make him Archbishop of Canterbury. At fifty Dunstan was a relatively old man, but now at last he was able to wield genuine power and his real career was just about to begin. He became Edgar's chief adviser in both religious and secular matters, and both men were deeply committed to strengthening the church. Together they founded over forty religious houses, encouraging learning and culture and supporting the monastic system throughout the land. Dunstan's experience in Flanders led him to introduce Benedictine discipline wherever possible. Edgar had a gift for appointing outstanding advisers, and in this great period of expansion he was also helped by Oswald, whom he made Archbishop of York, and Aethelwold, whom he appointed to be Bishop of Winchester.

These devout churchmen had a profound effect upon the time in which they lived; indeed, their work led to what has been called the 'tenth century reformation' – mostly thanks to the influence of Dunstan, the ex-hermit of Glastonbury. For us, however, the crucial importance of Dunstan in the history of English coronations is paramount. Dunstan crowned Edgar the Peaceful fourteen years after the king came to the throne.

DUNSTAN CROWNS AND ANOINTS KING EDGAR IN 973

Reigned 957–75, crowned May 973

A Thousand-Year-Old Tradition is Begun

Edgar stands out as one of the great Saxon kings: wise, innovative, devout, serenely sure of himself, and so much a king among kings that the famous occasion at which he was rowed in state on the River Dee by seven Welsh and Scottish kings has been depicted again and again by artists over the centuries. Therefore, it comes as something of a surprise to realise that he was aged only about fifteen when the Northumbrians and Mercians made him their king in 957 even while his elder brother, the wretched Edwy, was still on the throne. Two years later, in 959, Edwy's death ensured that Edgar became King of all England, still aged only seventeen.

Edgar's immediate recall of Dunstan from exile, making him Bishop of Worcester in 957, Bishop of London in 959 and then Archbishop of Canterbury in 960, showed that he knew exactly who he intended to rely on for advice. For the rest of his reign the two men must have been frenetically energetic in planning and founding dozens of abbeys and religious foundations throughout the kingdom. There were, of course, the other usual kingly jobs to attend to – fighting the Welsh; strengthening the navy; ridding the country of wolves; reorganising the circulation of currency by doubling the number of mints to sixty; marrying twice and begetting the necessary heirs. However, it is probably true to say that from the age of fifteen to thirty his main preoccupation was the peaceful settlement of the country with an ever-increasing number of monasteries.

However, during the first fourteen years of his reign, he still remained uncrowned. It was not until May 973 that King Edgar, by now aged thirty and with an exceptionally successful reign behind him, allowed himself to be crowned in a supremely magnificent ceremony at Bath. Naturally enough, the order of service of 973 was specially drawn up by Archbishop Dunstan – a very special service, worthy of such a pious and noble monarch. But at the time neither of them could know that this order of service would become the basis and foundation for all subsequent English coronation services for centuries to come – even to include the coronation of Elizabeth II, nearly a thousand years later, in 1953.

Why, then, did Edgar delay so long? What was it that was to make this coronation service so special? And what, in essence, did Dunstan devise, that could last so long?

Dunstan knew that on the continent, in the Frankish monarchy, a ceremony had emerged, sanctioned by the pope, which involved the sacred practice of anointing a new king. Up until then, kings in England had never as yet received this special distinction.[†] Crowned they may have been, but for Dunstan, as he

---

[†] Details of crowning ceremonies before the coronation of King Edgar are scanty. In England there was one example of the practice of anointing a new king from 785, when King Offa of Mercia had had his son Egfrith anointed and declared his successor. Egfrith survived his father by only four months and is almost totally forgotten nowadays. Nevertheless, he should be remembered here as he was probably the first king on English soil – albeit a very minor, local Saxon king – to be anointed. However, Edgar seems to have been the first king of all England to be anointed. The circumstances of Edgar's high-profile coronation gave solemn, added significance to this practice of anointing.

planned the coronation of his close friend, King Edgar, this was not enough. The addition of holy oil poured over a royal head and body would make the sovereign much more than a secular ruler. Anointed, a new king would become a priest as well. The implications of this were intriguing. Clearly, the prestige of kingship was being enhanced and at the same time a strong link between church and secular state was being forged, which arguably also enhanced the position of the church. Whatever else the ceremony signified, it made the king divine, unique, and such an anointing brought to mind biblical traditions which could be traced back to when King Solomon was annointed by Zadok the priest and the prophet Nathan.

The reason for the long delay before King Edgar's coronation can now be seen, for it was not until 973 that Edgar reached the age of thirty – the minimum age for the priesthood. It is now generally agreed that this 'coming of age' lay behind the coronation in which Archbishop Dunstan, assisted by Archbishop Oswald of York, solemnly anointed Edgar king in a service significantly containing the biblical text, 'Zadok the priest and Nathan the prophet anointed Solomon King,' – a text which has been recited and sung at coronations ever since. Handel's great anthem seven and a half centuries later served to remind later generations that the anointing is the crucially meaningful moment at a coronation.

Edgar entered the abbey wearing his crown, which he then laid aside as he knelt before the altar. Repeating words spoken by Dunstan, he took his three-fold oath: that the Church of God and all Christian people should enjoy true peace for ever; that he would forbid all wrong and all robbery to all degrees; and that he would command justice and mercy in all judgements. It must have been an impressive ceremony. *The Anglo-Saxon Chronicle* bursts into poetic rapture as it describes how

> In this year, Edgar, ruler of the English,
> Was consecrated king by a great assembly,
> In the ancient city of
> Acemannesceaster,
> Also called Bath by the inhabitants
> Of this island. On that blessed day,

Called and named Whit Sunday by the children of men,
There was great rejoicing by all. As I have heard,
There was a great congregation of priests, and a goodly
company of monks,
And wise men gathered together.

. . . Almost one thousand years had elapsed
Since the time of the Lord of Victories when this
happened.
Edmund's son, the valiant in warlike deeds,
Had spent twenty-nine years in the world when this took
place.
He was in his thirtieth year when consecrated king.

Bath is a city filled with memories and physical remains of Imperial Rome, lying about twenty-five miles from Cheddar Gorge and Glastonbury. The area was well known to both Dunstan and Edgar, and perhaps the choice of Bath came from a desire to remind everyone that this was a place where emperors had dwelt.

Sadly, nothing remains nowadays of the original abbey where that coronation took place. The present abbey was not begun until the eleventh century. However, there is a commemorative stained-glass window there, showing not only Edgar's coronation, but also the famous incident when he was rowed, shortly afterwards, on the River Dee by seven Scottish and Welsh kings. If that legendary event really did take place, there would have been no doubt in their minds that Edgar's sacred anointing invested him with unique authority, direct from God.

Unfortunately, Edgar lived for only another two years after his coronation, and died aged thirty-two. It had been an exceptionally important reign, and his early death was to plunge England into yet another period of chaos, made even worse by constant invasions by the Danes. However, Dunstan lived on, and having officiated at the funeral of King Edgar, burying him at Glastonbury, he survived into the reigns of Edgar's two sons, Edward and Ethelred, born of each of Edgar's two wives.

Edward (known as 'the Martyr') succeeded Edgar in 975, but he was only about twelve at the time, and was murdered at Corfe

Castle in 978, almost three years later, aged fifteen. It is unclear whether this unfortunate young king was ever crowned, although a coronation may have taken place at Kingston upon Thames. It is known, however, that Dunstan, now nearly seventy, having officiated at Edward the Martyr's funeral in Shaftesbury Abbey, went on to crown Edward's half-brother, Ethelred (known as 'the Unready') at Kingston upon Thames. Unfortunately, no details about this coronation survive.

However, Ethelred obviously had no time for Dunstan, who was now forced out of any active involvement in politics and retired to live quietly in Canterbury: teaching, reading, correcting manuscripts and visiting the tombs of Saxon saints in the middle of the night. It was a happy retirement, and when he died in 988 he was immediately revered as a saint. For centuries afterwards Canterbury schoolboys would pray to St Dunstan if ever they were in danger of being whipped. It has been said that the tenth century gave shape to English history and that Dunstan gave shape to the tenth century. He lived through the reigns of seven Saxon kings and achieved great things. Certainly, the most enduring of all St Dunstan's works was his Coronation Order of Service, from which, for almost a thousand years, all English kings and queens have been crowned and anointed.

EDMUND II ('IRONSIDE') AND THE DANISH KINGS

The death of Ethelred ('the Unready') in April 1016 heralded a period of uncertainty about the monarchy until the Danes finally gained full control. Ethelred's son, Edmund II, was chosen to be king by the members of the Witan (the Anglo-Saxon forerunner of parliament) resident in London, while the Witan majority at Southampton had little choice other than having to choose Canute (Cnut).

Records of the coronations of Edmund II and the Danish kings are understandably scanty. Westminster Abbey had yet to be built, and the growing tradition of holding coronations at Kingston upon Thames was broken. Edmund and the Danish kings who followed him were crowned at various locations:

KINGSTON'S 'CORONATION STONE'

Kingston upon Thames, about twelve miles west of London, is reputedly the place where Saxon kings had their coronations. In the middle of the town, visible for all to see, is a large lump of sandstone, surrounded by robust, blue-painted iron railings. The stone is roughly cube-shaped, about 4 ft square, resting on a seven-sided plinth. Boldly carved round the base of the plinth are the names of no fewer than seven Saxon kings who are said to have been crowned on Kingston's famous coronation stone: Edward the Elder, Athelstan, Edmund, Eadred, Eadwig, Edward the Martyr, Aethelred. Intriguingly, it has even been claimed that the very name Kingston derives from King's Stone.

However, apart from Edgar's famous coronation in Bath, it is simply not known where many of the Saxon kings were crowned. Certainly, *The Anglo-Saxon Chronicle*, which is our most reliable source of information, tells us of two coronations at Kingston: that of Athelstan in AD 925, and Ethelred the Unready in AD 979. The tradition that other kings were crowned at Kingston comes exclusively from the thirteenth-century Dean of St Paul's, Ralph de Diceto, who seems to have added the other kings to the list, without any evidence at all.

Edred, and possibly Edwy, may have also been crowned at Kingston – that is, if we can take the word of another medieval chronicler, Florence of Worcester. However, once again, the writer lived long after the events he was recording, and there is no complete certainty about his claims. John Leland in the sixteenth century makes the point that the citizens of Kingston claim 'certen knowlege of a few kinges crounid ther afore the Conqueste; and contende that 2 or 3 kinges were buried yn their paroche chirch'. But with the commendable scepticism of a true historian, he adds: '*but they can not bring no profe nor liklihood of it*'!

As for the coronation stone itself, there is no reliable information at all prior to 1850 when, in the words of Shaan Butters, who has recently researched the matter, it was rescued 'from obscurity and publicly inaugurated as an historic monument'. Sadly, there is no reference to a stone before 1793, when *The British Directory* claims that 'some of our Saxon kings were also crowned here; and close to the north side of the church is a large stone, on which, according to tradition, they were placed during the ceremony'. It was not until 1850 that it was moved to its present location and enclosed in the 'Saxon effect' railings that we can still see today.

Edmund II ('Ironside') (1016)	Crowned in Old St Paul's, London, April 1016
Canute (1016–35)	Crowned in Old St Paul's, London, 6 January 1017
Harold I ('Harefoot') (1035–40)	Crowned at Oxford, 1037
Hardecanute (1040–42)	Crowned in Canterbury Cathedral, 18 June 1040

At the death of Hardecanute, his half-brother Edward the Confessor – son of Ethelred the Unready and Queen Emma – was brought back from Normandy to become king, and he chose to be crowned in Winchester, the capital of Wessex, on 3 April 1043. It was to be the last coronation not in Westminster Abbey.

EDWARD THE CONFESSOR BREAKS HIS VOW TO GO TO ROME

When the last of the Danish Kings, Hardecanute, aged about twenty-three, choked himself to death at someone's wedding-feast in the summer of 1042, no one mourned. His was a short and brutal reign. He was probably poisoned.

The man who was now invited to become king could hardly have been more different – Edward, the monkish, saintly son of Ethelred the Unready and Emma of Normandy. Edward had been born in Islip, a tiny village in Oxfordshire, but when he was only ten the Danish invasion had forced his father Ethelred to flee the country and seek refuge in Normandy. Young Edward had gone with him and after his father's death he had continued to live there in exile throughout the Danish occupation of the English throne. To all intents and purposes Edward was now a Norman, although by birth he belonged to the ancient Saxon line of kings. Edward always realised that there was a slim chance of his becoming king of England, but he hardly realised how soon it would be. Hardecanute's sudden and unexpected death propelled him surprisingly quickly to the throne.

He was about thirty-nine, with an exceptionally red face, but otherwise snow-white skin, hair and beard. He was tall, and was described as having long, almost translucent fingers. It has been suggested that he was an albino. The most noticeable feature about him, however, was his deeply religious lifestyle. An early writer tells how he loved talking with monks and abbots, and particularly 'used to stand with lamb-like meekness and tranquil mind at the holy masses'. The very name that people gave him, 'Confessor', suggests that he was regarded more as a priest than as a king. Those long fingers of his were used to heal the sick, who came to him in large numbers to be 'touched' by them. Shakespeare mentions the Confessor's holy gift of healing in *Macbeth*. Early on in his life Edward had taken a vow of chastity, and was believed to have refused to consummate his marriage to Edith, daughter of Godwin, Earl of Wessex.

Edward the Confessor had also made another vow. He had sworn that if ever he were to be made king of England he would make a pilgrimage to Rome to visit the place where his favourite saint, St Peter, was buried. He hoped that St Peter's successor, the pope, would anoint him. Accordingly, when he came to the throne he announced his intention of going to Rome and fulfilling this vow. However, the members of the Great Council were horrified. They had just lost three Danish kings in quick succession and now that they had managed to get a king of the ancient Saxon blood-line, they certainly did not want to run the risk of losing him on a dangerous journey to Italy. They spelled out the perils: bad roads, rough seas, dangerous mountains, ambushes near bridges and fords, and above all the 'felon Romans, who seek nothing but gain and gifts.' At last the newly-crowned Edward gave way, and accepted a suggestion that a deputation should be sent to the pope to release him from his vow. The deputation duly set off, saw the pope, and returned with the good news that His Holiness would graciously allow King Edward to forego his oath, on the special condition that he would found or restore a monastery dedicated to St Peter, and that the king himself should become its royal patron. The project seized the Confessor's mind. The only matter left to decide was where this new abbey should be sited. The great monastery to which Edward the Confessor was to devote the rest of his life was Westminster Abbey.

Nowadays it is almost impossible to cast our minds back to visualise what the area must have looked like when he began this enormous project. The site was a swampy, boggy island situated between two rivulets running down to the River Thames. The island was so thickly covered by thorns and brambles that it had been given the name 'Isle of Thorns'. Far from being the densely built-up area we know today, it was completely desolate, miles from the small city of London, and apart from a couple of springs and a plentiful supply of fish from the Thames, it was without any apparently redeeming feature. Years before, King Offa of Mercia had seen this patch of marshy scrubland and had called it 'a terrible place'.

There had been some form of early settlement, possibly dating as far back as Roman times, and an earlier small monastery had grown up there, traditionally built in 616 by the newly-converted King Sebert, third king of the Saxon Kingdom of Essex. Dunstan, in the previous century, had helped to establish this more firmly, so that in his time twelve monks had dwelt and prayed there, prompting the citizens of London to call it the 'Western Monastery' or 'Minster of the West'. Thus the name of 'Westminster' was born. Even so, by the time Edward the Confessor came to the throne in 1042 this outlying religious settlement had been destroyed by the marauding Danes and had almost been forgotten. Quite by coincidence the ancient monastery had been dedicated to St Peter – the very saint in whose honour King Edward was bound to build or re-found a great new abbey. All sorts of legends connected with St Peter now began to be linked with this holy spot, embellishing the thought, in some form or other, that St Peter himself had founded it and was personally linked to the place. A bishop had a dream . . . a hermit had a vision . . .

Whatever the deciding factor may have been, Edward the Confessor began to construct a vast new abbey on this rather peculiarly-chosen site almost as soon as he came to the throne in 1042. Thereafter, for almost a quarter of a century, until his death in 1066, he spent vast sums of money and devoted boundless energy to creating what was, at that time, one of the largest abbeys in Christendom. Of equal importance, in order to supervise this great enterprise, Edward the Confessor now frequently began to live in Westminster rather than in the ancient capital of Winchester, so it was inevitable that a palace and other royal buildings should soon grow up alongside the new abbey. Thus abbey and palace developed together, so that Westminster gradually became what it is today, the centre of government as well as the focus of royal religious ceremony.

It is sad to record that Edward the Confessor never lived to see his new abbey take its central place in the life of the nation. After a lifetime spent on this great project he fell ill towards the end of 1065, just as plans were being finalised to consecrate the building.

He had arrived at Westminster and tried to take part in the Christmas celebrations, but it was clear to everyone that he had only days to live. His health collapsed on the Feast of St John, 27 December. Quickly he ordered that the consecration should be brought forward, to the following day, the Feast of the Holy Innocents. However, by then he was so weak that he could not rise from his bed. He only just managed to sign the Charter of the Foundation. His consort, Queen Edith, represented him at the consecration, accompanied by her two brothers, Harold and Gurth. It must have been a profound disappointment to the Confessor not to be there himself. He lay, slipping from delirium into unconsciousness over the next few days in his new Palace of Westminster, until at last, on 5 January, he died. . . . It was the fatal year, 1066.

1066 – A YEAR OF THREE KINGS

Within days of being consecrated, the newly-built Westminster Abbey received the body of its founder into its sacred keeping. He lies there still. England needed a new king, and although Edward had no son, it was apparent to many – but not all – that his brother-in-law Harold was the obvious choice. Throughout his reign the Confessor had relied heavily on Harold to rule the kingdom while he himself was busy with his religious building programme. As for Harold, he was only too keen to take over the throne – almost too keen, for he quickly gathered together all those members of the Witan who were at the old king's funeral and with indecent haste he managed to get himself elected, literally within hours of the Confessor's death. It was opportunism at its most blatant.

However, a few years earlier Harold had promised William, Duke of Normandy that he would support the future Conqueror's claim to the English throne. Indeed, he had made that promise in public, solemnly swearing fealty to William. It was an oath before God. Moreover, it was thought by many that before his death

Edward the Confessor himself had nominated the duke as his heir. The situation was clear. Everyone knew that Harold was seizing the throne in defiance of the Almighty; possibly in defiance of the wishes of the Confessor; and certainly in defiance of the warlike Duke of Normandy. It was a collision-course that was bound to lead to conflict. However, in January 1066, the fatal Battle of Hastings was still nine months away.

Immediately after the death of the Confessor Harold took charge of the situation and ordered the burial of the dead king for the very next morning. It has been said that in actual fact Harold had already reigned for thirteen years, and people naturally looked to him for leadership. The old king had carefully chosen the spot where he should be buried – in front of the altar of St Peter. Here, then, was where he was laid to rest, wearing a pilgrim's ring on one of his pale fingers and, possibly, the crown of England upon his snow-white head.

It was on the Feast of the Epiphany, Friday 6 January 1066, that the first of the year's three kings was buried. Bells tolled, black-robed Benedictine monks chanted psalms, and in the dark, early hours of the morning, just as dawn was breaking, the slow procession of churchmen and Saxon nobles bore the precious corpse to its final resting place. Westminster Abbey was now the home of England's most holy king. Miracles were expected as a matter of course. Then, as soon as the funeral rites had been completed, the little gathering returned to the palace buildings to prepare for a second ceremony – a coronation. Such preparations would necessarily be hasty, for Harold had decided to act swiftly, relying only on those Saxon supporters who were still around him. There was no need to invite nobles who dwelt in more distant parts of the kingdom. Who knows what their opinions might be about who should be king? Perhaps it would be wiser not to ask. Accordingly, about noon on that same Feast of the Epiphany, Harold and his supporters entered Westminster Abbey for a second time that day.

Details of this coronation are vague. Quite probably Harold was crowned by Ealdred, Archbishop of York. Stigand, the Archbishop of Canterbury, was held to be discredited because he had received his pallium (the holy vestment which symbolised the authority granted to him from the pope) from the antipope, Benedict X. Later on, the Normans spread the rumour that

Stigand had crowned Harold – thus rendering his coronation invalid. Whatever the details, Harold emerged from Westminster Abbey as king – the second king to rule England in the year 1066.

With hindsight, we can see that the importance of this first coronation in Westminster Abbey was not any particular detail, but the very fact that it took place where it did, thus setting a precedent for others to follow. Therefore, when William, Duke of Normandy, won his great victory at Hastings in the following October, becoming the third English king in that memorable year, it was inevitable that he should look to the most significant place in the kingdom in which he too could be crowned. What place could be more significant than Westminster, the resting place of his holy uncle, Edward the Confessor, and the site where his rival, the promise-breaking Harold, had been crowned?

So it was that on Christmas Day 1066, William, Duke of Normandy, duly came to Westminster to to be crowned in the Confessor's abbey. From Harold and William to Elizabeth II this line has been unbroken. Since 1066, with the two exceptions of the uncrowned Edward V, who was probably murdered in the Tower of London, and Edward VIII, also uncrowned, who abdicated to marry Wallis Simpson, every king and every reigning queen has been crowned and anointed there, all largely following the Order of Service devised by Archbishop Dunstan in Bath for the crowning and anointing of King Edgar in 973.

2

Coronations from William the Conqueror to Elizabeth II

WILLIAM THE CONQUEROR

Reigned 1066–87, crowned 25 December 1066, aged about 38

Panic and Fire!

William had won the Battle of Hastings in October, and in the ten weeks following he had moved cautiously, partly expecting to meet further resistance. However, at least for the time being, he had won total victory over the Saxons. All the same, he trod warily, taking Dover, so as to preserve his escape route should the need arise, and accepting the keys of Winchester and its treasury from Edith, widow of Edward the Confessor, who had retired to the ancient capital.

At length, after the Saxon nobles and church digitaries had gathered to discuss the situation urgently among themselves, William met them at Berkhamstead, where he received their submission and an oath of fealty from the one person who still had hereditary claim to the English throne – Edmund Ironside's grandson, Edgar the Atheling. Edgar was only fifteen, and to have continued opposing William at this late stage would have been sheer folly. After accepting this formal surrender, William pressed on to London and with the collapse of any further resistance, he found himself in full command of the country. Clearly, the inevitable next step was to have himself crowned. Although he himself would have preferred to wait until his wife Matilda could join him, his Norman entourage urged him to move quickly and arrange a coronation for himself. Only then could he claim legitimate kingship over the land he had just seized by force. Hence it was, on Christmas Day 1066, that Westminster Abbey witnessed its second coronation within a year.

A common idea about William, Duke of Normandy is that he

was a blustering but successful adventurer, an interloper rather like Napoleon would have been if he had managed to cross the channel. In fact, William considered that he had two claims to the English throne: firstly through his kinship with Emma, mother of Edward the Confessor, and secondly because both Edward the Confessor and Harold had promised him that he should be their successor. In William's eyes, it had been Harold who had been the promise-breaking interloper. Not only did William believe himself morally entitled to become king, but also the pope himself had given his holy approval to the venture. He had sent William a special banner, a sacred 'pallium', which he had personally blessed. With such support, William entered Westminster Abbey with an easy conscience, surrounded by his conquering companions. Stigand, the Saxon Archbishop of Canterbury, was not recognised by Rome, as he had received office uncanonically through the antipope, Benedict X, so William chose to be crowned and anointed by Eldred, Archbishop of York, with Bishop Geoffrey of Coutances helping to officiate. The discredited Stigand was allowed to be present – after all, William did not wish to cause offence.

A new crown had been made for the conqueror, the head of a new dynasty. However, to show continuity the coronation service followed the traditional form devised by Dunstan for King Edgar a century before. Only in one respect was it felt necessary to make changes, for the very practical reason that there were two groups of supporters in the abbey, Saxon and Norman, each with their own language. It was planned, therefore, that when the time came for the question asking the assembled congregation whether they were prepared to accept William as their lawful king, the 'Recognition' would be declaimed in *both* languages.

Archbishop Eldred put the question first in the Old English of the Saxons, and then this was followed by Geoffrey of Coutances asking the same question in Norman French. The resulting shouts were terrifyingly loud. Possibly, the two groups of people were trying to outdo each other; perhaps the Saxons were wanting to prove that they really did support the new dynasty; and quite probably the Normans were shouting with all the lusty support of a winning football crowd. Whatever the reason, the fierce acclamation 'Yea, yea, King William!' reached the Norman soldiers who were trying to keep order in the crowds outside. The shouts inside the abbey so alarmed the Norman soldiers standing guard outside that they drew the conclusion that the new king was being assassinated. It is a measure of the tension that surrounded the whole affair. Their immediate response was to set fire to all the thatched, wooden houses surrounding the abbey. Quickly a riot ensued. We have a near-contemporary account of the affair by a Norman chronicler, Ordericus Vitalis, whose father was probably an eye-witness:

> The armed guard outside, hearing the tumult of the joyful crowd in the church and the harsh accents of a foreign tongue, imagined that some treachery was on foot, and rashly set fire to some of the buildings. The fire spread rapidly from house to house; the crowd who had been rejoicing in the church took fright and throngs of men and women of every rank and condition rushed out of the church in frantic haste.
>
> Only the bishops and a few clergy and monks remained, terrified, in the sanctuary, and with difficulty completed the consecration of the king who was trembling from head to foot. Almost all the rest made for the scene of conflagration: some to fight the flames, and many others hoping to find loot for themselves in the general confusion.
>
> The English, after hearing of the perpetration of such misdeeds, never again trusted the Normans who seemed to have betrayed them, but nursed their anger and bided their time for revenge.

To do him justice, William was upset by this turn of events and is reported to have personally visited those who had suffered as a result of the fire.

Nevertheless, despite the shambles of this rather inauspicious beginning, William *had* been crowned and anointed. He had already demonstrated his military might, but now, after this momentous Christmas Day, he was divinely and legally empowered to rule. It now remained for him to bring his diminutive wife (Matilda was just over 4 ft tall) to be crowned and anointed as his consort.

MATILDA, QUEEN OF WILLIAM THE CONQUEROR

Dates as Queen 1068–83, crowned 11 May 1068, aged about 37

Enter Robert de Marmion, The Queen's Champion

It was not until April 1068 that William's wife Matilda crossed the channel to be crowned as his queen. She was crowned at a magnificent ceremony in the old Saxon cathedral in Winchester, soon to be wantonly pulled down by the victorious Normans in order to make room for the much bigger cathedral we see there today.

This old minster was one of the most beautiful buildings in the country, especially important because it was the burial-place of the Saxon kings and of the Danish King Canute. Legend has it that Canute had placed his golden crown above the altar here, to remind people that it was God alone, the King of Heaven, and no earthly king who could be presumed to rule the incoming tides. The sacred remains of many saints rested there too, chief among them being St Swithun, whose bones had caused such dramatic wet weather when, against his wishes, they had been moved inside the building. St Swithun's memory is still very much alive in Winchester today.

The coronation of Matilda was an important innovation in England. The wives of Saxon kings before the conquest were not usually honoured in this way, so this was something of a novelty. Whatever the onlookers may have thought, it was clear that William was willing to share power with his consort, as was the custom on the continent. Accordingly, his duchess was crowned and anointed on Whit Sunday, 1068. William took the opportunity to wear his own crown too, and 'crown-wearings' became one of his regular and looked-for customs. The conqueror regularly spent Christmas at Gloucester with his court, Easter at Winchester, and Whitsuntide at Westminster. Crown-wearings were a part of the ceremonies on all these occasions.

It was at the coronation of Matilda that yet another famous tradition was begun: the introduction of the king's (or in this case the queen's) champion. Just as the assembled guests were sitting down to the coronation feast after the cathedral service, the meal was interrupted by the arrival of a knight on horseback who rode into the hall boldly declaring: 'If any person denies that our most gracious sovereign, Lord William, and his spouse Matilda, are king and queen of England, he is a false-hearted traitor and a liar; and here, I, as Champion, do challenge him to single combat.' The challenge was repeated three times, but of course no one dared to meet it, and so in this manner Matilda became undisputed queen. The bold challenger was Robert de Marmion, one of William's entourage, and the office of 'Champion' was granted to him together with the lands of Fontenaye in Normandy and the manor of Scrivelsby, near Horncastle, in Lincolnshire. The custom of having a champion to make such a challenge was of Norman origin, and until this moment quite unknown in England. Luckily for Marmion, it was a hereditary office, which could be passed down even through the female line. The office of champion eventually passed in the fourteenth century to the Dymoke family, who have proudly been champions of England through the centuries, even taking part in the coronation of Elizabeth II in 1953.

William was in an expansive mood at that Whitsun coronation, even giving the manor of Addington to Tezelin, his cook, for devising a dish of specially delectable soup called *dillegrout* for the coronation banquet. Life was good for the royal pair: Duke and Duchess of Normandy; King and Queen of England; crowned and anointed with holy oil; three healthy sons; and Matilda was pregnant yet again. She was due to produce the future Henry I in the autumn. Two reigns later the timing of that pregnancy was to be specially significant.

WILLIAM II ('RUFUS')

Reigned 1087–1100, crowned 26 September 1087, aged about 31

'King Robert' Misses Out

William the Conqueror died in Rouen, France, on 10 September 1087, after sustaining severe internal injuries when his horse had reared and his vast belly had been thrust forward against the pommel of his saddle. The conqueror lay in mortal pain, deciding how to dispose of his estate, and finally wrote a will bequeathing Normandy to his eldest son, Robert, and England to the next son, red-faced, ginger-haired William Rufus. As for his youngest son, Henry, who was then aged only nineteen, he rather stingily gave him a mere £5,000 in silver.

Rufus inherited the throne of England. But it was a debatable choice. If the rights of eldest sons were to be upheld, surely it ought to have been Robert Curthose, and a number of the baronage would have preferred Robert to Rufus. The deciding mind was that of Lanfranc, appointed Archbishop of Canterbury by William the Conqueror as successor to the hapless and unrecognised Stigand. Even before William died, Rufus hastened across the channel to Lanfranc, carrying his father's will, and was able to persuade him that he should be crowned forthwith as the conqueror had wished. Robert was still in France, staying with his father's old enemy, King Philip, and had been estranged from his father for some years. To Rufus's relief, Lanfranc accepted the Conqueror's will, and before his elder brother Robert could mount a challenge, Rufus had himself crowned in Westminster Abbey.

For us, the important thing about this coronation is that it *was* in Westminster Abbey. It was the third time the abbey had been chosen, and henceforth was to become the accepted and traditional place for coronations, just as Rheims in France and Aachen in Germany.

Details concerning Rufus's coronation are scanty. William Rufus was not a favourite son of the church, but one supposes that a certain amount of hypocrisy on his part and expedient tolerance from the church enabled him to go through with the ceremony without too much display of principle on either side. In any case, Rufus was wary of the political worldlywise Archbishop Lanfranc, who was to live only for another two more years. In a sense he owed his crown to the archbishop, who had accepted his claim. However, when Lanfranc's successor, Anselm, became archbishop, Rufus was to quarrel openly and frequently with him. Anselm found it prudent to flee the country, and so for almost three years the archbishopric was left semi-vacant, or at least without an active leader. It must have been with a great sense of relief to the church when Rufus met his death, killed by an arrow in the New Forest and buried without rites in Winchester cathedral. In the absence of Anselm, the next coronation, that of Rufus's brother Henry, took place, somewhat controversially, without the services of an archbishop.

HENRY I

Reigned 1100–35, crowned 5 August 1100, aged 32

A Hasty Coronation as 'King Robert' Misses Out Again

No English coronation was carried out with such breakneck speed as that of Henry I. Fate had been kind to him when that arrow, perhaps well-aimed, felled his brother Rufus the 'Red King', in the New Forest on 2 August 1100. No one will ever know exactly what happened, or whether Henry himself had been implicated in a ruthless and successful assassination, but Henry rushed with almost indecent haste to Winchester in an effort to persuade an assembly of Norman nobles that he was now the rightful heir to the throne. Robert Curthose, his elder brother, was out of the country at the time in the Holy Land at the head of a crusade which had begun four years before. Robert had been highly successful in restoring the Holy City to Christian hands and had even turned down the offer of being made king of Jerusalem. It was now known that Robert would soon be returning to his lands in Normandy.

It was self-evident to many in Winchester that Henry's older brother Robert was the proper successor to Rufus. However, an ingenious argument was produced to support Henry, the younger of the two. It was put to the assembly that Robert had been born *before* his father had been crowned king of England, whereas Henry had been born *afterwards*. (Matilda had been carrying him when she was crowned in Winchester, and Henry had been born in Yorkshire later that year – the only son to be born in England.) Perhaps it was a specious argument, but probably the fact that Henry was energetically present and more than willing to become king swayed the assembly. Swiftly Henry took charge of the treasury and then galloped sixty miles to London. He was crowned two days later.

Clearly, he must have worked hard to get a coronation

organised in so short a time, and the ceremony itself must have been a less-than-magnificent occasion. Anselm, the Archbishop of Canterbury, was out of the country, hiding from the wrath of Rufus; to contact the Archbishop of York would have wasted time; so Henry arranged for Maurice, Bishop of London to officiate. Within a few days, Anselm hurried back to England, expostulating that he should have been asked to do the job, as only an archbishop could do it properly. But the deed was now done, and Henry simply pointed out that it had been necessary to be crowned as soon as possible. Anselm had to accept it as a *fait accompli*.

In any case, Henry was a popular figure. He had a reputation for learning, with nicknames of 'Beauclerk' (he could actually read), and also 'Lion of Justice'. In fact, at his coronation, his charters were especially important and significant, virtually anticipating Magna Carta. He promised to abolish 'the evil customs with which English law has been unrighteously oppressed' and to return to the happier times of Edward the Confessor. He promised to treat the church better than Rufus had done. In return, of course, he required explicit obedience, loyalty and assistance against his enemies. His brother Robert was probably forefront in his mind.

Anselm may have missed out on crowning Henry I, but his chance came later that same year when Henry decided to marry Matilda, sister of King Edgar of Scotland, and daughter of the Scottish King Malcolm (the Malcolm who makes the last speech in Shakespeare's *Macbeth*).

MATILDA OF SCOTLAND, FIRST QUEEN OF HENRY I

Crowned 11 November 1100, aged 20

Wrangling Priests

Matilda's coronation took place at the same time as her marriage to Henry. It was a popular wedding, for Matilda, or Maud (or Edith as she had been called by the Saxons), had an ancestry which went back to Alfred the Great: thus Normans and Saxons were being united in marriage. As a young girl Matilda had been brought up as a nun in Romsey Abbey, Hampshire, where her aunt was abbess. However, she was far from wanting to lead a religious life, stories are told that she only wore the veil in order to discourage unwelcome advances from unwanted suitors, and would tear it off and stamp on it if ever she was made to wear it on other occasions. Before the start of the service, Archbishop Anselm actually stood in the pulpit in Westminster Abbey and told the assembled nobles the truth about Matilda's nubility and assured them that she was genuinely free to marry, otherwise rumour might have spread that Henry was just about to marry a nun. To crown a nun would not augur well for the succession.

The thirteenth-century poet, Robert of Gloucester, enthused over Henry's choice of partner:

So that as soon as he was king, on St Martyn's-day I ween,
He spoused her that was called Maude the good queen,
That was *kind heir of England*, as I have told before.
Many were the good laws that were made in England
Through Maude the good queen, as I understand.

Henry had apologised to Anselm for not having asked him, as Archbishop of Canterbury, to officiate at his own coronation. He went on to butter Anselm up, saying that no one was dearer to him than Anselm, whose 'vicar' had had to be called in. So, when Anselm crowned Henry's consort, Queen Matilda, a second tradition was established that it was the prerogative of the Archbishop of Canterbury to officiate at English coronations.

Anselm dutifully put the crown on Henry's head at the traditional times of 'crown-wearings': Easter, Christmas and Whitsun. However, when he died in 1109, the Archbishop of York naturally expected the honour to devolve upon himself. However, to his annoyance, Henry passed him over at the Christmas crown-wearing and once again the Bishop of London, Richard de Belmeis, was given the task, on the excuse that he was suffragan of Canterbury. As usual, there was a sumptuous feast after the crown-wearing ceremony, but so much bitter wrangling went on at table between the two prelates over who was entitled to crown the king that Henry bluntly told them to shut up, push off and eat elsewhere!

All this may seem trivial and childish, but we must remember that in this post-Conquest world, people were still marking out their territory. It was not just a question of what happened at coronations, but who gave authority to whom. Feelings of precedence ran high over this issue. In fact, later that century the clash of personalities and hurt pride was destined to result in Christendom's most celebrated murder, that of Thomas Becket, several coronations later.

ADELA OF LOUVAIN, SECOND QUEEN OF HENRY I

Crowned 30 January 1121, aged about 18

'Take That Crown Off Your Head!'

Sadly, Henry I's first queen, Matilda, died in 1118, but even more grievous, perhaps, to Henry was the loss of his two legitimate sons by drowning, in the *White Ship* disaster in November 1120. He needed to produce more heirs urgently. So, early in 1121 he invited a teenager, Adela, daughter of Count Godfrey VII of Louvain, to be his second bride. They married at Windsor on 29 January 1121. Roger, Bishop of Salisbury, tried to claim the right to officiate because at that time Windsor was within his diocese. However, as always, the Archbishop of Canterbury was quick to jump to his own defence in claiming that marrying the king was *his* job. An ecclesiastical council was summoned and it was solemnly decided that in future, wherever a king and queen might be within the realm of England, they were to be considered as parishioners of the Archbishop of Canterbury. Accordingly, the Archbishop, Ralph d'Escures, now very old and tottery, performed the marriage service. The archbishop was so very old and weak that Henry asked Roger, Bishop of Salisbury, to officiate the following day, 30 January, at the coronation of his new wife.

An astonishing scene was now to take place. According to an account given by Eadmer, a contemporary chronicler and friend of Anselm, Bishop Roger began the coronation service at a somewhat early hour in the day – perhaps to circumvent the old archbishop. However, they did not reckon with the force of the old archbishop's determination. He arrived at the abbey halfway through the service and was aghast to find that Henry was already wearing his crown! 'Who put that crown on your head?' he demanded. Nonplussed, Henry tried to avoid giving a direct answer, and merely said that if anything had been done amiss, he would be willing to do anything the archbishop wished. At that, the archbishop took Henry's crown off the royal head, and then firmly put it back again. Once again, he had triumphed. However, the effort was almost too much for d'Escures, and he simply could not carry on with the rest of the service. He had to ask the Bishop of Winchester to complete the job after all – the See of Winchester was much older than that of Salisbury – but at any rate, he had made his point.

KING STEPHEN

Reigned 1135–54, crowned 26 December 1135, aged 38

Snatches the Crown From His Cousin

Stephen should never have been crowned at all. He was an unashamed usurper, taking the throne from his cousin Matilda, to whom his uncle Henry I had willed it. The two previous kings, Rufus and Henry I, had made a quick dash to the Archbishop of Canterbury to press their claims, and this one was no different. As soon as Henry I died in Lyons-la-Forêt, near Rouen, Stephen hastened across the channel to rally support for himself and persuade the church to accept him.

Luckily for Stephen, he was popular and well-liked, and to a large extent the nobles and church dignitaries were biased in his favour. There was, however, the sticky business of the oath of loyalty to Matilda which they had all made during Henry's reign. Oaths are oaths, even if they are in favour of a mere woman. Stephen's trump card, however, was the fact that his brother, Henry of Blois, the powerful Bishop of Winchester, was strongly behind him, and together they convinced the archbishop that making Stephen king would bring great advantages to both church and people. Added to this, one noble, Hugh Bigod, probably lying through his teeth, solemnly swore on the holy evangelists that Henry had disinherited Matilda on his deathbed, and adopted his 'most dear nephew Stephen' for his heir. At this Archbishop, William de Corbeil, saw his clear duty, and absolved the nobles of their previous oaths to Matilda. After all, oaths such as these were 'contrary to the laws and customs of the English, who had never permitted a woman to reign over them.' Within days, the good archbishop had crowned Stephen and anointed him.

Stephen's coronation took place on his name day, 26 December, the 'Feast of Stephen' when good King Wenceslas had 'last walked out'. Good King Stephen, however, somehow failed to materialise, and the promises he had made to the church in order to arrive at the throne were quickly broken. Even his brother Henry of Blois came to recognise that perhaps they had all made a mistake in choosing Stephen.

It is worth remembering that parliament did not exist in those days, and there was no constitution to refer to. For this reason, in the absence of a king or regent acting in his name, the authority of the church – in particular the head of the church – was paramount.

However, in 1139 Henry of Blois became even more powerful than an archbishop. Still Bishop of Winchester, he had also been granted the special office of papal legate. Feeling himself all-powerful, above king and archbishop, Henry of Blois welcomed Matilda to his palace in Winchester and solemnly declared her to be *Domina*, or 'Lady of the English'. It was a bold move, unique in history, and Henry accompanied his newly-appointed cousin-queen to London, intending to crown her. However, Matilda's coronation was destined to be a non-event: the citizens of London refused to accept her, storming the room in Westminster where she was enjoying a grand pre-coronation banquet. She fled: determined, however, to wage civil war.

HENRY II AND ELEANOR OF AQUITAINE

Reigned 1154–89, crowned 19 December 1154, Henry aged 21

'Curtmantle' Arrives – 'From the Devil He Came!'

The couple who walked up the nave of Westminster Abbey for this coronation were two of the most remarkable characters in history.

Henry II was a great-grandson of William the Conqueror, and son of Matilda who had been promised the throne on the death of Henry I, but who had been immediately ousted by her cousin

Stephen. The resulting wrangling and warfare between the two rivals brought the country to ruin. When finally, it was clear that Stephen would leave no heir, a compromise was arrived at by which Stephen was allowed to remain on the throne until he died, and then the crown would pass to Matilda's son, Henry of Anjou.

After the war everyone longed for a strong ruler who would bring peace and stability, so Henry's arrival was eagerly awaited. He was known to be a young man of ferocious energy who would dominate the kingdom with his presence. As for Eleanor of Aquitaine, it is impossible to describe this extraordinary woman in just a few sentences. Ravishingly beautiful, fabulously wealthy, she had already enjoyed a spectacular life of adventures: marrying the king of France; leading a 'ladies crusade' to the Holy Land; having numerous affairs; being ambushed and captured by would-be lovers. When she met Henry, ten years her junior, she promptly jilted her husband, the saintly King Louis of France, and married Henry in Bordeaux cathedral – five months pregnant with their first child.

Henry was superbly self-confident, but with a demonic temper. St Bernard once said of him: 'From the Devil he came, and to the Devil he will go!' It is said that when he was angry he could hardly prevent himself from clawing his opponent's eyes out. When news came that Stephen had died, Henry, then aged twenty-one, was busy besieging a rebellious castle in Normandy. His friends urged him to hurry to England lest there should be a revolt by the barons, but he replied contemptuously that they simply would not dare. He finished off the castle, taking his time to crush his enemy, and then six weeks later, arrived in England to take up the throne and enjoy what would easily be the most magnificent coronation that in London had seen.

No one in England had beheld such gorgeous costumes as those worn by Eleanor on that day. Her dress had been brought from Constantinople, consisting of a tight-fitting robe of gold cloth 'in many shades of gold upon gold'. and over this shimmering garment hung a royal mantle of violet silk, richly embroidered with gold fleur-de-lys and leopards, and edged with ermine. Her head-dress consisted of bands of wrought gold, blazing with huge pearls, rubies and emeralds; her hair was braided and coiled round her head; and over it all was loosely thrown an oriental veil of silver tissue, forming a kind of yashmak.

As for Henry, he shocked many of those present with his closely-cropped red hair, when the fashion was for long hair. He wore a fierce-looking moustache and had a shaven chin, defying the fashion for beards. He too was finely arrayed, wearing a doublet and his distinctive short cloak – possibly this was the time he acquired his nickname of 'Curtmantle' (short cloak).

Adding extra splendour to the occasion, the new queen also insisted that the archbishop and clergy were supplied with velvet and silk vestments, heavy with gold embroidery – and this was a notable innovation in itself. Eleanor had admired the fine robes of the Greek priests she had seen in the East, and felt that it was time for similar rich vestments to be worn in the Western Church. The Archbishop of Canterbury was assisted by the Archbishops of York and Rouen, and Henry was crowned with a splendid, large crown, which had probably been used by the Emperor, Henry V, who had been his mother's first husband.

The crowds in the streets were genuinely welcoming. For them, it was a new beginning. In fact it was the start of a new dynasty – for with Henry's arrival the Plantagenets were now on the throne, and one or other of them would remain in power until the fatal Battle of Bosworth Field in 1485, when the Tudors would take over.

Meanwhile, only sixteen years later, and almost half-way through the reign of Henry II, another coronation would take place – a highly unusual one, and with far-reaching repercussions – the coronation of Henry's eldest son, the fifteen-year-old Henry, known as 'the Young King'. This young man never lived to be king in solitary right, but for the twelve years following his coronation, England, oddly enough, had *two* King Henries. The next coronation, therefore, was hardly a change of reign, but it did result in a series of dramatic events, quite unforeseeable at the time. . . .

HENRY 'THE YOUNG KING'

Reigned 1170–83, crowned 14 June 1170, aged 15

A Murder and a Legend

It may seem crazy that Henry II had his eldest son crowned king during his own lifetime, but in fact this had long been common practice in France. The theory behind it was to enable a smooth succession in case the king died suddenly. It prevented a power-vacuum by having a 'spare king' already crowned and anointed. However, little did the king realise the complications which would arise from this decision. For one thing, the young king himself seems to have been throroughly spoilt and obnoxious, and arrogantly set himself up to provoke his father, asking for more and more powers and privileges until the relationship between the two burst out into open war.

Even at the coronation feast in Westminster Hall the older Henry must have seen the way things would go. When the trumpets sounded to announce the entry of the main dish – a boar's head – he paid his son a dramatic and unprecedented compliment. He knelt down before him and served the young man at table with the food. The Archbishop of York was sitting next to the young king, and made a remark which was intended as a compliment, but which backfired embarrassingly. 'Be glad, my good son,' he said. 'There is not another prince in the world that hath such a server at his table.' 'Why dost thou marvel?' replied the nasty young teenager. 'My father in doing it, thinketh it not more than becometh him. He being born of princely blood only on the mother's side, serveth me that am a king born, having both a king to my father and a queen to my mother.' Such a reply must have sent a shiver of horror round the hall – no one ever dared to speak to Henry II like that! The older man, with his notorious temper, must have found it almost impossible to swallow his pride. The incident was horrifying historians even three centuries later, for Raphael Holinshed, writing in the time of Shakespeare, commented: 'Thus the young man of an evil and perverse nature was puffed up in pride by his father's unseemly doing.'

However, the main problem associated with the young king's coronation was the question of who should perform the ceremony. The event took place at the height of Henry's monumental row with Thomas Becket, Archbishop of Canterbury, in which king and archbishop were at loggerheads over the powers of the church. Becket was in France, diplomatically distancing himself from Henry's wrath. In these circumstances Henry asked the Archbishop of York to do the crowning and anointing. Everyone knew that the Archbishop of York was being asked to overstep the mark, so to bolster him up in the task the bishops of London, Durham, Salisbury and Rochester were also present. But they all knew that they were obeying their king rather than the pope. It was then that the train of events was set in motion which led to Becket's death and martyrdom. It has been said that no coronation ever led to more disastrous consequences.

Becket was outraged when he heard that the Archbishop of York had crowned the Young King. Nowadays, it's difficult for us to appreciate the niceties of the precedence of the two archbishops, York and Canterbury, but for Becket himself there was no question about it. He and he alone, as Archbishop of Canterbury, had the right to perform the Coronation ceremony. Immediately he came back to England from Pontigny in France, and in the pope's name excommunicated the Archbishop of York and the bishops of London, Durham and Salisbury for taking part in this unholy coronation of the Young King. In fact he was reported as having said that he would 'tear the crown from the Young King's head!'

Naturally enough, it was now Henry II's turn to be outraged, and this was the moment when he finally exploded, shouting out to everyone within hearing distance: 'Will no one rid me of this turbulent priest?' Of course, everyone knows what happened next. Four knights galloped off to do what they thought the king wanted them to do; Becket was murdered within his own cathedral; Henry II publicly walked with bare and bleeding feet in penitence through the streets of Canterbury to kiss the stone where the archbishop had fallen; and soon a sumptuously rich shrine was built in Becket's memory to which hundreds of thousands of pilgrims came to venerate the 'holy, blissful martyr'. The lifestyle of England changed, and in the constant struggle between church and state, the church had triumphed – at least for the time being.

A couple of years later the Young King gave himself another coronation, this time in Winchester, when Rotrou, Archbishop of Rouen, came over to crown his wife, Margaret of France. She had not taken part in Henry's first coronation, and her father, King Louis VII of France, was somewhat displeased. The Winchester ceremony helped to smooth things over – but it's unlikely that the young king himself cared about pleasing the old French king – he was far too busy joining forces with his brothers, the future King

Richard I and the future King John, to make serious trouble for his own father, whom he had insulted so crudely at the coronation banquet. In 1183, after thirteen more years of puffed up pride young Henry was to die, still fighting against his father; so, perhaps luckily for England, he never came to the throne as a proper king.

The dramatic death of Thomas Becket took place just six months after the young king's coronation, and his martyrdom haunted the conscience of the age. His death symbolised the ultimate triumph of the church over the excessive power of the king. In later years a curious legend arose about a vision of the Virgin Mary which Becket is supposed to have had while in exile in France, and a miraculous gift of holy oil which she bestowed upon him for the anointment of future kings of England. A manuscript account of this legend, probably written in the fifteenth century, exists in the Bodleian Library in Oxford. Here is a translation from the original Latin:

> When I, Thomas, Archbishop of Canterbury, was fleeing in exile from England to France, I came to Pope Alexander, who was then at Sens, to show him the customs and abuses which the king of the English was bringing into the Church.
>
> And one night, as I was praying in the church of St Columba, I asked the queen of virgins to give to the king of England and his heirs a proposal and the will to amend their lives towards the Church of God, and that Christ of his great mercy would make the king love the holy Church with fuller love.
>
> Immediately there appeared to me the blessed Virgin with an eagle of gold in her bosom, and with a small phial of stone in her hand. She took the eagle from her bosom, and put the phial into it, placed the eagle and phial in my hand, and said these words: 'This is the oil with which the kings of England must be anointed, but not those wicked ones who now reign or will reign, and who, on account of their many crimes, have lost and will lose much.
>
> But kings of the English shall arise who will be anointed with this oil, who will be good and champions of the Church.

They will recover the lands lost by their forefathers as long as they have the eagle and phial.

Now there will be a king of the English who will be the first to be anointed with this oil: he shall recover by force the land lost by his forefathers, that is to say, Normandy and Aquitaine. He will be greatest amongst kings, and he it is that will build many churches in the holy land, and will put all the heathen to flight from Babylon, and will build many churches there. And as often as he carries this eagle on his breast he will have the victory over all his enemies and his kingdom will be ever increased. For thou art to be a martyr.

And then I prayed the blessed Virgin to show me where to keep so precious and holy a thing, and she said to me: 'There is a man in this town, a monk of St Cyprian's of Poitiers, who has been unjustly expelled by his abbot from his abbey. He is now asking the Pope to restore him to his abbey. Give him the eagle and phial for him to take to the abbey at Poitiers. And I would hide it in the church of St George by the church of St Hilary, and the western end of the 'chevet' (apse) of the church under a great stone, where it will be found at a convenient time.'

All these things were given to me by the blessed Virgin Mary enclosed in a leaden vessel.

RICHARD I (THE 'LIONHEART')

Reigned 1189–99, crowned 3 September 1189, aged 31

A King Needing a Second Coronation

Dying aged fifty-six, Henry II was enraged at the disloyalty of his sons, particularly Richard and John, who joined the King of France to defeat him in battle. Henry suffered a stroke, and on his death-bed his last reported words show how bitterly he regarded himself as a failure: 'Shame, shame on a conquered King!' There was no love lost between Henry and his eldest son Richard. Legend tells how when Richard I approached his father's dead body, the older man's corpse bled anew.

Within less than two months after Henry's death Richard had himself crowned in Westminster Abbey, ordering a splendid ceremonial for himself. Aged thirty-one, over 6 ft tall and with broad shoulders, Richard was at the height of his physical powers. He relished the kingship he had just inherited: it would enable him to seek untold adventures overseas, especially in the Holy Land fighting the infidel. He had no interest whatever in the welfare of England, so long as it was kept troublefree in his absence – and this would be most of the time.

At the coronation service he stood before the throne, a magnificent figure of a man, to be ceremonially disrobed down to his shirt and breeches. Special slits had been made in the shirt through which he could be anointed. Baldwin, the archbishop, who was to die in Palestine the following year on a crusade with Richard, consecrated him on the chest and hands and then dripped the holy oil on to his head, which was then carefully bound in a chrismale or linen coif. This would remain in place for eight days so that not one single drop of the precious mixture should be lost.

Richard was then solemnly dressed in tunic, dalmatic (a loose-fitting, wide-sleeved garment) and the cap of maintenance, which was pulled over the chrismale. Gold-laced sandals were placed on his feet; then came the spurs, sword, stole and mantle. After Richard had moved to the altar the oath was administered, in which he promised to uphold the laws of the kingdom (he would, in fact, be in England for only ten months of his ten-year reign). Richard himself then picked the crown up from the altar and passed it to the archbishop. The moment of crowning had come. Baldwin placed the crown over the cap of maintenance and chrismale. Richard was king. It remained for the ring to be put on his finger, and the sceptre and rod to be placed in his hands, and then, in regal state, the new king sat on the throne while the *Te Deum* was sung.

Apparently, all had gone well. It was a splendid event, attended by Richard's mother, the formidable Eleanor of Aquitaine, newly-released after spending sixteen years under house-arrest. Her husband Henry's death had brought her a welcome return to freedom and here she was, magnificently arrayed in a silken cape trimmed with squirrel-fur and sable. Richard's brother John was also there, with newfound wealth and expections. Furthermore, the importance of the occasion was emphasised by the presence of the Archbishops of Rouen, Tours, and Dublin.

As so often happened at coronations, however, there were several sinister omens, to be mulled over in later years. To begin with, the date chosen, 3 September, was one of the days marked by astrologers as an 'Egyptian day'. Nowadays, no one remembers these days of ill-omen, but medieval minds were fearful of such unlucky 'Egyptian days', two of which were supposed to occur in each month. They were also known as *dies mali* or 'evil days' – and we derive our word 'dismal' from this superstitious Latin phrase. As if to confirm that this was a dismal day, the congregation in Westminster Abbey was much alarmed during the coronation service by the appearance of a bat 'in the middle and bright part of the day'. It was 'inconveniently circling in the same tracks, and especially round the king's throne.' Yet another evil augury, 'hardly allowable to be related even in a whisper', was the peal of bells just before midnight, apparently without any agreement or knowledge of the ministers of the abbey. However, these three troublesome omens were as nothing compared with the very real troubles which were to take place at the coronation banquet held in Westminster Hall immediately after the service. The events triggered by this banquet constitute one of the blackest episodes in English history, with repercussions throughout the country.

The day before the banquet Richard had given orders that no woman or Jew should be present. To present-day minds such an order would be unthinkable, but in 1189 the strange medieval mixture of custom, religion, superstition and ignorance ensured that Richard's orders were accepted without question. Even Eleanor of Aquitaine, his own mother, was excluded from the coronation banquet, for the curious reason that Richard was still unmarried. All might have been well except for the fact that the Jewish community in London decided to ignore the king's command, and so came to the banquet bearing gifts. Little did they know what the results of this well-meaning but tactless disobedience would be. Even before they reached Westminster Hall they were set upon by the London mob, and their friends and relations back in the city were beaten up and killed, and their houses were burnt to the ground. In all fairness to Richard, this was none of his doing and the ringleaders of these disturbances were duly hanged.

Nevertheless, ugly anti-Jewish feeling had been stirred up, and this quickly spread to many other towns far from London itself. Stamford, in Lincolnshire, was the scene of terrible slaughter, in which Jews were 'y-beaten, y-slain, and y-spoiled,' and similar atrocities occurred at Lincoln, Norwich and Lynn. Worst of all these outbreaks of violence happened at York, where four hundred terrified Jews barracaded themselves inside one of the castle towers. There, after losing all hope of escape, the chief rabbi cut everyone's veins before slitting his wife's throat and then his own. It was a terrible start to Richard's reign. At the coronation feast itself Richard was oblivious of all the events taking place, and when he asked what the noises were that he could hear outside, the doorkeeper replied 'Nothing; only the boys rejoice and are merry at heart.' But when the king heard the truth of the matter, he had the doorkeeper dragged to death, tied to the tails of horses. Truly, the day turned out to be one of the most accursed of all the medieval *dies mali*.

Three months later Richard left for France, where he planned to join forces with King Philip of France and go on a crusade. The terrible events in England no longer concerned him, though the anti-Jewish demonstrations were still continuing. It has to be admitted that Richard was one of England's worst kings. He simply had not the slightest interest in the welfare of his realm, except as a source of income for his interminable wars. For Richard, life was just one long series of military adventures. Such a high-risk lifestyle was virtually bound to lead to ultimate disaster.

This is not the place to follow his ten-year reign in detail, but at least some mention should be made of the fact that en route to the Holy Land he married – almost incidentally – the bride chosen for him by his mother, Eleanor of Aquitaine. By this time Richard had already quarrelled with Philip of France, partly because he refused to marry Philip's sister, Alys. As soon as Eleanor arrived in Sicily with Berengaria of Navarre, Philip left the island in a rage. Very little is known of Berengaria: 'a lady of beauty and good sense', remarked one contemporary; 'sensible rather than attractive,' says another rather non-committally. Aged about twenty-six at the time Eleanor escorted her from her native Navarre to Sicily, Berengaria is the least-known of all English queens.

Eleanor did not stay in Sicily. She had done her duty by providing Richard with a wife, and so after three days she went back to England, leaving the pair to press on to the Holy Land, where they intended to marry. However, fate stepped in and on the way to Palestine Berengaria's ship was nearly seized by the Greek ruler of Cyprus, providing Richard with a perfect excuse for invading and capturing the whole island. So it was in the chapel of St George, at Limassol, in Cyprus, that Richard and Berengaria, almost complete strangers to one another, married – surely the most unlikely place for the wedding of an English king.

Immediately after the wedding service – on 12 May 1191 – followed the most unusual coronation of any English queen: unusual, because it is the only coronation of king or consort (apart from that of Matilda, wife of William the Conqueror) to have taken place anywhere other than in Westminster Abbey; the only coronation conducted by a foreign bishop; and Beregaria herself was the only queen never to be seen in England. Details are vague concerning this Cyprus coronation. It is not known what crown was used, if Berengaria was anointed, or if the Bishop of Evreux followed the order of service laid down by Dunstan. At this distance of time the whole affair seems almost hypothetical. Nevertheless, it is recorded that Berengaria wore a mantilla and Richard wore a mantle of striped silk decorated with gold crescents and silver suns, and on his head a scarlet hat embroidered with golden birds and beasts. On his feet were buskins of cloth of gold and gilded spurs. Three whole days of feasting followed, and within less than a month Richard continued on his way to the Holy Land, taking Berengaria with him.

When Richard eventually decided to return to England, after failing to capture Jerusalem, he sent Berengaria to sail on ahead without him; meanwhile he started to make his own way home by land. This proved to be a disastrous mistake. He was captured by his enemy, Leopold of Austria; sold to the Emperor, Henry VI, for 150,000 marks; held captive in Durnstein Castle on the banks of the Danube; and the ransom demanded for his release made it necessary for every man in England to pay a quarter of a year's income. Pigs were killed, sheep shorn, church plate sold. It was an expensive and humiliating business rescuing Richard.

When the 'Lionheart' eventually reached England, there was a general feeling among the barons that King Richard had lost something of his regality by this shameful period of imprisonment. It was remembered that in 1141 King Stephen had had himself re-crowned, or at least had worn his crown in a special ceremony at Canterbury after he had been released from captivity by Matilda. Somehow, Richard's royal dignity had to be restored, and so, rather reluctantly, he agreed to go through with a second coronation, to be held in Winchester Cathedral on Low Sunday (the Sunday following Easter) 1194. The choice of Winchester acknowledged the importance of the ancient Saxon capital of England. Edward the Confessor had been crowned in the old Saxon cathedral and so had the Conqueror's wife, Matilda. Even the new Norman cathedral, now just over a century old, was a place of deep significance, containing the bones of many Saxon saints and kings.

After dining in Winchester Castle on the Saturday, the day before his re-crowning, Richard went to the Priory of St Swithun, where he 'had himself bathed' before spending the night there. Then, on Low Sunday he went to the king's chamber in the monastery, where the regalia had been carefully set out on a fair cloth. He was robed and the golden verge tipped with the likeness of an eagle was placed in his left hand; the royal sceptre was placed in his right hand; and then Hubert Walter, Archbishop of Canterbury, solemnly placed the golden crown on Richard's head.

Now was the time for the re-crowned king to make his way to the cathedral, slowly and in procession with the two archbishops of Canterbury and Dublin, together with eleven other bishops, William, King of Scotland, and a multitude of earls, barons and knights. The ceremony to follow would not be a coronation but rather a crown-wearing, such as had been the custom of William the Conqueror and his immediate successors. No further act of anointing was necessary – once anointed, always anointed. The purpose of this crown-wearing was to imprint an indelible scene of majesty in the minds of the public. Richard sat high on a throne while the archbishop, wearing his sacred pallium, celebrated a special mass.

High in the triforium, looking down on her son, sat the Queen Mother, Eleanor of Aquitaine, now aged seventy-two, relieved to see Richard at the centre of power again – for it had fallen to her lot to help rule the kingdom in his absence, and more importantly to raise the enormous ransom needed for his release. She must have looked forward to this day of restoration with anxious longing.

Berengaria, who by rights should also have been watching this crown-wearing, was still in France. She had got as far as Aquitaine, but there she had stayed. Perhaps she never really wanted to get to England. After all, Richard was allegedly bisexual – a hermit had once warned him to 'remember the destruction of Sodom, and abstain from illicit acts', but the warning had been in vain. It was never a happy marriage for this neglected queen: she retired to a nunnery and spent the rest of her life caring for abandoned children and helping the poor.

After the ceremony in Winchester cathedral, Richard and the various notables processed back to his chamber in St Swithun's monastery. He exchanged his heavy crown and robes for lighter ones, and then they all tucked into a vast celebratory banquet in the monks' refectory. The following month Richard set sail for France and was never seen in England again.

JOHN

Reigned 1199–1216, crowned 27 May 1199, aged 31

'Lackland' Fails To Take The Holy Bread and Wine

Traditionally, historians have always given King John a rough ride. A near-contemporary chronicler, Matthew Paris, did not mince his words: 'Foul as it is, hell itself is defiled by the presence of King John.' Stories abound of his cruelty and selfishness – but at least he did try to govern England and improve its defences in appallingly difficult circumstances, which is more than can be said of his brother, Richard the Lionheart. John was the youngest of the eight children of Henry II and Eleanor of Aquitaine, so, as he came last, he was given none of the family wealth: he lacked money; he lacked land, hence his nickname 'Lackland.'

When a well-aimed arrow killed his elder brother King Richard, John was determined not to miss his chance, so despite the fact that he wasn't necessarily the next in line to the throne, he was naturally delighted when the elder statesmen of the country, including the Archbishop of Canterbury, agreed after some discussion, that they should offer him the crown. The alternative claimant was Arthur of Brittany, son of John's elder brother Geoffrey. The decision in John's favour was a near thing, so naturally one of the first things John felt he had to do, after his coronation, was to have his nephew Arthur murdered. Some say he did the deed himself.

John had already been married for ten years to a wealthy heiress, Isabella of Gloucester, when he came to be crowned, but he had no use for her now. They had had no children, but he had her money. So, although he was still married, John had himself crowned alone, and Isabella's existence was ignored. He soon divorced her.

Little is known of King John's coronation. The fact that it was an elective succession rather than a strictly hereditary one gave rise to argument and protest. The Archbishop of York absented himself, and the bishop of Durham protested on his behalf that the Archbishop of Canterbury was going ahead with the ceremony without him. Reportedly, the Archbishop of Canterbury even addressed the congregation to stress the fact that John had been elected – but whether Matthew Paris was embellishing history in recording this will never be known. It is, nevertheless, interesting to see in this the beginnings of a constitutional monarchy, especially in view of the future restraints which Magna Carta would impose on the king.

In the coronation ceremony itself, a new tradition was begun. As a reward for the help given to John by the Cinque Ports in his constant journeying to and from Normandy, the five Barons of the Cinque Ports were granted the honour of carrying the canopy over the king as he entered Westminster Abbey, and also to hold it over him when he was unclothed for the process of anointing. This honour has belonged to the Barons of the Cinque Ports at every coronation since. The 'Cinque Ports' (the name is simply the French *cinq* meaning five) were the five Kent and Sussex seaports of Hastings, Sandwich, Dover, Romney and Hythe, which were given special privileges in recognition of the fact that they provided ships and men for the defence of the English Channel. Winchelsea and Rye were added to the number later, but 'Cinque' never changed to 'Sept'.

Afterwards, there was the customary banquet in Westminster Hall. John was fond of his food, and it would be partly due to gluttony that he would die, seventeen years later. However, the conversation at the table, behind John's back, must have centred on the fact that he had declined to partake of the holy bread and wine during the coronation service. This omission was tantamount to an open display of Godlessness. What sort of a reign would this new king inflict upon them? People must have wondered at the truculent wickedness of such outrageous behaviour.

ISABELLA OF ANGOULÊME, QUEEN OF JOHN

Dates as Queen 1200–16, crowned 8 October 1200, aged 13 or 14

A Teenager Becomes Queen of England

John met Isabella in France when she was about twelve, and he quickly made it plain to her father, Count Audemar of Angoulême, that he was going to marry her. Of course, she immediately gave up the lover she wanted to marry: no one argued with John. In those days girls were indispensable commodities to help settle political differences or form alliances, and this was an area in France – a fiefdom nominally under John's control – that was constantly giving trouble.

All the same, Isabella seems to have been an exceptionally nubile youngster. The pair were married in Angoulême in August 1200, and people wryly observed that for a while John's lifestyle underwent a remarkable change and he seldom got out of bed until noon. A somewhat shocked Victorian historian moralised that 'his young queen shared some of this blame, as the enchantress who kept him chained in her bowers of luxury.'

After a honeymoon in Normandy they returned to England at the end of September, and almost immediately afterwards, on 8 October, Isabella was given a separate coronation, crowned Queen of England. It has been said that John's treatment of his first wife created as much public hostility as George IV's treatment of his wife Queen Caroline, so Isabella's public appearance cannot have been easy for her. The coronation itself was not an elaborate affair – for despite his infatuation, John was not keen to spend out unnecessarily.

Some of the accounts relating to the event have survived. Three cloaks of fine linen, one of scarlet cloth, and one long grey mantle were provided for her at the modest cost of £12 5*s* 4*d*. It may be argued that this sum represents much more in modern currency, but when we find that a chorister was paid £1 5*s* for singing the hymn *Christus vicit* 'at the unction and crowning of the said lady queen', or that someone else was paid £1 13*s* simply for spreading rushes on the floor of Westminster Hall for the banquet afterwards, we can realise that relatively speaking Isabella's coronation clothes were not considered much of a priority. However, the ceremony passed off without any untoward incident, and now that she was anointed and crowned, Isabella was ready to face the future as England's queen. Her life was to prove full of incident, and she was destined to play an alarmingly central role in the next coronation to take place in England.

HENRY III

Reigned 1216–72, crowned at Gloucester 28 October 1216,
crowned in Westminster Abbey 17 May 1220, aged 9

A Child Crowned in Desperate Haste

Henry III was only nine years old when his father, King John, died unexpectedly, possibly from food poisoning. Many believed that it was a deliberate poisoning. Politically, the country was in chaos. John had been travelling around East Anglia, struggling to gain the upper hand over the rebellious barons, and he had suffered the miserable indignity of losing virtually all his treasure as wagon-loads of bullion and jewellery sank in boggy marshes near the North Sea.

John was already suffering from dysentery as he arrived at Swineshead Abbey in Lincolnshire, and he was foolish enough to indulge himself too freely on the monks' hospitality there, gorging himself on peaches and new cider. Sick and depressed, he dragged himself on to Newark in Nottinghamshire. Realising he was mortally sick, perhaps even poisoned, he just managed to dictate his will, asking to be buried in Worcester Cathedral, near St Wulfstan, his favourite saint, before he died, aged only forty-nine.

His Queen, Isabella of Angoulême, was in Gloucester at the time of John's death. She was now about twenty-nine, and had five children to look after, the eldest of whom, the nine-year-old Prince Henry, was now king. Unfortunately, however, it wasn't quite as obvious as all that to everyone. The fact is, London was occupied and being ruled by the French.

The barons had become so fed up with John's chaotic rule that in despair they had invited Louis Capet, son of King Philip II of France, to come and take over as king. Louis had arrived with an army and settled into London and Winchester. In effect there was civil war, aggravated by a Scottish invasion deep into England, and it was debatable whether the barons, the French, or John himself had been in control of the country when he died.

This then was the fraught background to young Henry III's first coronation. It says much for his mother Isabella's swift presence of mind that Henry was crowned at all. He was not in London; no crown was available; and there was not an archbishop in sight. Nevertheless, with swift decisiveness Isabella ordered that Prince Henry should be proclaimed king in the streets of Gloucester and sent her younger son, Richard, then aged seven, to Ireland to keep him out of harm's way – he was next in line to the throne if anything should happen to Henry – and then, just nine days after the death of King John, she organised a hasty coronation in the Benedictine Abbey at Gloucester (now the cathedral).

Peter de Roches, Bishop of Winchester, undertook to crown the young boy, but he drew the line at anointing him as this would have infringed the rights of the Archbishop of Canterbury. A problem arose over the crown, as John had probably lost it in the mud-flats of Lincolnshire, and King Edward's Crown was a hundred miles away, locked up in Westminster Abbey. But there was no time to waste, so Isabella lent one of her own pieces of jewellery, either a chaplet – (a head garland), or perhaps it was a golden collar and Henry was, at least provisionally, crowned.

Solemnly, the nine-year-old swore the oath, that he would 'give honour, peace and reverence to God and His Holy Church all the days of his life'. Then he swore to show justice to the people committed to him and destroy evil laws and unjust customs. However, rather more controversially, he paid homage to the most holy Roman Church and to Pope Innocent for the kingdoms of England and Ireland and undertook faithfully to continue to pay the pope the thousand marks per annum which his father had promised to do.

This last promise was political dynamite. King John, his father, had tried to outmanoeuvre the barons by 'giving' England to the pope and then buying it back again at a fixed yearly sum. It was an outrageous agreement to put into the little king's speech, especially as he probably hardly knew what he was saying. The citizens of Gloucester were somewhat dubious about what was happening. There were divided opinions. Those who were loyal wore white crosses, cut in cloth and pinned on their clothes, or else they were asked to wear chaplets themselves, to signify that they agreed the king really was crowned. How many of them owned chaplets? There can't have been many. For a nine-year-old, this must have been an exciting and rather frightening period, but of course there were plenty of people ready to take up the reins of power and tell him what to do and what to say.

The Crown of St Edward Reappears

When eventually the French were persuaded to leave England and go back home, Henry made his state entry into London. At last, England now had its own king again. It was obvious to all that it was time to give him a proper coronation, now that things were getting back to normal. So it was on that Whit Sunday 1220, Henry III came to Westminster Abbey for his second crowning. He was now aged twelve, growing up and by now quite used to being king. However, he was growing up without his mother, for Isabella of Angoulême had left England within a year of that difficult first coronation in Gloucester. She went back to live in her native part of France, where she married the man she had been forced to give up so many years before, when King John had intruded into her life.

Henry, then, was maturing fast, but it must have been a lonely existence, so he immersed himself deeply in his historical and artistic pursuits. Enlarging and embellishing Westminster Abbey was to be his life's work. When he died in 1272 the abbey had been changed almost beyond recognition thanks to his patronage, and his enthusiasm for honouring the memory of his favourite saint, Edward the Confessor, resulted in the creation of a magnificent shrine, which was the wonder of Christendom when it was completed.

Even at the tender age of twelve, Henry was already beginning his great task of rebuilding Westminster Abbey, but as he grew older he actively supported a host of other church building projects, such as the construction of Salisbury Cathedral, which had begun only one month before this second coronation. By the end of his life he proved himself to have been one of the greatest patrons of church architecture that England has ever known, though he had a poor reputation as a king.

Henry was anointed and crowned with 'a crown of pure gold adorned with precious stones' at his second coronation by Stephen Langton, one of the greatest of all medieval archbishops of Canterbury, whose name had headed the list of John's counsellors in the preamble to Magna Carta. Also present at his coronation was the great theologian and universal sage, Robert Grosseteste, later to become Bishop of Lincoln. Henry took the opportunity to ask him an unusually difficult question: 'What was the precise grace wrought in a King by the unction?' It was an esoteric enquiry by a precocious youngster. Grosseteste hesitated before he replied, and then came up with his answer: that it was 'the sign of the King's special reception of the sevenfold gifts of the Spirit, as in Confirmation'. Whatever the answer, certainly the question tells us much about the mentality of the new monarch – obviously a king for whom the niceties of theology were far more important than swashbuckling warfare.

During Henry III's reign, important changes were made to the coronation regalia, partly as a result of his concern to enlarge Westminster Abbey and provide a new shrine for its saint, Edward the Confessor. The Confessor, who had founded the abbey, had been buried there within days of its completion. It was not until 1163 that he was canonised and at that ceremony his relics were translated to another more elaborate tomb. However, Henry III was determined to provide a shrine of unparalleled magnificence for his saintly predecessor, who was venerated as the Patron Saint of England. This involved yet another translation of St Edward's bones, in 1269, after many years of work on the new shrine.

Importantly, and associated with this growing cult of St Edward, the Confessor's ancient regalia was brought out at this time for future use. Quite how this happened is somewhat obscure. One supposition is that on opening the Confessor's tomb, it was discovered that he had been buried with his crown, and this was now brought out for future coronations. Another explanation may be that when the Confessor died, his crown and other coronation ornaments were hidden away by the monks as precious relics. From this time onwards there were *two* distinct sets of regalia: St Edward's Regalia, for use only at the coronation ceremony; and the Royal Regalia, for use partly at coronations but also on other state occasions. In the history of coronations, therefore, the reign of Henry III has particular importance. Although he was crowned twice, Henry was the last monarch *not* to have been crowned with 'St Edward's Crown' – but in his veneration for the Confessor he made it possible for all his successors to be crowned with it.

ELEANOR OF PROVENCE, QUEEN OF HENRY III

Dates as Queen 1236–72, crowned 26 January 1236, aged 14

Extravagance and Luxury for a Young Queen

Henry was twenty-eight when he married Eleanor – just twice her age. He had tried to find himself a wife for quite a while: in fact had been turned down no fewer than five times by other prospective brides, but at last his younger brother suggested Eleanor, who was reputed to be beautiful and intelligent. She was certainly well connected, for her elder sister was Queen of France. Henry was delighted, and did his best to make her welcome when she arrived at Dover.

They were married in Canterbury within a few days of her arrival, on 4 January 1236, and then travelled on to London, where an elaborate and magnificent coronation was being planned for her. As they reached London they were met by 360 of the leading citizens of London 'clothed in long garments broidered about with gold . . . every man bearing golden or silver cups in his hand and the king's trumpeters before them sounding.' Thanks to Matthew Paris, a monk from St Albans, who was the official abbey chronicler, we have a detailed account of all the splendours of Eleanor's coronation – especially concerning the banquet held in Westminster Hall afterwards. He tells us of the 'profusion of dishes which furnished the table, the abundance of venison, the variety of fish, the diversity of wine, the gaiety of the jugglers, the comeliness of the attendants.' The good monk describes the streets of London hung with different-coloured silks, garlands and banners, and with lamps lighting them up by night. And these streets had actually been cleaned up – all the lumps of mud and filth which normally made the roads virtually impassable were scraped up for the occasion.

Henry was nothing if not lavish in his gifts, and spent enormous and extravagant amounts of money on jewellery, sumptuous clothes and redecorations in the Palace of Westminster in her honour. The jewellery alone cost nearly £30,000, for she was given no fewer than *nine* chaplets for her hair, made of gold filigree and clusters of precious stones. Her golden crown, also set with gems, was worth £1,500. As for Henry, he was dressed in a robe of golden tissue, so that, in the words of Matthew Paris, he 'glittered very gloriously'. Paris hardly mentions the service in Westminster Abbey, except to note that his own abbot took precedence over all the others. The actual crowning was performed by Edmund Rich, Archbishop of Canterbury, later to be canonised, whose name is still perpetuated by St Edmund Hall at Oxford.

After the coronation in the abbey the king and his newly-crowned queen walked to Westminster Hall upon a carpet of 'striped English burel' – i.e. fine felt – the longest carpet to have been seen in England up to that time. New luxuries were to be seen everywhere, and the celebrations lasted well into the following week, with eight days of jousting taking place in Tothill Fields.

It was quite clear to everyone that Henry was going over the top in trying to please his teenage bride. In fact, he used up all his treasury in gifts and banquets which seemed to go on and on incessantly. When at last he asked the lords for a thirtieth part of all his subjects' property to help get out of of his financial difficulties, they told him quite bluntly that 'they had amply supplied funds both for his marriage, and that of the empress (Henry's sister's wedding) and as he had wasted the money, he might defray the expenses of his wedding as he could.'

Henry III's spendthrift lifestyle was demonstrated as never before in this coronation, and it was inevitable that Eleanor's own initial popularity soon disappeared, as she was associated with her husband's extravagance. In fact she became one of the most hated of all the queens of England, with a reputation for being proud and grasping. In one incident, later in her life, the disgruntled citizens pelted her boat with mud and garbage as she was rowed under London Bridge. The mob yelled at her: 'Down with the witch! Let's drown her!' Little wonder that when Henry died after his long reign of fifty-six years she retired to a nunnery, living out her days in Amesbury Abbey, near Stonehenge, in Wiltshire, where it is said that she 'despised the withering flower of this world'. Perhaps by then she had learned her lesson about extravagance. It was a sad end to a life which was so happy and filled with such promise on her coronation day.

EDWARD I AND ELEANOR OF CASTILE

Reigned 1272–1307, crowned 18 August 1274, aged 35

Feastings Galore and Horses For Free

Edward's coronation was a wildly popular event. It was the first time that an English king and queen were crowned together. They were both young and well-liked; the succession was secure; and there was more than a touch of devil-may-care extravagance in the festivities which took place over many days.

The royal couple were abroad in Sicily, coming back from a crusade in the Holy Land, when they heard that they had succeeded to the throne. The story goes that two successive messengers came to them, each bringing bad news from England. The first told them that their son and heir, Prince John, aged only five, had died. The second told them that Edward's father, the ageing Henry III, had died. They were being entertained by Charles of Anjou at the time, who was astonished by Edward's different reactions to these two deaths: the loss of his young son left him quite unperturbed, but the loss of his father left him inconsolably grief-stricken.

Charles asked why he had been so calm to hear of his son's death, but so upset to hear of his father's. Edward replied that though it was easy enough to beget further sons, 'when a man has lost a good father, it is not in the course of nature for God to send him another.' In the event, it was not quite so easy as he supposed: Eleanor was to bear him fourteen children in all, but the son to succeed him, the future Edward II, was the fourteenth child – and the only son to survive.

One would have imagined that on hearing of the death of Henry, Edward and Eleanor would have quickly hurried back to England to claim their thrones, but in fact they took their time over their return. Clearly, Edward was confident that England was his, and without danger of rebellion. After all, he had already beaten off and killed his enemy Simon de Montfort, and he enjoyed a formidable reputation for military skill and toughness. In such circumstances, further rebellion was unlikely. The leisurely way in which they returned to England is quite remarkable. Eleanor even had time to produce another son, Alphonso,[†] named after her brother, before they finally arrived.

It was not until 2 August 1274 that Edward and Eleanor, together with nine-month-old baby Alphonso, finally landed at Dover, and seventeen days later they were crowned by Edward Kilwardby, Archbishop of Canterbury. Preparations must have been intense, for the feastings and celebrations that were laid on for them had never before been seen on such a scale in England. Old Palace and New Palace Yards in Westminster were filled with wooden, improvised buildings to serve as temporary kitchens, open at the roof so as to let the smoke of the cooking-fires escape. An enormous amount of food was prepared: 440 cows and oxen, 430 sheep, 450 pigs, 16 fat boars, 278 flitches of bacon, 22,460 'capons and other poultry' had been ordered as far back as February, when rumour had it that the king and queen were on their way. As Edward and his wife rode into London every street was hung with rich cloth-of-gold, arras and tapestry. It was reported that the aldermen and burgesses threw handfuls of gold and silver out of their windows to show how pleased they were to see them back in England, and the conduits ran with white and red wine, 'that each creature might drink his fill.'

This coronation was the first to take place in the newly-enlarged Westminster Abbey, an enterprise which had been the life-time preoccupation of Edward's father, Henry III, and the first to use

---

[†] Alphonso died in August 1284, aged ten, just four months after his brother the future Edward II had been born. England was destined to have no King Alphonso. Edward II was the only surviving son of Edward and Eleanor.

the ancient crown of Edward the Confessor since before the conquest.

By far the most extraordinary and exciting feature of this coronation, in most people's memories, happened at the coronation feast. King Alexander III of Scotland arrived to pay his respects, accompanied by an entourage of a hundred knights, all on well-harnessed horses. Astonishing everyone, after they had dismounted, these Scottish knights set their horses free and allowed anyone who could catch one to keep it as a gift! Naturally there was a mad free-for-all as people scrambled to find free horses for themselves. Equally remarkably, this gesture by the Scottish knights triggered off a chain-reaction of generosity among the English nobles; first the king's brother, then the Earl of Gloucester, and then the Earl of Pembroke and the Earl of Warenne followed suit and gave up their own horses – and a hundred English knights all relinquished theirs as well! In the end, the mad fighting for free horses must have led to many a bloody tussle. What the English and Scottish knights must have felt when they woke up sober the next day to realise that they had given away their horses is not recorded. In our own times it would have been comparable to throwing their car-keys into the midst of a rabble. As for the common people, even those who did not manage to get horses enjoyed a fortnight of free food, as the royal kitchens continued to serve up daily banquets to all and sundry for the next two weeks.

King Alexander of Scotland was related by marriage to Edward I, and relations were still cordial. However, the keen-eyed Edward noted with anger that Llewellyn ap Gruffyd of Wales had absented himself from this coronation, and quickly sent a sharp message to him to demand why he had not come to pay homage to himself and Eleanor. Clearly, once the coronation jollifications were over, some serious business needed to be done.

Edward's grief was great when Eleanor died in 1290, quite suddenly, in the little Nottinghamshire village of Harby, on her way north to support him in his Scottish campaigns. The beautiful series of 'Eleanor Crosses' which he erected at the twelve stopping-places of her body as it was carried back to Westminster give testimony to this great royal partnership. Nine years later he married Margaret of France. They were married in Canterbury Cathedral and from there they travelled up to London. Margaret

The Origins of the Stone of Scone

Before Edward I stole it from Scotland in 1296, the Stone of Scone – otherwise known as the Stone of Destiny – had been used in coronations for a long time. It is by far the oldest object connected with British coronations, and no one knows the full truth of its ancient past.

Legend tells of how this was the stone on which Jacob rested his head and had the vision of angels ascending and descending the ladder to heaven, as described in Genesis 28:11. According to the legend the stone was carried successively to Egypt, Sicily, Spain, and eventually to Ireland, where it was thrown on the seashore as an anchor. Then it became the *Lia Fail*, or Stone of Destiny, on which the kings of Ireland were crowned on the sacred Hill of Tara. Apparently, if the new king was a false pretender it would let out a thunderous groan.

The story continues that Fergus Mor mac Erc, a founder of the Scottish monarchy, took the stone to Dunstaffnage in Argyll. Here fable merges imperceptibly with history when Kenneth MacAlpin moved the centre of his kingdom from Dalraida, and established the stone in Scone, where he was crowned king of Scotia in AD 843. For the next 400 years all subsequent kings of Scotland were crowned on it.

By the end of the thirteenth century the Stone of Scone had acquired such a mystique that anyone who wished to conquer the Scots would need to remove this ancient symbol of their past. Edward I, the Hammer of the Scots, seized the stone and took it in triumph to Westminster when he deposed John Balliol in 1296.

Edward was delighted with his prize and planned to incorporate it within a bronze chair. However, in the end he ordered Master William Durham to design and construct the present oak chair at a cost of 100s. It was completed in about 1300, and the precious stone was set in the place that it would occupy for the next 700 years.

was given a great welcome as she entered the capital: wine again flowed from the conduits, and cloths of gold hung from the windows along her route. However, Edward was still far too preoccupied with his never-ending Scottish campaigns to give her the coronation she might have hoped for.

EDWARD II AND ISABELLA OF FRANCE

Reigned 1307–27, crowned 25 February 1308, aged 23

The Stone of Scone is Used for the First Time in England

There had been no love lost between Edward I and his son. One of the main causes of contention was young Edward's infatuation with his homosexual lover, Piers Gaveston. 'I do not remember to have heard that one man so loved another,' wrote one chronicler of Edward II's relationship with Gaveston. Indeed, such was the hold that his Gascon partner had over the young king that people were beginning to think that Piers must have been a sorcerer.

Surprisingly, despite this attachment, and only six months after his father's death, Edward II married Isabella, daughter of Philip III of France. She was just sixteen at the time, and could hardly be aware of the embarrassing and tumultuous life she was about to lead as she came to England to be crowned as Edward's queen. Certainly, she would have been surprised to know that she would be come to be known as the 'She-Wolf of France.'

Piers Gaveston had been banished from England by Edward I, who could barely conceal his contempt for him. However, one of the first acts of Edward II, after his father's death, was not merely to bring Gaveston back, but to honour him by creating him Earl of Cornwall. To bestow such an honour on so worthless an upstart deeply shocked the nobility. It was especially shocking because this title traditionally belonged to members of the royal household – indeed even today the Duchy of Cornwall is held by the present Prince of Wales. Worse was to come. When Edward went to France in January 1308 to marry Isabella in Boulogne cathedral, he appointed Gaveston as his regent! As has been pointed out many times, if

Edward had deliberately set out to alienate his lords he could hardly have done it more successfully. Their lordships were incensed at the ennoblement of such a posturing nobody.

Edward married on 25 January 1308. One month later, on 25 February, having brought his bride back to England, he arranged to be crowned, together with Isabella, in Westminster Abbey. However, since the Archbishop of Canterbury was in exile, banished by Edward I, the officiating prelate who crowned Edward and Isabella was Henry Woodlock, Bishop of Winchester. (The feelings of the Archbishop of York are not recorded.) Edward II's coronation was a complete disaster from start to finish, almost exclusively because of Piers Gaveston, who had been placed in charge of the event. By now the members of the king's council were at boiling-point, incensed at having to take second place to him. On the day of the coronation, just before the service, they met in high dudgeon. And in the very presence of Edward and Isabella they threw down an ultimatum: unless Edward were to banish Gaveston forthwith, they would all boycott the coronation and refuse to attend.

It must have been a tense moment. Edward had to think quickly. If the coronation did not take place properly, with the requisite oaths of allegiance paid to him, there would be open rebellion throughout the country. His somewhat evasive response was that if they would allow the coronation to continue he would promise to obey the next parliament. Somewhat mollified, the council agreed. So it was against this background of near-revolution that the coronation went ahead. And what a shambles it was!

Piers Gaveston, dazzlingly dressed in purple clothes sewn with costly pearls, took first place. His ostentatious finery eclipsed everyone. To universal indignation, and despite the opposition of the nobility, Edward had appointed him to carry, on a velvet cushion, the sacred Crown of St Edward – the most important piece of the regalia, and he was further given the honour of clipping the ceremonial spur upon the King's heel. One of the earls present was so outraged by all this that he had to be restrained from slaying Gaveston there and then, even within the abbey itself. The crowds, pushing and shoving to get a better sight of what was going on, didn't make things any easier. In fact a brick wall in the abbey was completely pushed over, crushing a knight, Sir John Bakewell, who was trodden to death in the mad scramble.

Isabella must have been horrified to witness all this. But what was most personally upsetting to her was to see Gaveston actually wearing some of the jewellery which had been given to Edward as a part of her dowry. Her father, King Philip III of France, had presented a huge amount of costly rings, brooches, jewels and precious heirlooms to Edward at the time of their marriage, just a month before. It was now plain to everyone that her new husband was insulting both herself and her father by publicly bestowing these on his beloved favourite. Accompanying Isabella as guests to the coronation were many nobles and members of the French court, including two of her uncles, Charles, Count of Valois and Louis de Clermont, Count of Evreux. They too were deeply offended by the transfer of jewellery to Gaveston, and quickly reported these insults to Isabella's father when they returned home.

After this unsatisfactory ceremony in Westminster Abbey a successful coronation banquet would have been one way of sending the guests away in better spirits, but as the day wore on it was clear to everyone that Gaveston's organisational skills were minimal. The coronation did not finish until three o'clock in the afternoon. Everyone was getting hungry and irritable. But even when they got to Westminster Hall no food appeared until well after dark; and when, at last, it did arrive on the tables it was found to be badly cooked. The meat was either raw or boiled to a tasteless pulp and the sweet dishes were declared unfit to eat. In these circumstances most of the food was left untouched. Queen Isabella was devastated, and wrote home in disgust.

This was probably the worst coronation in our history, but one new element was introduced into the ceremony that would henceforth be repeated at all subsequent English crownings, for it was at this event that the Scottish 'Stone of Scone' or 'Stone of Destiny' was first used. Edward's father, later nicknamed the 'Hammer of the Scots', had seized this symbolic prize in 1296 during one of his many attempts to subdue Scotland. His orders had been that this should be 'transported to London as a sign that the kingdom had been renounced and conquered'. He had arranged for the stone to

be incorporated into a specially-made throne, and now, twelve
years later, it was making its first appearance in the English
coronation ceremony.

EDWARD III

Reigned 1327–77, crowned 29 January 1327, aged 14

A Fourteen-Year-Old Takes Over After a Forced Abdication

The position of the monarchy at the coronation of the teenager
Edward III was precarious to say the least. Edward's father,
Edward II, had become so unpopular and had ruled so badly that
on 20 January 1327 he had been made to listen to a catalogue of
his misdemeanours and forced to abdicate. Now, just nine days
later, his fourteen-year-old son was crowned in Westminster Abbey
in a service which, perhaps understandably, lacked much of the
usual pomp and ceremony. Circumstances were far from normal.
After all, the new king's father was still alive, locked up as a
prisoner in Kenilworth Castle.

No English king had been made to abdicate before. Arguably,
the nobles who had forced the issue were guilty of treason and
Edward III, the newly-crowned youngster, was a usurper. The
transfer of power, therefore, was a delicate matter. Just two
days before his coronation Edward III had issued a
proclamation which he must have known to be utterly false,
stating that his father had abdicated 'of his own good will and
by common consent of the prelates, earls, barons and other
nobles, and the community of the realm'.

However, as the nobles knew full well, Edward II's departure
was not the result 'of his own good will'. In fact the events
leading to Edward II's deposition culminated in a scene of
unparalleled humiliation for any English king. It took place in
Kenilworth Castle, where Edward was being held prisoner. A
group of twelve commissioners, comprised of nobles and
churchmen, held a kind of ceremonial court. Adam Orleton,
Bishop of Hereford, acted as their leader and spokesman and
he demanded the king's abdication, requiring him to deliver up
his crown, sceptre and the rest of the regalia into their hands.

Edward burst into floods of tears as Orleton harangued him, listing all his faults and failings.

Significantly, Bishop Orleton spelled out the conditions which they were intending to impose on him. Edward could either agree to go, in which case they would allow his son (the future Edward III) to succeed to the throne; or, if he refused to go, they would choose someone else, outside the royal blood-line. Edward fainted, he lay stretched out on the floor 'as one dead'. Whether he was just pretending or not no one can say. The Earl of Leicester and the Bishop of Winchester managed to bring him back to some degree of consciousness, whereupon Orleton continued relentlessly to press him to abdicate. Eventually Edward withdrew to another room and when he returned, dramatically dressed in black, he ceremonially handed over the regalia. (Edward II was murdered in Berkeley Castle later that year.)

Such was the background of Edward III's coronation. His mother, by now the former Queen Isabella, pretended to weep throughout the coronation ceremony. But she had long since been estranged from his father and was openly living with her lover, Roger Mortimer, Earl of March. Clearly the nobles, Queen Isabella and above all Roger Mortimer were eagerly anticipating a situation in which they would be the ruling powers behind the throne. A fourteen-year-old king is always a sure recipe for political intrigue.

The Archbishop of Canterbury, Walter Reynolds, helped to assuage any uneasy consciences. He preached to the general assembly convened in Westminster Abbey to discuss the transfer of power, using the somewhat dubious text, *Vox populi vox Dei* (the voice of the people is the voice of God). Finally, to reassure anyone who might still have any doubts, medals were struck and thrown into the crowd. On one side young Edward III was shown resting on a cushion of hearts, with the inscription *He gives laws to a willing people:* and on the other side was a hand taking a crown falling from heaven, with the inscription *Non rapit sed accipit* – 'He does not snatch it – he receives it.' Even then, public relations were important. As the French historian Jean Froissart put it, 'as it was agreed by all the nobles, so it was accomplished. And then was crowned with a crown royal at the palace of Westminster beside London, the young King Edward the Third, who in his days after was right fortunate and happy in arms.' A sense of wariness and conspiracy, however, must have hung over this coronation.

PHILIPPA OF HAINAULT, CONSORT OF EDWARD III

Married 24 January 1328, crowned March 1330, aged 16

A Quiet Coronation for a Pregnant Teenager

Philippa of Hainault was the daughter of Count William of Hainault, in Flanders – no connection with Hainault Forest in Essex. She seems to have been a good-looking youngster, tall and fair-complexioned. Everyone spoke well of her. She was to make a splendid consort and bore her husband twelve children. Edward III had married her just a year after he had come to the throne and they had had a brilliant wedding at York. Edward was fifteen and Philippa still only thirteen.

At the time of their marriage the young king and his bride were still very much under the dominance of his mother and Roger Mortimer. Edward was biding his time, growing in self-confidence and waiting for the opportunity to seize real power for himself. It seems strange that Philippa should have to wait for two years before being crowned, but the probable reason was that Mortimer and Isabella were too preoccupied with other matters, and in any case they had run out of money. Even in 1330 the coronation seems to have been a muted affair. Perhaps it was arranged at that time because Philippa was pregnant with her first baby, due to be born in three months' time. It would be good to get the coronation over with before she gave birth. Apart from the fact that she was crowned by Simon Meopham, Archbishop of Canterbury, there are few records about this coronation. After all, Philippa was only a girl, and Isabella and Mortimer were not inclined to waste money unnecessarily.

However, one curious document relating to the coronation has survived. It states that Robert de Vere, Earl of Oxford, being hereditary chamberlain to the queens of England, therefore had the traditional right to be given the bed in which the queen had slept, her shoes, and three silver basins, one in which she washed her head and two others in which she washed her hands. No similar record exists, so one begins to wonder whether someone was simply trying his luck with the young Flemish queen. After all, she would hardly be able to query the genuineness of such a claim. No one knows whether the good earl managed to get his silver basins. So Philippa was crowned. Three months later she duly gave birth to a baby boy who would grow up to become the Black Prince.

RICHARD II

Reigned 1377–99, crowned 16 July 1377, aged 10

A Boy-King Falls Asleep

More than fifty years had elapsed since the last king had been crowned – Richard's grandfather, Edward III. The Black Prince, Richard II's father, had died just a year before, probably of cancer, thus leaving the succession to his ten-year-old son. Obviously, the boy-king was very much a puppet in the hands of his mother, Joan of Kent, and all his many uncles and cousins.

England had developed greatly in many ways in the fifty-year reign of Edward III, and record-keeping was much more systematic. Contemporary accounts of Richard II's coronation, therefore, give us the fullest description of any coronation up to this time. Also, thanks to Edward III, a sense of royal grandeur and public ceremony had become much more pronounced; for example, the Knights of the Garter were now established. One of Westminster Abbey's most precious documents, the *Liber Regalis* – the Royal Book – written by an Abbot of Westminster, Nicholas Littlington, was used for this occasion. This beautifully illuminated volume is the 'Book of the Royal Offices to be performed and observed according to the use of the Royal Church of Westminster.' It is quite small, with just thirty-eight leaves of vellum, and apart from the actual text it contains four elaborately-worked illluminations on a ground of burnished gold with scrolls, showing the crowning of a king, the crowning of a king and a queen consort, the crowning of a queen, and finally a king lying in state. The *Liber Regalis* is of crucial importance in the history of coronations as it prescribes the order of service in the greatest detail. It has been the basis of all coronations from that time to the present and is believed to have set the standard in France as well. A comparison between Nicholas Littlington's Order for the Coronation Service used at the crowning of Richard II in the fourteenth century and that of Elizabeth II in the twentieth century shows very few changes, apart from the language used.

However, the celebrations marking Richard's coronation included several innovations. For the ordinary citizens of London, perhaps the most important of these was the cavalcade from the Tower of London – a huge and jolly affair which was greatly enjoyed by everyone along the route from the Tower to Westminster, and which became a feature of all subsequent coronations for several centuries to come. The tradition grew up that the king or queen who was due to be crowned would stay at the Tower for a few days beforehand, and then make a triumphant progress to Westminster through the crowded streets on the day before the coronation itself.

In 1377 Richard must have enjoyed being the centre of attention as he rode bareheaded on a white charger under a canopy of blue velvet carried on silver poles by eight knights in armour. He had long golden hair and was dressed completely in white – the colour of innocence. It was a glorious morning in July and all the buildings along the route were hung with decorations, painted cloths, cloths-of-gold, cloths of silver, flags and tapestries. Ropes were strung across the streets to carry colourful banners. Conduits ran with wine, and opposite Foster Lane a kind of castle was constructed with four turrets surrounding a dome in the centre. In each turret stood a little girl aged ten – the same age as Richard himself – and as he passed by the girls blew showers of gold leaf down upon him and sprinkled imitation gold florins under his horse's hooves. Having emptied their baskets of florins they ran down from the towers and presented Richard with wine from a golden goblet. Then, to everyone's astonishment, a mechanical gilt angel appeared from out of the dome, holding a crown above the future king.

Trumpets blared as the procession continued on its way down Fleet Street as other spectacles were awaiting them. A giant Hercules, complete with mace, wished the king health and strength. As they reached Temple Bar they were entertained by a dancing spectacle by men wearing animal masks of bears, wolves, lions and leopards. Oddly enough, seated on a rock in the middle of all this was a boy dressed with a tiger-skin round his loins, representing John the Baptist. Nearby was another boy sleeping with his head on a closed book and with a lamb at his side, supposed to be representing the holy Christ-child. Even more oddly, the goddess Minerva then appeared, delivered a speech on the repression of injustice to the young king, and finally presented him, in the city's name, with a golden tablet bearing a representation of the crucifixion. Such were the bustling jollifications. And from this time onwards the citizens of London produced similar and even more spectacular pageants to entertain their future sovereigns as they processed along the customary route from the Tower to be crowned at Westminster. Having arrived at Westminster, Richard was given a ceremonial bath, symbolically washing away sins and impurities. Newly-created knights were also given baths before dressing themselves and accompanying the king to his palace.

The following day, at the coronation itself, Richard wore shirt and tunic with special slits in them for the anointing. He was met at the door of the abbey by the clergy, and then, barefooted, he walked over a carpet of striped worsted towards the high altar while a canopy was borne above his head by the Barons of the Cinque Ports. It was a long ceremony. The Bishop of Rochester delivered a sermon in which he warned Richard about excessive taxation; the oath was administered; Archbishop Simon Sudbury asked him whether he would keep the laws of the country, defend the church, and be just in his judgements; another bishop asked him if he would defend the privileges of bishops and abbots; and of course the young king promised everything required of him. After all, he had a Council of State who would deal with all this, and it probably meant very little to him. Then came the consecration, at which standing behind a curtain of cloth-of-gold, Richard was anointed on six places, as the slits in his specially-made shirt were opened: on his hands, his breast, shoulders, back, elbows and head. Now came the time for all the insignia of royalty to be solemnly produced and given to the newly-anointed king: the alb, the tunicle, buskins, spurs, sword, armilla, the imperial mantle, and the crown of St Edward. Next, the thrice-blessed ring. Then the sword *Curtana* was ungirt and Richard offered it to the altar. It was redeemed by John of Gaunt for 100s, who then carried it naked before the king for the rest of the ceremony. The final moments had arrived for Richard to be given the rod and sceptre. He kissed the bishops, and at last, to the accompaniment of a sung *Te Deum* he was lifted on to the throne built by his great-great-grandfather, Edward I. It had been placed on a raised platform in the centre of the abbey, at the crossing of the transepts and nave.

Richard was so exhausted by all this that after it was over he could hardly keep his eyes open. He had to be carried, fast asleep, out of the abbey by his tutor, Simon Burley. In the process, one of the ceremonial slippers fell off his royal foot and was lost for ever.

Yet another innovation at the coronation of Richard II was the appearance of Sir John Dymoke as the king's champion. The office of champion was not new, as we have already seen that the Marmion family had been champions to the Dukes of Normandy, and a Marmion had held that office at the coronation of Matilda, wife of William the Conqueror. However, this was the first of many appearances of members of the Dymoke family as king's champion. In fact, Sir John Dymoke claimed the office because of his descent from the Marmions. Sir John had had to contest the right to be champion with Baldwin de Freville who also claimed descent from Marmion. Fortunately for him, Sir John Dymoke had won his cause, and from the coronation of Richard II to that of George IV various succeeding Dymokes duly fulfilled their ceremonial duty at English coronations. (Since then, Dymokes have continued to play a part in coronation ceremonies. At the coronation of Elizabeth II a Dymoke bore the Union Jack.)

On this first occasion Sir John apparently did not know quite when to make his challenge, so he decided to make a grand appearance just as everyone was coming out of the abbey. According to custom surrounding the office of champion, he was wearing the 'second best' suit of mail in the royal armoury and the 'best but one' horse from the royal stables. Thus suitably caparisoned he came, accompanied by his spear-bearer and his shield-bearer, waiting for the king and nobles to appear. One can imagine his discomfiture when the Earl Marshal told him to take his armour off and rest for a while and not to make his entry until later, during the coronation banquet. Rather deflated, he did as he was told.

Thus it was that at the coronation feast in Westminster Hall that he entered, fully armed and on horseback, escorted by the Earl Marshal and the High Constable, and dramatically threw down his gauntlet on the stone floor to challenge anyone who dared to dispute Richard's II's right to the throne. The herald returned the gauntlet to the champion, who then repeated the challenge twice in the centre of the hall before advancing to the royal dais, where the king greeted him. Later, it became the custom for the king to pledge his champion in a gold cup, which was then handed to him as his fee.

ANNE OF BOHEMIA, FIRST QUEEN OF RICHARD II

Married 20 January 1382, crowned 22 January 1382, aged 14

Chaucer is Present at These 'Mighty Feastings'

Anne was only fourteen when she came to England to marry Richard II, and he was only fifteen, having been king for five years, but still not old enough to rule. She came from Bohemia – now the Czech Republic – a distant country of whose very existence most people were totally unaware. This geographical ignorance was reciprocated by Anne's mother, widow of the Holy Emperor Charles IV, who actually sent an ambassador to inspect England before she would consent to the marriage of her daughter, to find out whether it was a suitable place for Anne to live. On hearing that it was acceptable, she gracefully gave her permission, and Anne was duly brought to England, bringing with her all kinds of fantastical fashions: those huge horned head-dresses which adorned ladies at court at this time; the rather curious and dangerous practice of riding side-saddle; astonishing shoes with long pointed turned-up toes; and strange and unheard-of new cuisine.

Richard and Anne, both teenagers, revelled in these exotic affectations and enjoyed a luxurious and ostentatious lifestyle throughout their marriage. Anne was given a magnificent coronation just two days after their wedding. She was crowned by William Courtenay, Archbishop of Canterbury who followed the order of service laid down in Abbot Littlington's newly-written *Liber Regalis*. By now the citizens of London were used to royal junketings and the wedding and coronation celebrations flowed into each other with 'mighty feastings', as Froissart records. Both Froissart and Chaucer were present to see the events for themselves.

However, far more memorable than any coronation feastings in the minds of Londoners was Anne's personal intervention in urging Richard to issue a general pardon to those who were still suffering reprisals after Wat Tyler's rebellion. The Peasants' Revolt of 1381 had led to barbarous executions on an unprecedented scale, and Anne's responsibility for granting this amnesty to mark the occasion of her coronation led her to be called 'good Queen Anne' for many years to come.

Their marriage was to last for twelve years and Anne was only twenty-eight when she died of the plague, childless, in her palace at Sheen, in present-day Richmond. She was given the most extraordinary funeral yet seen in the country. A vast sum was spent on wax candles and torches, specially imported from Flanders, and the roadways of Fleet Street, the Strand, and Charing Cross were flaming with light as the long procession passed along towards Westminster Abbey. All the peers and their wives were commanded to attend and to wear long-trained black cloaks and hoods. Her husband Richard was devastated at Anne's early death, but made the oddest choice of a second wife, Isabella, the seven-year-old daughter of King Charles VI of France. Once again, therefore, a child was to be at the centre of coronation celebrations.

ISABELLA OF VALOIS, SECOND QUEEN OF RICHARD II

Married 4 November 1396, crowned 8 January 1397, aged 8

An Exquisitely-Dressed Little Eight-Year-Old Becomes Queen

As one may well imagine, the entry of little Isabella into London to marry the king was marked by huge crowds who turned out in astonishment to welcome their new child-queen. In fact nine people were crushed to death on London Bridge as they scrambled to see her as she processed from Kennington to the Tower of London. She spent one night there and then the following morning her procession moved ceremonially to Westminster, where Richard was waiting to receive her.

It was, of course, a political marriage, and to mark the increased friendship between France and England Isabella brought a vast dowry of 800,000 francs in gold, to be paid in yearly instalments. She also brought a wardrobe of many rich clothes, and an immense collection of jewellery: coronets, rings, necklaces and clasps. Added to all this were heavy tapestries to decorate her rooms, embroidered with elaborate scenes of country life and shepherdesses.

A few months after the wedding, now aged eight, she was given a splendid coronation led by Thomas Arundel, Archbishop of Canterbury. However, always Isabella seems to have been merely an exquisite little pawn in the elaborate political chess-games of the times. She was to enjoy her status as queen-consort for less than three years before being widowed aged eleven and packed off back to France.

HENRY IV

Reigned 1399–1413, crowned 13 October 1399, aged 33

Uniquely Holy Oil Has a Remarkable Effect

As a usurper, crowned while Richard II was still alive and being kept prisoner in Pontefract Castle, Henry Bolingbroke, styling himself Henry IV, had every need to make his coronation as conspicuously correct and majestic as possible. Thomas Arundel, his archbishop, had formerly been archbishop during Richard II's reign and had crowned the little queen Isabella. However, he had fallen foul of Richard and had been impeached and banished to St Andrews where he became its bishop. Henry Bolingbroke quickly brought him back and reinstated him as Archbishop of Canterbury. Arundel therefore had the satisfaction of crowning him king.

Anniversaries and festal days were crucially important in the Middle Ages, so it was with solemn significance that Henry chose

THE 'KNIGHTS OF THE BATH'

A marvellously detailed and contemporary description of Henry IV's coronation was written by Jean Froissart, the French chronicler and poet.

Froissart was born in Valenciennes, Hainault, and as a young man he had served Queen Philippa as clerk of her chamber. He spent a lifetime in royal circles, serving the Black Prince in Aquitaine, visiting King David of Scotland and enjoying the hospitality of Richard II when he returned to England. Everywhere he went he made it his business to record his experiences, and as he was particularly interested in chivalry and courtly ceremonial his voluminous *Chronicles* provide us with a wealth of closely-observed detail of his times. He was sixty-seven at the time of Henry IV's coronation, and nearing the end of his life. Although we cannot say for certain whether he attended it in person, it is quite likely that he was present to see it for himself.

His *Chronicles* were translated in the time of Henry VIII by John Bourchier, Lord Berners, whose sixteenth-century prose captures the mood of Froissart's own medieval French.

> The Saturday before his coronation he [Henry IV] departed from Westminster, and rode to the Tower of London with a great number; and that night all such esquires as should be made knights the next day, watched, who were the number of forty-six. Every esquire had his own bayne [bath] by himself; and the next day the Duke of Lancaster [the future king – Froissart correctly avoids calling him 'king' because he had yet to be crowned] made them all knights at the mass-time. They had they long coats [mantles?] with strait sleeves, furred with mynever like prelates, with white laces hanging on their shoulders.

It has been said that with his coronation Henry IV inaugurated the Knights of the Bath. Strictly speaking this is not quite true, for the Order was not established until 1725 by George I, who in that year 'revived' the Most Honourable Order of the Bath. Nevertheless, it is true to say that Henry IV did give special emphasis to the custom of creating a number of new knights in the Tower of London as a mark of grace, and this custom continued for 250 years. Charles II was the last monarch to keep up the tradition of residing at the Tower before being crowned at Westminster.

to have himself crowned on the feast day of the translation of St Edward the Confessor, that is to say the anniversary of the day in 1163 when the Confessor's bones and relics were reverently placed in a new shrine in the abbey and he was formally canonised as a saint. It was the most important day in Westminster Abbey's calendar, and arguably one of the most important days in the English year, for at that time Edward the Confessor was still held to be England's patron saint.

Remembering the great festivities and tableaux that had accompanied Richard II's coronation twenty-two years before, Henry arranged to have a similar procession from the Tower of London to Westminster. Once again the houses and shops were hung with tapestries and the conduits spouted red and white wine. Once again, dozens of knights were newly created for the occasion, having ceremonial baths before being robed with elaborate costumes.

Henry did his very best to make his coronation even grander and more charged with holy significance than any of his predecessors. The ceremony itself was to begin at nine o'clock in the morning, but Henry arrived late, making known that he had already heard three masses and had spent long hours with his confessor. He was no ordinary usurper. Froissart tells us that as he entered the abbey the Barons of the Cinque Ports bore a rich canopy over him – 'a cloth of estate of blue with four bells of gold'. His son, 'Prince Hal' – the future Henry V – walked before him, carrying *Curtana*, the Sword of Mercy. Two archbishops and ten bishops then took part in the service, which proceeded with the utmost pomp and ceremony, matching the splendour which had been arranged for young Richard II twenty-three years before.

But Henry had a trump card to play, for he let it be known that he had discovered an especially sacred oil which was to be used for his anointing. The extrordinary rumour was spread that the Virgin Mary herself had given a golden eagle filled with holy oil to St Thomas of Canterbury when he was in exile in Sens. She had appeared to him as he was praying in the church of St Columba, holding this eagle and a small phial of stone and had made the promise that any kings of England anointed with it would be merciful rulers and champions of the church. She even went on to say that the first to be anointed with this oil would be a king who would regain Normandy and Aquitaine, build churches in the

Holy Land, and put the heathen to flight from Babylon. She added that it should be hidden in the Abbey of St Cyprians at Poitiers, where it would be discovered when the time was ripe.

A hermit had revealed the whereabouts of this sacred oil to the Black Prince, who then had it placed for safe keeping in the Tower of London, ready for the time when his son, Richard II, should be crowned. The story went on to say that Richard had not discovered it until the last year of his reign, and had then taken it with him to Ireland, asking Archbishop Courtenay to anoint him with it. The archbishop had refused to do this, saying that he could not be anointed twice. On his return from Ireland, therefore, Richard gave up the ampulla to the archbishop, prophetically announcing that it was obviously 'meant for some more fortunate King.' Clearly, the Virgin Mary's oil had been destined for none other than Henry Bolingbroke. However, not everyone was impressed. William of Usk, a Welsh historian, maliciously reported that when the oil was poured over Henry's head, all the headlice ran out.

JOANNA OF NAVARRE, QUEEN OF HENRY IV

Married 7 February 1403, crowned 26 February 1403,
aged about 33

Musicians at Cheapside Earn 13s 4d

It was a second marriage for both Henry and Joanna. Henry's first wife, Mary de Bohun, had died in childbirth having already produced seven children, notably the future Henry V. As for Joanna, she had been married to the Duke of Brittany and had already produced an heir for her deceased husband. Because of her position as dowager Duchess of Brittany she is sometimes referred to as Joan of Brittany.

Joanna had led an eventful life even as a child. She was the daughter of King Charles II of Navarre, known as Charles the Bad, and when she was only eleven she had been captured by the French and held hostage as security for her father's good behaviour. She probably enjoyed living in Paris, and had acquired sophisticated tastes. Henry IV, then, was marrying a woman who was used to the royal life and to political intrigues. They had their wedding well outside London – in Winchester Cathedral – and then he was able to bring her as his wife, to be crowned in Westminster Abbey about three weeks later.

The citizens of London gave her a fair welcome. Six minstrels were hired from Suffolk and they were paid no less than £4 to ride out to Blackheath to greet her. Then the mayor, aldermen and sheriffs accompanied her to the Tower, where she rested for the night. Joanna's procession from the Tower to Westminster, by now a traditional event, took place the following day, and the Suffolk minstrels earned themselves another 13s 4d for playing as the new queen passed through Cheapside. A contemporary drawing of Joanna shows her to have been tall, dignified and elegant, and Henry paid her the compliment of having her enthroned alone elevated on a high platform under a rich, emblazoned canopy and holding a sceptre in her right hand and an orb surmounted by a cross in her left. Such symbols of sovereignty, if she really did hold them, must have been allowed as a mark of very special favour.

Thomas Arundel, Archbishop of Canterbury, officiated at the coronation. He holds a record for having crowned two kings and two queens. He had already crowned little Queen Isabella and Henry IV, and after this coronation he would go on to crown Prince Hal as Henry V. However, Arundel's mark in history was made by his determination to stamp out heresy, particularly that of Lollardry, and the introduction, in 1401, of the punishment of public burnings of anyone suspected of being a heretic.

Little did Joanna realise that in the next reign, her new stepson, the future Henry V, would arrest her on suspicion of being a witch. Luckily, she was released after four years of imprisonment. But the terror of being burnt alive must have been acute. Such was the penalty of being a queen in those days.

HENRY V

Reigned 1413–22, crowned 9 April 1413, aged 25

A Snow-Storm Symbolises The New King's Purity and Mercy

Despite his popularity and military achievements, Henry V, the victor at Agincourt, seems to have been something of an enigma.

Shakespeare has given us an unforgettable account of his early years as the roistering 'Prince Hal', the young man-about-town who enjoyed the lowest of company and who gained a reputation for being a ne'er-do-well. There was the story of how he tried on the crown even before his father, Henry IV had died. People must have had serious misgivings about this wild young prince as he came the throne, a disreputable son of a usurping king. However, Shakespeare carries on with his story of Prince Hal, showing his extraordinary change of character as he assumes his new role of king. Falstaff and the rest are peremptorily ignored ('I know thee not, old man') and suddenly we have a noble and majestic 'warlike Harry' guiding England's destiny ('Cry "God for Harry, England, and Saint George!"'). Of course, much of this is Tudor propaganda, but the fact is that Henry does seem to have turned over a new leaf, consciously and conspicuously, as soon as he was crowned.

The weather conditions on the days surrounding Henry V's coronation were dramatically memorable. On this Passion Sunday, 9 April 1413, the entire country suffered from heavy blizzards. A thick blanket of snow covered England, burying animals, men, even houses, and the snow and arctic conditions stretched south even to Paris. Henry's procession from the Tower of London to Westminster had to ride through a blizzard so intense that the silken canopy held over his head had to be shaken several times to get rid of the snow falling on it. The snow was so appalling that people were led to find divine or occult meanings behind it. Could it be that some dreadful doom was awaiting England now that a new usurper was taking the throne? After all, everyone knew that Edward Mortimer, Earl of March, was the rightful claimant. Nevertheless, other soothsayers confidently pointed out that the whiteness of the snow signified the new king's purity, and its softness his mercy.

In the abbey itself the coronation passed off without incident. Harry sat on his throne, elevated on the scaffold known as 'the theatre' which was draped with cloth-of-gold and was crowned by Arundel. To judge from his behaviour after this sacred anointing, he must have taken his vows with ferocious intensity. Henceforth, apart from his interminable wars with France, his life was to be filled with pious acts of devotion: fastings, pilgrimages, endowments of religious houses, abstinence from illicit sex, swearing, drinking or carefree merry-making; and he was punctilious in hearing no fewer than three masses each day. Even at the coronation feast Harry sat moodily aloof, seated on a marble chair, not even eating or sharing in the rich food being served. Indeed, it was reported that for three days afterwards he still continued to fast, preparing himself for his new life of dedicated majesty. Aged twenty-five, he was taking upon himself a divine role. Dymoke, his champion, duly rode into the hall to deliver the challenge, but who would dare to confront this God-fearing king? Thus the warlike Harry began his reign.

Henry V's coronation is the only one to be depicted in Westminster Abbey itself. The ceremony is sculpted on each side of his chantry and it shows the king newly crowned, sitting on his throne with two churchmen or nobles on either side of him. His helm and crest are carved just beneath.

CATHERINE OF VALOIS, QUEEN OF HENRY V

Married 2 June 1420, crowned 24 February 1421, aged 19

Roast Porpoise and Fried Minnows

Henry V had been king for seven years when he married Catherine of Valois, daughter of King Charles VI of France ('The Mad'). In those seven years he had swiftly re-asserted the English monarchy's claim to rule France and had proved his point by inflicting a crushing defeat on the French army at the Battle of Agincourt in 1415. He had then proceeded to reconquer Normandy, 1417–19, march into Paris in 1419, and finally impose his will over the French court at the Treaty of Troyes in 1420, in which the French were forced to recognise him as the next king of France. Meanwhile, he was to act as regent, during the period of Charles VI's increasingly numerous periods of insanity.

It was a resounding success and, to cap it all, Charles's daughter, Catherine, was a part of the booty. The wedding of Henry and Catherine took place just twelve days after the Treaty of Troyes had been signed, and naturally it was a supremely triumphant affair, attended by nobles and royalty from both England and France, and King James I of Scotland, a long-term but honoured prisoner in England, was also present. The wedding and coronation which followed would turn out to be unexpectedly lucky for him too.

Henry, of course, had to rush off afterwards to continue waging war, but now, at last, seven months later, he had brought his French bride to London. It was time to give her a coronation with all the feastings appropriate to the occasion. After all, any son born to them once they had both been regally anointed would happily and unarguably unite the two countries in his future reign. Henry, now aged thirty-two, was at the height of his popularity and the coronation of his attractive nineteen-year-old queen was a cause for great rejoicing. A contemporary French chronicler, Enguerrand de Monstrelet, remarked that from the time that Catherine arrived at Dover 'she was received as if she had been an angel of God.'

At the coronation she was escorted from Westminster Palace to the abbey by two bishops, and was crowned by Henry Chichele, Archbishop of Canterbury, who had been appointed by Henry V and who had strongly supported him in his French wars.† However, the most memorable aspect of this event is the account of the banquet held afterwards in Westminster Hall. The menu included roast porpoise and fried minnows. Luckily, we have a fascinating and detailed account of this, written by Robert Fabyan, an English chronicler and sheriff of London in 1493. Although he was writing well after the event, it is clear that memories of this extraordinary feast were still vivid. No meat could be eaten as the banquet was taking place during Lent, so the cooks had to think up a menu with the main courses entirely made up of fish dishes.

Fabyan tells us that the first course included *dead* eels stewed! For the second course came 'jelly coloured with columbine flowers; white pottage, or cream of almonds; bream of the sea; conger; soles; cheven, or chub; barbel, with roach; smelt, fried; crayfish, or lobster; leche, clear jelly, damasked with the king's motto or word, flourished, (decorated) UNE SANS PLUS; lamprey,

---

† Chichele speaks the first words in Shakespeare's *Henry V* and is made to utter fulsome praise of the king in his sudden transformation from his former youthful wildness. However, the sincerity of his admiration for Henry V is shown by the fact that fifteen years after Henry's death he founded All Souls College, Oxford, in which prayers were to be offered for the souls of Henry V and all Englishmen who had been killed in the French wars. All Souls College, in fact, is a kind of war memorial for Henry.

fresh baked; *flampayne*, flourished with a scutcheon-royal, and therein three crowns of gold planted with fleurs-de-lis and flowers of camomile, all wrought of confections' (confectionery). The third course, though it's hard to see how these courses could be considered separate from one another, consisted of 'white leche'; dates 'in compost'; mottled cream; carp; turbot; tench; perch; with gudgeon; fresh sturgeon, with whelks; porpoise, roasted; crabs; prawns and eels roasted with lamprey. The dessert seems to have been a kind of marzipan, and 'tartes'.

No less memorable were the table decorations, called 'subtleties', which contrived to impart symbolic meanings. For example, there was an image of St Katherine, the queen's patron saint, disputing with the doctors of the church; next to her was 'a pellican sitting on hir nest with hir birds' holding a message in its beak:

> This sign to the king
> Great joy will bring.
> And all his people
> She (madame the queen) will content.

This fishy meal with its subtleties obviously made a great impression, but perhaps the most important event that day was Catherine's dramatic act of mercy on behalf of James I of Scotland, an honoured guest, but nevertheless a prisoner of state.

At the banquet Catherine had been sitting with King James on her left. He was now aged twenty-five, but he had been held captive in England since 1406, when as an eleven-year-old he had been captured by English pirates. Henry IV had been kind to him and had treated him well in Windsor Castle, giving him a careful education there. All the same, he was still a prisoner, and now at this coronation banquet he must have appealed to Catherine's sense of justice, for as soon as the meal was over she publicly begged Henry V to give James his freedom. Amid great cheering, her request was granted.

Memorable in many ways, then, this wedding and this coronation held out great hopes for the future, but only two years later Henry was dead and Catherine was a widow with a nine-month-old baby to look after – the luckless Henry VI.

HENRY VI

Reigned 1422–61 and 1470–71, crowned 6 November 1429,
aged 7, 16 December 1431 and 13 October 1470

'Beholdyinge the Pepylle All About Saddely and Wysely'

Henry VI is unique in having had no fewer than three coronations. He was given the first of these in Westminster Abbey when he was just a month short of his eighth birthday; following this, just over two years later, he was crowned in Notre Dame, Paris, as King of France; and then, having been deposed in 1461 by Edward IV he was restored to the throne in 1470, having his second English coronation in St Paul's Cathedral, London. This second period of kingship was to last only 187 days, however, before he was again deposed and murdered, aged forty-nine, in the Tower of London on 21 May 1471. It was a miserable reign, during which he can hardly be said to have been in control of the events happening around him.

The archbishop officiating at the first of Henry's coronations was Henry Chichele, who had already crowned Henry's mother, Catherine of Valois eight years before. However, this coronation was a very different affair, for young Henry, looking around him 'sadly and wisely', was symbolically carried into the abbey by the Earl of Warwick (the 'Kingmaker'), who was really in charge. The little king was so small that the crown was far too big for his head, and so heavy that it had to be supported on each side by a bishop holding it. However, young as he was, Henry was already showing the seriousness and piety which marked his character. He must have been pleased to know that he was being anointed by the holy and miraculous oil which had allegedly been given to Thomas Becket by the Virgin Mary, and which his grandfather Henry IV had so conveniently discovered.

Of course, everyone knew that Henry was really too young to be crowned, but at this time Joan of Arc was making a mockery of the English forces in France. On 17 July 1429 the dauphin had been crowned as Charles VII, and it seemed as if Henry V's efforts to claim the French throne had come to nothing. As a desperate measure, it was proposed to crown the young Henry VI in France, giving him an impressive coronation in Paris, as this might drum up a sense of loyalty to the English.

However, before he could be crowned in France, it was necessary that he should first be crowned in England. Thus it was arranged that Henry's English coronation should be rushed through as soon as possible. The date chosen was Sunday 6 November, St Leonard's Day. As he was the sixth Henry, this number appealed to the medieval mind as being appropriate. New Knights of the Bath were created the previous day – thirty-two of them being ritually washed. However, the traditional procession from the Tower of London to Westminster was not much enjoyed by Londoners, who had come to expect free wine gushing from the conduits and wildly improbable merry-making in the streets. No such treats were in store for them this time. Instead, pious inscriptions were placed around the streets, and people were rationed to just one cup of wine per person.

At the abbey Henry, dressed in 'a clothe of scharlet furryed' (scarlet cloth edged with fur) was led to the high platform 'and there the King was sette in hys sete in the myddys of the schaffold there, beholdyinge the pepylle all about saddely and wysely.' The ceremony was appallingly long and exhausting, but the young king did everything that was expected of him, lying down prostrate, 'longe tyme lyying stylle,' and allowing himself to be 'strypte . . . owte of hys clothys in to hys schyrte' for the anointing. And at the mass which followed, Henry was noted to be 'knelynge with humylyte and grete devocyon'. Finally, at the feast which followed, he was given his favourite dishes: 'roast meat fritters' and jelly.

Second Coronation
Parisian Mobs Grab The Food

From one point of view, this coronation was a great success. From another, it was an abysmal failure. Five months after his English coronation, in April 1430, Henry the boy-king was taken across the channel to Calais in preparation for his coronation in France. But the state of things was so chaotic that he had to stay in Calais for three months before it was considered safe for him to proceed further towards Paris. Joan of Arc, then aged nineteen, had been captured and her trial and ultimate punishment of burning at the stake had still to take place. Oddly enough, on his way to Paris Henry stayed at the same castle in Rouen where Joan was being held captive. Did they ever meet? At all events, on 30 May Joan was publicly burnt in Rouen market place.

Henry finally reached the French capital in December 1431 to be given his ostentatious coronation in Notre Dame, crowned this time by his uncle, the powerful Cardinal Beaufort, Bishop of Winchester, who had taken part in the condemnation of Joan of Arc. The French, of course, were insulted by not having any of their own churchmen invited to take part in the ceremony: it was to be an all-English affair. Naturally, much umbrage was taken, and Henry's own grandmother, Queen Isabel, did not attend, although she was in Paris at the time.

As Henry had entered Paris he had been preceded by representations of the 'Nine Worthies' – Hector, Caesar, Alexander, Josua, David, Judas Maccabaeus, Arthur, Charlemagne, Godfrey of Bouillon – but the crowds were moved by curiosity and greed rather than any loyalty to this child being paraded before them. Early on the day of the coronation the people forced their way into the great hall where the feast was to take place, and grabbed as much food and drink as they could so that when the time came for the feast to be served, there was utter confusion.

Henry was hustled out of France before the end of the month, but his big moment came when he was received back in England in February 1432. Here he was given a tumultuous reception. After all, he had been out of the country for almost two years, and now that he was returning as 'King of France' the citizens were prepared to honour him as never before. The celebrations as Henry entered London were probably among the happiest of his unlucky reign.

The gentlemen and commoners of Kent, all arrayed in red hoods, met him on Barham Downs, between Dover and Canterbury, and escorted him all the way to Blackheath, where he was met by the citizens of London, who presented him with a loyal address. Riding on to Deptford, he was met by a concourse of clergy, and then, taking the route from Deptford through Southwark to the City of London, the royal procession went straight to St Paul's for a service of thanksgiving. Another cavalcade then took him back to his palace at Westminster. Two days later the citizens of London sent the ten-year-old Henry a deputation to present him with a gold casket containing £1,000 as a token of their devotion and loyalty.

Third Coronation
'Utterly Dullyd With Trubbles'

The chaotic reign of Henry VI cannot be summarised here. Battles, periods of mental paralysis, civil war, imprisonments: poor Henry hardly knew what was happening to him for much of the time. When he was fully conscious he was pious, gentle and generous – but these were not the qualities needed to hold the kingdom together in the troubled period vaguely referred to as the 'Wars of the Roses'.

Most of the last five years of Henry's life were spent as a prisoner. He was arrested at Islington by Warwick 'The Kingmaker' on 24 July 1465, and with his feet bound to his stirrups and his spurs removed, a symbol of knightly degradation, the ex-king was escorted under armed guard through Cheapside and Cornhill to the Tower of London. It was not until October 1470 that his fortunes were reversed. Warwick had changed sides yet again in this wretched civil war and gave orders to release Henry. A contemporary, John Warkworth, Master of Peterhouse, Cambridge (1473–1500) wrote that:

> in the beginning of the month of October, the year of Our Lord 1470, the Bishop of Winchester, by the assent of the Duke of Clarence and the Earl of Warwick, went to the Tower of London where King Herry (*sic*) was in prison by King Edward's commandment, and there took him from his keepers, which was not worshipfully arrayed as a prince, and not so cleanly kept as should seem such a prince; they had him out, and new arrayed him, and did to him great reverence, and brought him to the palace of Westminster, and so he was restored to the crown again.

Henry needed to be given some sort of public recognition. Not much is known of the coronation but it must have involved the putting on of a crown, but it is unlikely that he would have been anointed. After all, as Shakespeare's Richard II says, 'Not all the water in the rough-rude sea / Can wash the balm from an anointed king.' (*Act III ii*). The ceremony did not take place in Westminster Abbey, but in St Paul's Cathedral. Riding there in a long gown of blue velvet, Henry did as he was told and duly received his crown again, 'of the which he took no great rejoice'. Not surprisingly, he was described as 'a man amazyd and utterly dullyd with trubbles and adversitie.' Henry's second period of kingship was to last for less than half a year. In April 1471 Edward IV was back on the throne. The following month Henry VI was murdered.

MARGARET OF ANJOU, QUEEN OF HENRY VI

Dates as Queen 1445–61 and 1470–71, crowned 30 May 1445, aged 15

Daisy Flowers and Noah's Ark on London Bridge

Although Margaret is known as Margaret of Anjou, she was in fact the daughter of King René of Sicily and niece of the queen of France, and she was educated at the French court as well as in Naples. Henry VI was delighted to be marrying her, as it brought a truce with France, which was urgently needed in the aftermath of the wars waged during the reign of his father, Henry V, and the subsequent political chaos.

At the time of their marriage Henry was twenty-four and Margaret just turned fifteen. Young, pretty, well-educated, cosmopolitan but desperately poor, Henry's bride-to-be landed at Portchester on the Hampshire coast in April 1445. Henry married her immediately, at Titchfield Abbey in the New Forest, near Southampton, and then she was escorted to London and given a rather more splendid coronation than Henry could really afford. In fact Henry had to beg for loans to pay for it, for he was almost as impoverished as Margaret. She was given a tremendous welcome as she made her royal entry into London. Everyone, including the French and English nobility wore a daisy (marguerite) for this was her emblem-flower. Henry VI even had daisies enamelled and engraved on his royal plate.

Triumphal arches had been erected over the route she took, and, as a near-contemporary historian, Robert Fabyan writes, 'many costly pageants were made ready of divers old histories, to her great comfort'; and John Stow, the Elizabethan chronicler of London, describes it all in some detail, giving us a splendid picture of a typical medieval public royal occasion:

> On the 28th of May, queen Margaret was met at Blackheath by an equestrian procession, consisting of the mayor, aldermen, and sheriffs of the city of London, in scarlet, and the crafts of the same, all riding on horseback, in blue gowns, with embroidered sleeves and red hoods, who conveyed her with her train through Southwark, and so on to the city of London, which was then beautified with pageants of divers histories and other shows of welcome, marvellous costly and sumptuous, of which I can only name a few.
>
> At the bridge-foot towards Southwark was a pageant of Peace and Plenty; and at every street corner, in allusion to the text of the parliamentary sermon, two puppets, in a moving pageant called Justice and Peace, were made to kiss each other. Noah's ship (the Ark) was upon the bridge, with verses in English, likening their young queen to the dove that brought the branch of peace. At Leadenhall, madam Grace, the chancellor of God. At the inn in Cornhill, St Margaret. At the great conduit in Cheapside, the five Wise and Foolish Virgins. At the cross in the Cheap, the Heavenly Jerusalem, with verses. At Paul's-gate, the General Resurrection and Judgement, with verses accordingly, all made by John Lydgate.

After the traditional crowning and anointing in Westminster Abbey by John Stafford, Archbishop of Canterbury, the pageantry continued with jousting for another three days.

So, after such celebrations, it really did seem that the wars with France might finally have come to an end. Margaret wrote to her uncle, King Charles VII of France, expressing 'the happiness her lord king Henry and herself feel in the repose from war, and hoping the blessing of peace may be firmly established between them.' Perhaps tactlessly, however, she signed herself 'Margaret, queen of France and England' – so the tensions between the two countries had by no means disappeared completely. In fact it was not until 1 January 1801 that England ended the pretence that it owned France, and

George III, after forty years on the British throne, ceased to use the ancient title 'King of France'.

However, Margaret's part in the Wars of the Roses, which were just about to start, makes dramatic reading. It was not long before she was to realise that her husband, Henry VI, was completely out of his depth, and for decades she did valiant work in helping him and in waging war against his Yorkist rivals. However, these problems were still in the future.

In the light of the later tragic events of Margaret's life as Henry VI's queen, it is worth remembering that her reception in England and her early years as queen were marked by genuine affection on the part of her subjects.

EDWARD IV

Reigned 1461–70 and 1471–83, crowned 29 May 1461, aged 19

A Strange Superstition

Edward was a usurper, as he took the throne from Henry VI – but then, Henry VI's grandfather had also been a usurper, taking the throne from Richard II, so it could be argued that this coronation was merely putting things straight again. The Wars of the Roses was a family feud, but this is not the place to go into details. In essence Henry VI was descended from a Duke of Lancaster whereas Edward IV was descended from a Duke of York. Both 'Lancastrians' and 'Yorkists' were ultimately descended from Edward III.

Henry VI proved to be so incompetent that his weakness as king amounted to a power-vacuum. Inevitably, the Yorkist claimants to the throne seized whatever chance they could. Several battles ensued, but in March 1461, after victory at the bloodiest battle in English history – fought in a blizzard just outside the Yorkshire town of Towton – Edward Mortimer, Earl of March, found himself able to claim the throne. His father and elder brother had both been killed three months earlier at the Battle of Wakefield, so Edward, aged only eighteen, had become the head of the Yorkist faction. After the Battle of Towton he was in a position to be crowned as Edward IV.

His coronation took place on 28 June 1461, three months after that decisive battle. The Archbishop of Canterbury, Cardinal Thomas Bourchier, was a staunch Yorkist, and so was quite willing to crown and anoint Edward, despite the fact that Henry VI was still alive, although held under lock and key. On the Friday 26 June Edward rode from Lambeth to the Tower of London, attended by the mayor and aldermen in robes of scarlet, and by 400 supporters 'well-horsed and clad in green'. Then, having settled into the Tower, he created twenty-eight new Knights of the Bath, including his own two younger brothers, George and Richard, later to become Richard III.

The next day there was the customary procession through the streets of London, with the new knights riding ahead of the king 'in blue gowns, and hoods upon their shoulders like to priests.' And then, on the Sunday the coronation was held. This was the day when he would be duly anointed and the rich crown of King Edward the Confessor would be solemnly placed on his head. The usurpation would then be complete; he had no qualms about taking over the kingdom.

However, some people were more worried about the date on which he would be crowned. It was noticed, with misgivings, that it was the twenty-eighth of the month. Some calendar dates had acquired horrendous significance in the medieval mind. There were, for example, the *dies mali*, or 'accursed days' two of which occurred every month. But worse even than these was the horror attached to 'Childermas', or Holy Innocents' Day, when Herod had killed all the 'little childer' – 28 December – and especially so when this day fell on a Sunday. If it did, then the twenty-eighth day of every month throughout the following year was considered to be a seriously unlucky day. It so happened that Childermas *did* fall on a Sunday in the year 1460, so clearly to be crowned on 28 June in 1461 was tempting providence.

It is astonishing that a man such as Edward, who could hack his way to the throne through countless pieces of human flesh and bone, could allow himself to be worried by such a superstition. Nevertheless, he felt it prudent to go again to the abbey the next day in thanksgiving. Some accounts of this time state that the coronation was actually deferred until the Monday. Afterwards, he returned to St Paul's, and to the huge delight of the crowds, he was 'incensed' by a mechanical angel with golden wings that flew down from the roof 'by means of a rope and alighted at his feet' to pay him homage.

The crowds watching all this must have been relieved to think that the civil war seemed to be over. Edward was an extremely well-made man, probably the tallest of all English kings. Thomas More wrote that he was 'princely to behold, of body mighty, strong and clean made.' The Speaker of the House of Commons complimented him, in a formal speech, on his 'beauty of personage' and even a French chronicler admitted that Edward was 'the handsomest Prince my eyes ever beheld'. At this coronation time, Edward IV was the darling of his new subjects: a lover of art, science, food, wine and women. But most of all he loved power – and this is what he now possessed.

ELIZABETH WOODVILLE, QUEEN OF EDWARD IV

Dates as Queen 1465–70 and 1471–83, crowned 26 May 1465, aged about 28

A Lancastrian Widow Becomes a Yorkist Queen

Three years after he had become king, Edward IV, then aged twenty-one, married a young widow, Elizabeth Woodville, in very great secrecy, in the village church at Grafton in Northampton-shire. The reason for such secrecy was that Elizabeth was a mere commoner. True, her mother had been a princess of Luxembourg, and Elizabeth herself had been one of the ladies-in-waiting at the court of Margaret of Anjou, Henry VI's wife. Nevertheless, at the time of Elizabeth Woodville's marriage she was a relatively obscure and poor young widow.

Strictly speaking, Elizabeth Woodville's name was Lady Grey. Until Edward IV had seized power she had been living quite comfortably with her husband, John Grey, in Bradgate Park, Leicestershire, where they had been happily bringing up their two young sons. However, Sir John Grey had been an active supporter of Henry VI, leading the cavalry and helping to win the second Battle of St Albans. It was one of the few Lancastrian successes in the Wars of the Roses.

Unfortunately, Sir John Grey was seriously wounded during that final cavalry charge and died shortly afterwards. As for Elizabeth and her young sons, they were forced from their home at Bradgate, her sons were disinherited, and they were all living in poverty in Grafton.

According to tradition – and there is no real reason to doubt it – Elizabeth was determined to get her property back, and so she contrived to meet the young King Edward IV as he was hunting in Whittlebury Forest, near Grafton. The story goes that she waited behind a large oak tree which she knew he would pass, and then dramatically stepped out in front of him and accosted him with her pitiful tale of injustice. She relied not only on her powers of persuasion, but also on her ravishingly beautiful looks. Her charms worked, and for the nineteen-year-old king it was lust at first sight. 'My liege, I know I am not good enough to be your queen,' she is supposed to have said, 'but I am far too good to be your mistress.' It was a classic ploy. Two generations later, Anne Boleyn would say the same to Edward's grandson, Henry VIII – and with exactly the same result. Both Henry VIII and Edward IV married their commoner-wives in secrecy, and then, when the news had to come out, they both gave their wives the most brilliant coronations possible, almost as if to compensate for the hole-in-corner weddings they had forced on them.

As with so many other coronations, the background against which Elizabeth Woodville was crowned is almost as important as the event itself. It took four months before Edward found himself compelled to confess that he was married. A great meeting of state councillors had assembled at Reading, and one of the topics on the agenda was to persuade the king to marry a French princess. In a state of some embarrassment, Edward had no option but to come out with his secret. His news was met with consternation. Everyone was horrified. The assembly told the king that Elizabeth Woodville 'was not his match, however good and fair she might be, and he must know well that she was no wife for a prince such as himself.' As for Edward's family, they were bitterly offended. His mother and his brothers could hardly find words to express their contempt for this commoner-wife. Matters were not made any better when people realised that she was the widow of a prominent supporter of Henry VI. Despite all this, Edward was unrepentant and on Michaelmas Day, 1464, he escorted Elizabeth his wife into Reading Abbey and presented her to all his nobles as their sovereign lady and queen. They did their duty, gritted their teeth, knelt before her and paid her homage.

So Elizabeth Woodville's coronation eight months later, on Whitsunday 1465, splendid as it was, provoked deep undercurrents of resentment among the king's own family and throughout the nobility. It was noted with sour amusement that the new queen was arranging extraordinary weddings for her numerous brothers and sisters, so that they could marry into wealthy and aristocratic families. For example, one of her brothers found himself marrying the eighty-year-old dowager Duchess of Norfolk – 'a diabolical marriage', according to William of Worcester.

The coronation itself provided Edward with the opportunity for a huge public relations exercise. He invited as many as possible of Elizabeth's near-royal, almost forgotten, distant relatives from Luxembourg to the event – he was keen to make it appear that Elizabeth *was* truly well connected. And he went to considerable expense to provide new scarlet and crimson robes for the heralds and kings of arms; and jewellery, gold cups and basins, and costly cloth-of-gold were all lavishly on view to convey the necessary aura of opulence and regality.

At the Tower of London, on 23 May, Edward created forty new Knights of the Bath – this was more than he had created on the occasion of his own coronation – and of course among them were the queen's brothers and new brothers-in-law. Pageants were staged; banquets were eaten, chivalric tournaments were held: and at the end of it all no one could be left in any doubt that Elizabeth Woodville, the ex-Lancastrian widow, was now a genuine Yorkist queen.

Elizabeth herself brazened it out, even insisting that her own brother Anthony had to get down on bended knee when he spoke to her in public. She soon learned how to make her presence felt, and the rest of Edward's family despised her – especially her husband's brother Richard, who was to become king himself, much sooner than anyone expected. So when, quite unexpectedly, Edward IV suddenly died, Elizabeth Woodville's upstart pride was remembered with a vengeance. Her sons were to bear the brunt of Richard's thrusting enmity.

RICHARD III AND ANNE OF WARWICK

Reigned 1483–85, crowned 6 July 1483, aged 30

A Young King Mysteriously Disappears

Everyone has heard of the mysterious disappearance of the two young 'Princes in the Tower' – Edward, aged twelve, and Richard, aged nine. They were the two sons of Edward IV and Elizabeth Woodville. When their father died it was obvious that the elder boy, Edward, who was being brought up in Ludlow Castle at the time, should succeed him as King Edward V. However, both Edward and his younger brother were brought to the Tower of London by their uncle Richard, Duke of Gloucester, and after a few weeks there, they both vanished.

Edward V reigned for seventy-seven days, but it was a very hypothetical reign. In theory it began at the death of his father, Edward IV, on 9 April 1483, but it ended abruptly when his uncle suddenly had himself proclaimed King Richard III by parliament on 26 June. Richard III was crowned just ten days later, by Archbishop Bourchier, on 6 July. No one dared ask awkward questions, especially after an incident when one nobleman, Lord Hastings, who was known to have misgivings about the way things were being handled, was arrested at a council meeting, taken outside and, in the words of Sir Thomas More, 'his head was laid down upon a log of timber and there striken off' (*sic*).

Very much like Henry IV, a previous usurper, Richard III was keen to give himself an exceptionally splendid coronation, hoping to prove to everyone how right and proper everything was. The more pomp and ceremony there was, the more acceptable it would appear in the eyes of the public. Indeed Richard did prepare his public with care, first of all arranging that an outdoor sermon should be preached outside Old St Paul's Cathedral in which the speaker, Dr Ralph Shaa, took the curious text 'Bastard slips shall not take root' – obviously referring to Edward V. Public sermons were often used in those days as a method of spreading political propaganda and influencing people's attitudes. The secret marriage between Edward IV and Elizabeth Woodville was now being questioned, so that the legitimacy of their children was put in doubt. Richard had always hated the Woodvilles, and now at last he was determined to crush them. Elizabeth Woodville, now living in poverty, was referred to as 'Dame Gray, lately calling herself queen of England.'

At this crucial time, Richard was staying at Baynard's Castle, an old Norman fortress which used to stand in Upper Thames Street in London. He had taken the precaution of bringing a huge number of supporters down from the north of England, where he was genuinely popular. So it was at Baynard's Castle on 26 June that the final stage in his take-over took place.

It was all carefully planned. First, a deputation from parliament, led by the Duke of Buckingham, arrived at the castle with a petition to beg Richard to take the crown. Then Richard pretended to be surprised and showed great reluctance. Then shouts of 'King Richard! King Richard!' were dutifully made. Next, nobles moved forward to take their oath of allegiance. And then, accepting this 'surprising' offer of being elected king, Richard rode with 6,000 of his northern supporters – virtually a private army – to Westminster Hall, where he sat in the royal chair. Finally he went to Westminster Abbey, where after being greeted by the abbot, he made offerings at the sacred shrine of Edward the Confessor. The take-over was complete. All it needed was a coronation.

Luckily, everything was prepared. (It was to have been Edward V's coronation, but no one mentioned it too openly, at least not in Richard's hearing.) Wildfowl were ready for the banquet, and dresses of velvet, cloth-of-gold and ermine had been made for the guests. At the ceremony, Richard, wearing 'Robes of Purple Velvett' and his wife, Anne of Warwick, wearing a 'rich Coronett set with Stones and Pearle' walked with bare feet into the abbey for what has been described as the most magnificent coronation of the century.

For Richard's queen, Anne of Warwick, this must have been the highlight of her short but eventful life. She was the second daughter of Richard Neville, Earl of Warwick – 'the Kingmaker' – who had been so rich and powerful that whichever side he supported during the Wars of the Roses achieved at least momentary success. The trouble was, he switched sides, and poor Anne was caught up in all those complicated events as a useful pawn, to be married off as and when convenient. She had already been married to the Lancastrian Prince of Wales, Edward, son of Henry VI, but he had been killed at the Battle of Tewkesbury and she had been left a widow at fifteen. After her father had been killed at the Battle of Barnet she married, perhaps somewhat unwillingly, the Yorkist Duke of Gloucester, Richard. At the time of their coronation, they had one child (yet another Edward, Prince of Wales) who was aged ten – about the same age as his Woodville cousins, the Princes in the Tower.

One contemporary account of this coronation contains the astonishing statement that both Richard and Anne 'put off their robes, and stood all naked from their waists upwards till the bishop had anointed them.' This would certainly have made a noteworthy sight – and vastly different from Queen Victoria's coronation, at which anointing on the breast was omitted altogether, 'from motives of delicacy'. At the mass which followed, they were 'both housled with one host devided betwene them', they shared a piece of communion bread, and the service ended as they both made an offering at the shrine of Edward the Confessor. Everything was done with an eye for gaining approval both from church and state.

The banquet afterwards in Westminster Hall began at four o'clock and lasted well into the evening. As expected, the king's champion, Sir Robert Dymoke, entered the hall, his horse draped with white and crimson silk; but, with sharp memories of what had happened to Lord Hastings less than a month before, it isn't surprising that no one dared pick up the gauntlet which Sir Robert flung down before the guests. However, there must have been *some* guests at that banquet whose minds were haunted by the thought of two young boys, now spending what would be their last few days of life, securely under guard in the Tower of London.

HENRY VII

Reigned 1485–1509, crowned 30 October 1485, aged 28

Crowned Beside a Hawthorn Bush

The Battle of Bosworth Field, fought on 22 August 1485 about twelve miles west of Leicester, was one of the great turning-points in English history. The long line of fourteen Plantagenet kings, which had lasted 330 years, came to an abrupt end when Richard

III was killed, and the victorious Henry Tudor, Earl of Richmond, seized power. The battle was a cliff-hanger right up to the last moment, for no one knew which side the equivocating Stanleys – Thomas, Lord Stanley, and his brother Sir William Stanley – would support. In the event, they sided with Henry, and as a result Plantagenet dominance came to an end.

The circumstances were dramatic: it was, of course, the replacement of one usurper king by another. Legend tells how, after the battle, Richard's crown – or some sort of golden circlet which he had worn around his helmet – was found under a hawthorn bush, and that Lord Stanley himself placed it on Henry Tudor's head. Henry literally owed his crown to the Stanleys' last-minute support. No one will ever know the precise details, but such a moment of high significance may well have taken place. Today, visitors to the battlefield site may stand on what has been known since that day as 'Crown Hill'. Later in life, Henry was to adopt the crown and hawthorn as his personal badge and this emblem appears on his tomb in Westminster Abbey: clearly Henry was keen to perpetuate the event in people's memories.

The new king was determined that the Battle of Bosworth was not to be just another skirmish in the seemingly never-ending struggles between Lancastrians and Yorkists, so, only twenty-three days after his victory on the battlefield, and in order to make his position safe and unassailable Henry created a special protective, personal bodyguard. They were to be known as 'Yeomen of the Guard of Our Lord the King' and were charged with keeping daily attendance on the king's person. The present-day Beefeaters, seen at the Tower of London, are a reminder of these, though strictly speaking the Yeomen Extraordinary of the Guard, who are wardens of the Tower of London, are a separate body of guards, created in the sixteenth century by Edward VI.

Henry VII took personal care in founding his original Yeomen of the Guard; for him, they were a necessary safeguard. They consisted of fifty archers, 'hardy, strong and of agility' and they were given the special Beefeater uniform which is the basis of what we still see them wearing today. Their duties included attending the king at meals and tasting his food lest it should contain poison, and when Henry went to bed they had to examine the royal mattress to make sure it contained no hidden daggers or knives: 'Then shall they lay on the bed of down and one of the

Yeomen to tumble up and down the same for the search thereof, and to beat it and lay it even and smooth.' Evidently, Henry was taking no chances.

Then, just ten weeks after the Battle of Bosworth, still unmarried and aged only twenty-eight, Henry had himself crowned at his formal coronation in Westminster Abbey. The 81-year-old Archbishop Bourchier was called into service yet again – he had previously officiated at the coronations of Edward IV, Elizabeth Woodville, Richard III and Anne of Warwick.

Henry's assumption of regal authority was performed with supreme self-assurance. In hindsight we know that he was establishing a remarkable royal house, but it takes an effort to remember that here was a young man who had seized power after a lengthy period of chaos, and that assuming the reins of power he was accepting a difficult challenge. In the event he was to rule with skill and success for the next twenty-four years, but at the time of his coronation he needed, and displayed, cool courage of a very high order.

The coronation was held on Sunday 30 October, one of the simplest and most economical on record, mainly because the prolonged civil war had somewhat depleted the treasury. The new Yeomen of the Guard were very much in evidence, in case of sudden last-minute opposition. Henry knew, as did everyone else, that his legal claim to the throne was somewhat flimsy, but once he had been crowned and anointed there would be few who would dare to challenge him.

Henry made an interesting innovation in the wearing of his crown that has been continued in all subsequent coronations. As crowns are heavy, cumbersome and uncomfortable to wear, especially for long periods at a time, he wore the crown *over* the 'Cap of Estate'. Edward III had begun the custom of wearing the softer and more comfortable alternative to the crown. It was made of velvet with a flattened top and the base turned up with 'miniver' or white fur, and was a distinctive badge of rank. It became the custom of a king who was about to be crowned to wear a scarlet robe and the Cap of Estate (sometimes called a Cap of Maintenance) before the anointing. Nowadays, crowns worn at coronations and state occasions have an internal velvet lining that was originally an entirely separate form of headgear.

Henry must have been immensely relieved when his coronation was over. However, the ceremony which perhaps was of even more importance to him was his intended marriage to Elizabeth of York, daughter of Edward IV and niece of the slain Richard III. Indeed, Francis Bacon wrote that 'His marriage was with greater triumph than either his entry or his coronation'. The point was, of course, that with this union he would strengthen his claim to the throne, and certainly his heirs would be able to claim unarguable royal descent. Within twelve weeks of his coronation, on 18 January 1486, the aged Archbishop Bourchier was pressed into service once more to link the Houses of York and Lancaster in marriage. It was reported that 'His hand held the sweet posie, wherein the white and red roses were first tied together.' Considering that it was in the depth of winter, this must have been a remarkable bouquet for those times.

Whatever the truth of the matter, the 'Tudor Rose' was soon to be seen everywhere, symbolising the new royal House of Tudor. As an emblem, it appealed to the imagination of the people, and of course Henry was not slow to encourage its use. He incorporated it in a collar with a pendant of St George and the Dragon, which he gave as insignia to the Order of the Garter, and it became the custom to surround the Royal Arms with a circle of these roses. Popular verses appeared, such as 'A Crowne-garland of Golden Roses gathered out of England's loyal garden: a princely song made of the red rose and white, royally united together by King Henry VII and Elizabeth Plantagenet'. One of its verses ran:

These roses sprang and budded faire, and carried such a grace,
That Kings of England in their armes afford them worthy place,
And flourish may these roses long that all the world may tell
The owners of these princely flowers in virtues doe excell.

Despite her importance in Henry's royal schemes, it is somewhat surprising that Elizabeth of York herself was not given a coronation for almost another two years in November 1487 – a coronation far more magnificent than Henry's. In the meantime she was to give birth to Henry's son and hoped-for heir – the ill-fated Prince Arthur.

ELIZABETH OF YORK, QUEEN OF HENRY VII

Dates as Queen 1486–1503, crowned 25 November 1487,
aged 21

A Tudor Dragon Spouts Flames into the Thames

Although Henry VII's own coronation had been somewhat strained, the coronation of his queen, Elizabeth of York, was a particularly splendid and happy occasion, with celebrations lasting four whole days.

Henry himself must have been much more relaxed and confident. He had married an English princess who had given much-needed extra credibility to his royal position; he now had a son and heir, Prince Arthur, who would inherit the Tudor crown; and earlier in 1487 he had successfully defeated the rebel army led by the Earl of Lincoln on behalf of the imposter Lambert Simnel at the bloody Battle of Stoke Field, near Nottingham. The earl had been killed, but the naïve little ten-year-old, Lambert Simnel, who had been pushed into the limelight to be crowned[†] 'King Edward VI' in Christ Church, Dublin, was now working as a scullion in the royal kitchens in Westminster. Henry quickly realised that young Lambert, by himself, posed no threat to anyone, so in honour of his queen's impending coronation he had magnanimously forgiven him, promoting him to the honourable position of turnspit. Later, Lambert was to become one of his falconers.

Elizabeth's coronation must have been a wonderful moment for her. Her teenage years had been fraught with danger and tragedy. Her mother, Elizabeth Woodville, queen of Edward IV, had spent desperate weeks with her children, claiming sanctuary in Westminster Abbey while her brother-in-law, the Duke of Gloucester, was busy making himself King Richard III.

The former queen had no furniture, only primitive toilet and

[†] Lambert Simnel was crowned as 'Edward VI' in Christ Church Cathedral, Dublin, the Bishop of Meath performing the ceremony with a crown taken from a statue of the Virgin Mary. He had claimed first to be the son of Edward IV and then he changed his story, making out that he was the son of the Duke of Clarence who, according to notorious rumour, had been drowned in a butt of malmsey wine.

washing facilities, and relied on the embarrassed monks to feed her. Her youngest child, Bridget, was only three; Katherine was four; Cicely six; Anne eight; Richard nine; and her eldest had been Elizabeth of York herself, then aged seventeen. During that period of humiliation Elizabeth of York had witnessed the anguish of her mother, the widowed queen, who had been forced to yield up her son Richard to join his elder brother in the Tower of London. These two boys were shortly to disappear for ever, probably murdered on the orders of Richard III. As the eldest in the family, Elizabeth of York would have had to help take charge of her younger siblings in these desperately emotional circumstances.

All this had happened only five years ago. Now, aged twenty-two, married to the King of England and already the mother of the heir to the throne, Elizabeth of York must have had some mixed feelings as she entered Westminster Abbey again, this time to be crowned and anointed queen in her own right.

Henry VII gave his young queen a coronation of exceptional splendour. Festivities began on a Friday as Elizabeth left Greenwich Palace, rowed in a magnificently-decorated barge to the Tower of London, accompanied by Margaret Beaufort, the Countess of Richmond. Following her came the 'Bachelors' Barge' of the gentlemen-students of Lincoln's Inn, which carried a red dragon, the ensign of the new House of Tudor, 'spouting flames of fire into the Thames.' Musicians in the Bachelors' Barge played music to entertain the royal party, and many other barges provided 'pageants, well and curiously devised to do her highness sport and pleasure withal.'

According to John Leland, the 'king's antiquary' under Henry VIII, Elizabeth was wearing a kirtle of white cloth-of-gold damask and a mantle of the same material furred with ermine, fastened on the breast with a great lace of cordon, curiously wrought of gold and silk, finished with rich knobs of gold and tassels. 'On her fair yellow hair, hanging at length down her back, she wore a caul of pipes (a piped net-work) and a circle of gold, richly adorned with gems'. Like her mother, Elizabeth Woodville, the new queen had beautiful blonde hair, and clearly she knew how to make the best of herself.

The citizens of London thronged the streets the next day as Elizabeth made the customary progress through the city to Westminster. She was seated on a litter drawn by eight white horses, and in Cheapside she was greeted by a crowd of children dressed as angels and saints, singing her praises. Velvet and cloth-of-gold hangings hung out of windows all along the route. Lord Stanley, who had played such a crucial part at Bosworth, was now high constable and was in attendance, together with eleven newly-created Knights of the Bath.

The coronation was on the Sunday. This time Elizabeth was dressed in a kirtle of purple velvet, furred with ermine bands in front, and on her hair she had a circlet of gold, set with large pearls and coloured gems. The route from Westminster Hall to the abbey was carpeted with a striped cloth, and the crowds were so impatient to get hold of pieces of this traditional perquisite that some were even trampled to death in the scramble. It was a brief but unhappy incident and the queen's ladies were momentarily 'broken and distroubled'.

Inside the abbey the service was conducted by John Morton, Archbishop of Canterbury, who had recently been appointed Lord Chancellor, and was soon to become notorious for his tax-gathering skills. However, the centre of attention, very properly, was on Elizabeth herself, with her sister Cicely, now eleven, as her train-bearer, and supported by the Bishop of Winchester on one hand and the Bishop of Ely on the other. Henry VII himself took no part in the ceremony, and discreetly watched the coronation from behind a latticed balcony specially constructed in the choir, accompanied by his mother, Margaret Beaufort, who as great-great-granddaughter of Edward III was crucial to his royal pretensions.

This early version of 'God save the King' may have been sung at her coronation:

> God save King Henerie whereso'er he be,
> And for Queene Elizabeth now pray wee,
> And for all her noble progenye;
> God save the Church of Christ from any follie;
> And for Queene Elizabeth now pray wee.

Henry also took a back seat with his mother on a 'goodly stage' set up on one side of the main table at the stately banquet in Westminster Hall which took place afterwards. The newly-crowned queen sat alone at her coronation feast, eating 'pheasant royal, swan with chawdron (a sauce made of chopped entrails and spices), capons of high grease (specially fattened), and pike in latimer sauce.' Lord Fitzwalter acted as her 'sewer or dapifer' (one who brings food) and 'came before her in his surcoat with tabard-sleeves, his hood about his neck, and a towel over all, and sewed all the messes' (served all the dishes). Meanwhile, mistrels both royal and 'of other estates,' provided background music; there were 'three distributions of largesse'; and the lord mayor of London ceremonially presented fruit, wafers and 'hypocras' (wine).

Festivities continued the following morning, the fourth day of coronation celebrations; Elizabeth and Henry attended mass in St Stephen's Chapel, after which 'she kept her estate' – (sat in royal pomp, under a canopy) in the parliament chamber. Guests were received and after another banquet there was a ball at which the queen and her ladies danced. It must have been the happiest time in her life. Little did she know of the savage Tudor century which lay ahead.

HENRY VIII AND CATHERINE OF ARAGON

Reigned 1509–47, crowned 24 June 1509, aged 17

Tudor Magnificence on a Midsummer's Day

Boundlessly energetic, superbly self-confident, and with all the physical strength and restlessness of a young teenager, Henry VIII gave himself and his newly-wed queen a splendidly flamboyant coronation. He adored showing off, and now that his miserly father was dead he knew he could do just what he liked. Hardly any king of England came to the throne in such a mood of sheer animal *joie de vivre*.

Just thirteen days beforehand, he had married Catherine of Aragon, six years his senior, and widow of his much-lamented older brother, Arthur. Now, at twenty-three, she was delighted to be given recognition and attention again. As a mere widow at court, she had been shamefully treated by her father-in-law, and had desperately wanted to return to Spain. In fact, her belongings were being packed up just as Henry VII fell ill and died. Now, at last, fortune's wheel had turned and fate was being kind to her.

With hindsight we take it for granted that Henry was to marry Catherine, as a kind of necessary and smooth sequel to the death of Arthur; but in fact the young uncrowned Henry VIII was dramatically defying his dead father's wishes by marrying her. True, he had been betrothed to Catherine a year after the death of Arthur. The actual treaty of this betrothal had been signed on 23 June 1503, when young Henry was a few days short of his twelfth birthday. However, politics being politics, two years later, the day before his son's fourteenth birthday, Henry VII had made him formally repudiate this betrothal to Catherine in order to be engaged to the seven-year-old Eleanor of Austria. Such a sudden switching of international allegiance put Catherine in an appallingly difficult situation, and although she proudly and obstinately still regarded herself as Henry's future bride, Henry VII treated her with virtual contempt, only grudgingly allowing her food and accommodation. Thus for almost four years Catherine had lived in a limbo of neglect.

The death of Henry VII must have come as an enormous relief to Catherine, and of course for Henry VIII it meant an unexpectedly early assumption of absolute power. The old king had died on 21 April and one of Henry VIII's first acts was to abandon his father's political manoeuvring with Austria and to make immediate preparations for an early marriage with Catherine of Aragon. In marrying his brother's widow Henry was certainly going against the rules of the church, and even Archbishop Warham himself had misgivings. Nevertheless a dispensation had already been sought, and obtained, from the pope when the pair had first been engaged. No one at the time was overly concerned by the fact that this dispensation implied the possibility that Catherine and Arthur had consummated their marriage. Catherine knew that this was not true and Henry was soon to find that she was indeed a virgin.

Henry, then, was impatient and in love and he wanted a companion to share his coronation, fixed to take place on Midsummer Day. In view of the impending coronation, their marriage was a small and private affair at Greenwich. However, in constrast, the coronation festivities were planned on a large and extravagant scale. It was to be the most splendid double coronation of a king and queen since that of Edward I and Eleanor of Castile.

By now, the tradition that kings about to be crowned should spend the previous night or nights before the coronation at the Tower of London had lasted for many reigns. Originally it had been a necessary precaution to stay in an impregnable fortress where rivals could not penetrate. However, it had long become a convenient place from which to stage an elaborate procession through the streets of London, winding its way to the Palace of Westminster and thence to the abbey. It was a chance for the citizens to see the new king and his consort, and make merry with demonstrations of loyalty and drink free wine.

Henry and Catherine arrived at the Tower from Greenwich on 21 June. The next day Henry created twenty-four new knights to accompany him and then, on 23 June the couple proceeded in state to Westminster. Henry wore a robe of crimson velvet furred with ermine and even his horse wore trappings of golden damask edged with ermine. Catherine was dressed in white, as a royal bride, with her hair hanging down her back almost to her heels – a symbol of virginity. Around her head was a coronet set with rich jewels. She was seated in a litter of white cloth of gold, borne by two white horses, and following her came attendant noble ladies carried two by two in open carriages called 'whirlicotes' – a newly-fashionable chariot-like vehicle. Then, close behind, came nine children dressed in blue velvet, representing Henry's territorial possessions: England, Cornwall, Wales, Ireland, Gascony, Guyenne, Normandy, Anjou, and France.

As usual, the streets of London were lavishly decorated for the occasion, and as Henry and Catherine passed along Cornhill, maidens dressed in white lined the route carrying artificial palms of white wax, while priests dressed in their richest robes blessed the royal couple, swinging silver censers. It was all very gratifying. Edward Hall, a contemporary historian, went into ecstasies: 'If I should declare what pain, labour and diligence the tailors, embroiderers and goldsmiths took both to make and devise garments for lords, ladies, knights and esquires and also for decking, trapping and adorning of coursers, jennets (small Spanish horses) and palfreys it were too long to rehearse; but for a surety, more rich, nor more strange nor more curious works hath not been seen than were prepared for this coronation.'

The ceremony in the abbey followed the traditional order of service and after it was over, the participants moved into Westminster Hall to embark on the serious business of eating and drinking. The banquet was memorable. According to Edward Hall the wedding feast was 'greater than any Caesar had known', with Henry and Catherine sitting at an elevated stage in Westminster Hall. 'The trumpets blew up' as the first course, 'sumptuous with many subtleties, strange devices, with several posies and many dainty dishes,' was ushered in by the Duke of Buckingham and the Lord Steward, both on horseback.

At the second course the king's champion cried out the traditional challenge in three different places in the hall: 'If there be any person of what estate or degree so ever he be, that will say or prove that Henry the Eighth is not the rightful inheritor and king of this realm, I, Sir Robert Dymock here, his champion, offer my glove to fight in his quarrel with any person to the utterance' (*à l'outrance*). However, by then the troublesome years of Lambert Simnel and Perkin Warbeck were well and truly over.

Finally, after all the feasting, the royal couple and their guests moved to the courtyard outside Westminster Hall to enjoy displays of jousting. The great fountain there had been transformed into a decorated castle with its roof 'embattled with roses and pomegranates gilded, and under and about the said castle, a curious vine, the leaves and grapes thereof gilded with fine gold.'

Henry's lifestyle in the early years of his reign seems to have consisted very largely of riding, hunting, tilting, wrestling, singing, leaping, dancing, and dressing up fantastically to surprise and delight his new and adoring wife. Catherine herself described it all, as she wrote to her father, as 'continuous feasting'. The coronation jollifications went on for days, and were only brought to a conclusion by the sudden illness and death of Henry's grandmother, Margaret Beaufort, Duchess of Richmond, who had just managed to survive into this turbulent reign.

ANNE BOLEYN, SECOND QUEEN OF HENRY VIII

Dates as Queen 1533–6, crowned 1 June 1533, aged 25 or 26

'The Concubine' Wears St Edward's Crown

Henry VIII had married his second wife, Anne Boleyn, with the utmost secrecy in the darkness of an early January morning. It was a sticky situation; after all, he was committing bigamy. But the fact of the matter was that Anne was pregnant. One of the royal chaplains, Dr Rowland Lee, had received a sudden command on St Paul's Day (January 25) 1533, to celebrate mass in a little-used turret of Whitehall. Somewhat to his surprise, when he got to the required place he found the king with two of the grooms of the chamber and Anne Boleyn with her train-bearer Anne Saville, waiting for him. Immediately he was told to perform the nuptial rite between Henry and Anne in the presence of the three witnesses.

This bizarre situation was hardly steeped in royal splendour, and not unnaturally Lee was somewhat hesitant at first to undertake such an important task. However, Henry assured him that the pope had agreed to the divorce between himself and Catherine of Aragon and that he had a dispensation for a second marriage in his possession. As events would prove, Henry was gambling on the arrival of papal approval which he hoped would soon be on its way. In the circumstances, the chaplain had no choice other than to comply.

When the ceremony was over, all went their several ways, silently, still in the early morning darkness. News of the marriage did not come out until about a fortnight afterwards and the precise date, perhaps in view of Anne Boleyn's condition, was kept obscure. For a while, even Thomas Cranmer, the ever-compliant Archbishop of Canterbury, was kept in total ignorance of the marriage. As for Anne's baby, the future Queen Elizabeth I, she was to be born just eight and a half months later.

Although Anne was known as 'the Concubine', this was hardly fair on her, for she had held out against Henry's advances for months. For her, it was to be marriage or nothing, and this very reluctance inflamed the king's desire for her into a mad lust.

Before the marriage Henry wrote desperately love-lorn letters to her. Once, after not seeing her for a full fortnight he pined for her: 'Mine own sweetheart, these shall be to advertise you of the great elengenes (loneliness) that I find here since your departing. . . . I would not have thought it possible that for so little a while it should have grieved me, but now that I am coming toward you methinketh my pains been half released. . . . Wishing myself (specially an evening) in my sweetheart's arms, whose pretty dukkys (breasts) I trust shortly to kiss. Written with the hand of him that was, is, and shall be yours by his will.'

It seems that Anne did eventually give in to his lusty advances sometime towards the end of 1532 and the pair of them enjoyed a full sex life in anticipation of a formal marriage. The resulting pregnancy required swift action, lest any future heir should be born out of wedlock.

Such was the situation then at the beginning of 1553: Henry was used to getting what he wanted. Confidently, he expected the pope's approval of a divorce, and grew more and more impatient when it did not come. Meanwhile, he needed to display his new queen to the world at large. Preparations were made to give Anne the most lavish coronation possible. Perhaps it was a way of making amends for having married her in such a hole-and-corner fashion; perhaps it was an act of defiance against the pope; perhaps it was to bolster his self-confidence that the marriage *was* legal and morally acceptable: perhaps it was in anticipation of Anne giving birth to a bonny bouncing son; at all events, Archbishop Cranmer's crowning of Anne on 1 June, just four months after their marriage, was one of the most splendid and colourful events of his reign.

Permission for Henry's divorce was still not forthcoming, even less than a month before the date planned for Anne's coronation, so Henry urgently pressed Cranmer to speed up proceedings. Accordingly, Catherine of Aragon was summoned to attend an ecclesiastical court at Dunstable in Bedfordshire – well away from London and about six miles from Ampthill, where she was then living.

Catherine flatly refused to acknowledge the very existence of this court and predictably failed to appear. Henry was not there either, as he was too busy preparing Anne's coronation. Hence it was that Cranmer, in front of just two notaries in the Lady Chapel of Dunstable Priory, solemnly declared Catherine to be 'contumacious'; that her marriage to Henry was null and void; and that both Henry and Catherine were henceforth free to marry elsewhere if they chose.

The busy and dutiful archbishop then hastened back to London where, just one week later, he was to place St Edward's Crown on the head of Anne Boleyn. It is worth noting that Anne is still the only English queen consort to have been granted the honour of being crowned with this almost sacred crown – a measure of Henry VIII's determination to establish his new wife with emphatic firmness as the undisputed queen of England. None of his four later wives were given coronations.

Events leading up to Anne's Whitsun coronation began with the customary procession through the city streets from the Tower of London to Westminster, and these celebrations were exceptionally costly and elaborate even by Henry's standards. The lord mayor of London, Sir Stephen Peacock, was charged with the task of conveying Anne from Greenwich to the Tower. Fifty gaily-decorated barges accompanied him: some filled with scarlet-clad city gentlemen, some with guns firing ferociously, one with a dragon spouting flames, another with a bevy of virgins singing the queen's praises, and yet another with a band, playing on 'shalms' and 'shag-bushes'.

Henry himself met her at the Tower, which had just undergone a massive rebuilding programme, including a new gallery for the queen. Then, after spending two nights there, Anne set out for Westminster on the Saturday morning. Edward Hall, who was himself an eye-witness, provides a detailed account of her open litter:

> The litter was covered with cloth of gold shot with white, and the two palfreys which supported the litter were clad, heads and all, in a garb of white damask, and were led by the queen's footmen. Anne was dressed in a surcoat of silver tissue, and a mantle of the same, lined with ermine. She wore her dark tresses flowing down her shoulders, and on her head a coif, with a circlet of precious rubies. A canopy of cloth of gold was borne over her by four knights on foot. The queen's litter was preceded by her chancellor, and followed by her chamberlain, lord Borough; William Cosyns, her

master of horse, led her own palfrey, trapped down to the ground with cloth of gold. After came seven ladies, in crimson velvet, trimmed with cloth of gold, riding on palfreys, and two chariots covered with red cloth of gold; in the first of which were the old duchess of Norfolk and the marchioness of Dorset, and in the other chariot were four ladies of the bedchamber. Fourteen other court ladies followed, with thirty of their waiting-maids on horseback, in silk and velvet; and then followed the guard, in coats ornamented with beaten gold.

Along the route were all kinds of pageants, fountains running with wine, children declaiming verses, banners in Latin proclaiming such sentiments as 'Proceed, Queen Anne and reign prosperously!' or 'Queen Anne, when thou shalt bear a new son of the King's blood, there shall be a golden world unto thy people!' – and the aldermen of London presented her with a purse containing a thousand marks of gold 'which she very thankfully received with many goodly words.' Finally arriving at Westminster Hall, she was welcomed with wine, comfits and sugar-plums.

But the ordinary people of London were muted in their expressions of loyalty. After the procession Anne is reported to have remarked to the king that she had seen 'a great many caps on heads and saw but few tongues', in other words there were few caps raised in her honour and not much cheering. Both Henry and Anne knew that she had to battle to win popularity. Some people even believed she had used witchcraft to obtain power over the king, and there was still much sympathy for Catherine of Aragon, banished from London, but not from people's memories. Henry's and Anne's initials, H and A were widely used in the coronation decorations (they are also to be found in King's College, Cambridge) and HA! HA! was a source of sniggering humour behind the royal backs.

However, despite coolness in certain quarters, Anne put on a brave face. Her moment of triumph came on the Whitsunday in Westminster Abbey, when Thomas Cranmer anointed her on the head and breast, put the crown of St Edward on her head and gave her the golden sceptres to carry.

Afterwards, the usual banquet in Westminster Hall took place.

Henry stood apart and watched his new queen from a distance, allowing her to be the sole focus of attention. Anne behaved with exemplary table-manners, for throughout the meal the Countess of Oxford stood at her right and the Countess of Worcester on her left, both charged with the task of holding a 'fine cloth before the queen's face, whenever she listed to spit or do otherwise at her pleasure'.

It is not recorded whether a champion came forward to demand if anyone challenged her right to be queen. But then, if a Dymoke *had* put this awkward question, who would possibly have dared to reply?

This day saw the pinnacle of Anne's fortunes. Now she would look forward, perhaps with some concern, to September when everyone knew she was duty-bound to produce Henry's longed-for son and heir.

EDWARD VI

Reigned 1547–53, crowned 19 February 1547, aged 9 years

'King Edward Upspringeth From Puerility and Towards Us Bringeth Joy and Tranquillity'

At the age of nine, little Edward was small enough at his coronation to be able to lie face-down on the altar in Westminster Abbey and be anointed on his back by his godfather, Archbishop Thomas Cranmer. The good archbishop must have been relieved to see such a young and apparently harmless lad on the throne, after the appalling turmoil and bloody executions he had witnessed during Henry VIII's reign. Also, he knew that the new king, young though he was, nevertheless had very firm religious opinions – Protestant ones.

In view of the king's age and tender years, the coronation service was greatly abridged, partly 'for the tedious length of the same' and partly because 'many points of the same were such as, by the laws of the nation, not allowable.' Indeed, the old form of election did not form a part of the service, as the archbishop simply presented the young prince as 'rightful and undoubted inheritor'. The consent of the people was asked only to the ceremony of the coronation.

Unusual, too, was the fact that the crown was held by 'my Lord Protector, the Duke of Somerset', Edward Seymour, as well as the archbishop. For the first time in history three crowns were used: St Edward's Crown and the King's Imperial Crown were briefly placed on his head, and a third, a 'rich crown made purposely for his grace', probably specially made to fit his head, was also worn. Unfortunately, the last crown disappeared at the time of the Commonwealth and no detailed records of it remain. Also this may have been the first coronation at which a copy of the Bible was presented to the Sovereign.

According to the nineteenth-century Dean of Westminster, Dr Arthur Stanley, Cranmer's short address was 'perhaps the boldest and most pregnant utterance ever delivered in the abbey. He warned the young king against confounding orthodoxy with morality. He insisted on the supremacy of the royal authority over both the Bishops of Rome and the Bishops of Canterbury.' Then, taking as his text, 'The wiser sort will look to their claws, and clip them,' and describing the coronation service itself, the archbishop pointed out to his young monarch:

> in what respect the solemn rites of coronation have their ends and utility, yet neither direct force nor necessity; they be good admonitions to put kings in mind of their duty to God, but no increasement of their dignity: for they be God's anointed – not in respect of the oil which the bishop useth, but in consideration of their power, which is ordained; of the sword, which is authorised; of their persons, which are elected of God, and endued with the gifts of His Spirit, for the better ruling and guiding of His people. The oil, if added, is but a ceremony: if it be wanting, that king is yet a perfect monarch notwithstanding, and God's anointed, as well as if he was inoiled. Now for the person or bishop that doth anoint a king, it is proper to be done by the chiefest. But if they cannot, or will not, any bishop may perform this ceremony. – He described what God requires at the hands of kings and rulers – that is, religion and virtue. Therefore not from the Bishop of Rome, but as a messenger from my Saviour Jesus Christ, I shall most humbly admonish your Royal Majesty what things your Highness is to perform.

Cranmer then required the nine-year-old sitting before him:

> like Josiah, to see God truly worshipped, and idolatry destroyed; to reward virtue, to revenge sin, to justify the innocent, to relieve the poor, to procure peace, to repress violence, and to execute justice throughout your realms.

It was a tall order, but Edward VI was old beyond his years, already a prodigy of precocious wisdom, who before he was twelve would write a tract in French against the pope. He was about to take his Protestant duties, as outlined by the archbishop, with terrifying sharpness.

The coronation itself took place on 19 February, a Shrove Tuesday, traditionally a day for merry-making. Naturally enough, the main business for his majesty's subjects on the previous day was to produce pageant after pageant to amuse him as he made the traditional progress through the streets of London from the Tower to Westminster.

Edward rode a white pony caparisoned with silver, and wore a white velvet waistcoat and cloak slashed with Venetian silver brocade, embroidered with pearls. Over him was carried a white silk canopy, fringed with silver. On either side of him rode his two uncles, his dead mother's brothers Edward Seymour, Duke of Somerset, now his 'Protector'; and Thomas Seymour, Lord High Admiral, who would shortly become his step-father by marrying the dowager queen, Catherine Parr. Within a few years, uncle Edward would execute uncle Thomas for treason, and a few years later it would be uncle Edward's turn to have 'his head cut off', as the young king would record in his private journal. However, the future must have seemed filled with limitless power and riches for both of them as they accompanied their nephew through the decorated streets.

The boy king met 'Faith', 'Justice' and 'Truth' in Fleet Street, each of whom recited a lengthy poem in his honour, and Faith held a Bible in her hand – still a rare and valuable item, but one which Edward himself held to be supremely important. Temple Bar was 'new painted in dyvers colours' and hung with cloth-of-arras and decorated with innumerable flags and standards. As the procession passed under the arch of Temple Bar a fanfare 'blew sweetly', played by seven French trumpeters and a choir of children sang an anthem for the new monarch. An 'Angel' descended from a triumphal arch at Cheapside, and presented Edward with a purse containing £1,000; and a 'Giant' welcomed him at London Bridge.

Entertainment followed entertainment – so many so that Edward became too impatient to watch or listen to some of them. It was noted that he spurred his horse to escape an old man dressed up as Edward the Confessor, who was hoping to declaim a long ode in Latin. Probably the sight which captivated him the most was a Spanish acrobat who performed a dazzlingly dangerous display of rope-dancing and then glided on his chest down a tightrope, without using hands or feet, all the way down from St Paul's steeple to the pavement near the deanery gate. After prostrating himself and kissing the king's feet he nimbly climbed all the way back up again to the top of St Paul's.

Then there were numerous popular songs, many composed in an extraordinary kind of doggerel verse. But they possessed an innocent exuberance, probably much more acceptable to the king than formal Latin odes. A jolly example was:

> King Edward upspringeth from puerility,
> And towards us bringeth joy and tranquillity;
> Our hearts may be light, and merry our cheer,
> He shall be of such might that all the world may him fear.
> > Sing up, heart; sing up, heart; sing no more down,
> > But joy in King Edward that weareth the crown!
> His father, late our sovereign, each day and also hour,
> That in joy he might reign, like a prince in high power,
> By sea and land, hath provided for him eke (also),
> That never King of England had ever the like.
> > Sing up, heart; sing up, heart; sing no more down,
> > But joy in King Edward that weareth the crown!
>
> He hath gotten already Bullen (Boulogne) that goodly town,
> And biddeth sing speedily up and down,
> When he waxeth weight, and to manhood down spring,
> He shall be without fail of four realms the King.
> > Sing up, heart; sing up, heart; sing no more down,
> > But joy in King Edward that weareth the crown!

Ye children of England, for the hour of the same,
Take bow and shaft in hand, learn shootage to frame,
That you another day so do your parts
As to serve your King as well with hands as with hearts.
        Sing up, heart, sing up, heart; sing no more down,
        But joy in King Eward that weareth the crown!

The usual banquet in Westminster Hall followed after the coronation, and the challenge was made without being taken up. Joustings brought the day to a conclusion.

True, there were some grumblings. Trade had suffered because very few women had been present, and so the tailors and jewellers and embroiderers had not been able to cash in on the event. It was also noticed that although the streets had been thronged with people, there had been very little cheering. People were moved by curiosity rather than any genuine sense of loyalty: after all, the boy-king was an unknown personality. In any case, the very fact that the event occurred only three weeks after the death of Henry VIII meant that much of the preparations had to be done in a hurried, makeshift manner. Nevertheless, we can sense a feeling of smug satisfaction in the words which Edward wrote in his diary that night: 'it was asked of the people "whether they would have him to be their king"; and they answered "Yea, Yea." '

MARY I

Reigned 1553–8, crowned 1 October 1553, aged 37

Here Present is Mary, Rightful and Undoubted Inheritrix

Stephen Gardiner, Bishop of Winchester, who had been personally rescued from imprisonment in the Tower of London by Queen Mary, officiated at this autumn coronation. It was now the turn of the Archbishop of Canterbury, Thomas Cranmer, to be incarcerated there, as he had been implicated in the plot to put Lady Jane Grey on the throne. In any case, his Protestant theological beliefs were abhorrent to the new queen. The Archbishop of York, Robert Holgate, had also been stripped of his rank and imprisoned for the heinous crime of being married. Luckily for him, however, he obtained his release by declaring that he repented of his marriage and that he had only married for fear of being thought a papist. He offered to put his wife away, obey the queen's laws and pay £1,000. His wealth was enormous, but he loyally made no mention of his wife in his will.

Gardiner it was, then – Henry VIII's highly-valued private secretary – who had the unusual honour, as a mere bishop, of crowning the new queen. For him it was a happy and unlooked-for change of fortune, for he had suffered much under the reign of Edward VI. In June 1548 he had been required to preach before the king (then aged ten) to make his theological position clear. He thought he had done so without offence, but the very next day he had been arrested, deprived of his bishopric, and sent to the Tower, where he was held for the next five years, until the accession of Mary.

One of Mary's first acts on entering London, in the immediate aftermath of the Duke of Northumberland's plot to put Jane Grey on the throne, had been to go directly to the Tower of London and to release the high-profile captives. It is said that Mary burst into tears as she recognised old friends, kneeling before her in front of the Chapel of St Peter-ad-Vincula. 'Ye are my prisoners!' she said; and raised them one by one, kissed them and gave them their liberty.

Now, three months later, Bishop Gardiner, now Lord Chancellor, was standing before her and beginning the coronation service with words heavily pregnant with meaning in the light of recent events:

Sirs – Here present is Mary, rightful and undoubted inheritrix, by the laws of God and man, to the crown and royal dignity of this realm of England, France and Ireland; and you shall understand, that this day is appointed by all the peers of this land for the consecration, unction, and coronation of the said most excellent princess Mary. Will you serve at this time, and give your wills and assent to the same consecration, unction and coronation?

Yes, indeed, Mary *was* the 'undoubted inheritrix'. The scheming Duke of Northumberland and his fellow-traitors had now been sent to the block and there must have been a palpable sense of relief among Catholics and traditionalists to know that normal religious beliefs and practices were now being restored. And so, although it was unique to have a queen on the throne, reigning in her own right, Queen Mary's coronation demonstrated a clear and obvious succession. Hopefully, the protestant movement would now wither away, and in one of her first pronouncements the new queen commanded 'her good and loving subjects to live together in Christian charity.' In view of 'Bloody' Mary's later reputation perhaps it needs something of an effort to remember that in these early days of her reign she enjoyed genuine popular affection – after all, she was Bluff King Hal's daughter, and many people still had happy memories of her mother, Catherine of Aragon, before the arrival of Anne Boleyn.

The atmosphere in London, then, was one of relief and unfeigned rejoicing as Queen Mary made the traditional progress from the Tower of London to Westminster. As a queen, she was habitually attended by women, and on this occasion she was accompanied by seventy ladies on horseback, all dressed in crimson velvet. Five hundred gentlemen, nobles and various ambassadors and dignitaries went before her; and Mary herself was seated in a splendid litter covered in cloth of silver and supported between six white horses. She was dressed in a gown of blue velvet, furred with ermine, and on her head was a caul of gold network, enriched with pearls and precious stones. John Stow, the contemporary London historian, remarked that this headpiece was so heavy 'that she was fain to bear up her head with her hand.'

Following just behind Mary, riding in an open carriage decorated with crimson velvet came the Princess Elizabeth – later Elizabeth I – accompanied by Henry VIII's only surviving widow, Anne of Cleves. Both of them were dressed in robes of cloth of silver with large hanging sleeves. Anne of Cleves, now aged thirty-eight, had lived in comfort since being summarily divorced for being an unsuitable wife for Henry. As for Elizabeth, she had lived in obscurity and poverty. At twenty, she was enjoying the first happy public event of her life. Seeing her in splendour for virtually the first time, Londoners must have marvelled at what a beautiful young woman she had now become.

As in all the Tudor coronation processions the city was highly decorated, and pageant after pageant presented extraordinary entertainments for the coronation guests. 'Giants' were seen and an anonymous eye-witness gives us a hair-raising account of an acrobat, 'Peter the Dutchman', who performed amazing dare-devil antics on the top of the spire of Old St Paul's: apparently he had 'made two scaffolds upon the top of Paul's steeple, the one upon the ball thereof, and the other upon the top thereof above that . . . and he himself standing upon the very top or back of the weathercock, did shake a little flag with his hand, after standing on one foot did shake his other leg, and then kneeled on his knees upon the said weathercock, to the great marvel and wondering of all the people which beheld him, because it was thought a matter impossible.' When we remember that this spire was 489 ft from the pavement – 85 ft higher than Salisbury cathedral's – we can share the 'wondering' of the crowds who were watching.

Queen Mary and her attendants pressed on to the royal residence in Whitehall. A great fire had destroyed the king's apartments in the Palace of Westminster in the last years of Henry VIII's reign, but he had already acquired Wolsey's 'White Hall'. This was now the centre of an ever-expanding complex of royal buildings, tilt-yards, tennis-court, bowling green, cock-pit, and countless apartments for court officials.

The climax of all these festivities came at the coronation itself on Sunday 1 October. Blue cloth was laid from a marble chair in Westminster Hall to Westminster Abbey, and the altar there was covered with cloth of gold. The queen was dressed in crimson robes and walked under a canopy borne by the barons of the Cinque Ports, supported on her right hand by the Bishop of Durham and on her left by the Earl of Shrewsbury. Her half-sister, the red-headed Princess Elizabeth, walked immediately behind her. Following after Elizabeth came Anne of Cleves, who had been given a position of honour as befitted a former queen (albeit briefly) of England.

Mary was met in Westminster Hall by Stephen Gardiner together with ten other bishops, all wearing their mitres and copes of gold cloth, and then, after being censed and sprinkled with holy water, the procession wound its way into the abbey for the elaborate, lengthy and traditional coronation service. After making her coronation oaths, swearing upon the Host to observe and keep them, Mary prostrated herself before the high altar and remained there motionless while Gardiner sang the hymn of invocation to the Holy Ghost, beginning *Veni, Creator Spiritus*, with the choir and organ joining in.

Like her half-brother, Mary wore three crowns during the service: St Edward's Crown, the Imperial Crown of the realm of England, and a third crown specially made for her. A fanfare of trumpets blared out as Gardiner placed each of these on her head. Elizabeth I was the last sovereign to be crowned with three crowns.

Having been anointed and invested with Ring, Jewelled Bracelets, Sceptre, St Edward's Staff, Spurs, Ball of Gold and 'Regall', the queen was brought to St Edward's Chair and received the homage of the bishops and nobility present as they approached her one by one and kissed her on her left cheek. It was the triumphant culmination of her life, after decades of neglect and abuse.

The banquet which followed was equally impressive. The queen's champion, Sir Edward Dymoke, threw down his gauntlet with the challenge that if there be any manner of man that will say that our sovereign lady Queen Mary is not the rightful and undoubted inheritrix . . . 'I say he lieth like a false traitor!' However, this was not the time for strife or rebellion. Many must have had vivid thoughts about the Duke of Northumberland and Lady Jane Grey: but no one picked up the gauntlet. The last Catholic coronation to take place in England was now over, and Queen Mary settled into her task of re-converting her realm and cleansing it of such misguided heretics such as the wicked and wretched Archbishop Cranmer.

ELIZABETH I

Reigned 1558–1603, crowned 15 January 1559, aged 25

A Soothsayer Chooses the Most Auspicious Date for the New Queen's Coronation

Elizabeth was sitting under an oak tree in the grounds of Hatfield House when a messenger arrived from St James's Palace bringing her the news that Mary had died and that she was now queen. According to tradition, she had been studying her psalter at the time.

Although she was first in line to the throne, Princess Elizabeth had been held under virtual house arrest throughout most of Mary's reign: indeed for two months she had been a prisoner in the Tower of London, held under suspicion of treason; and then for almost a year after that she had been held closely guarded at Woodstock, near Oxford. Her only hope had been to dress soberly, and to behave with conspicuous piety, so as not to attract attention to herself. These were years when suspicion of disloyalty or Protestant sympathy could bring death by execution or burning. Elizabeth had known her kinswoman Lady Jane Grey well: she had been executed. Archbishop Cranmer had counselled her mother, Anne Boleyn: he had been burnt.

News of her accesssion, therefore, was a moment of exquisite joy and freedom for Elizabeth. 'It is the Lord's doing,' she exclaimed, 'and it is marvellous in our eyes.' She held her accession council in the timbered Great Hall at Hatfield House, and one of the first acts of her reign was to appoint William Cecil to be her chief minister. She had an uncanny eye for judging those who would serve her best, and Cecil, afterwards Lord Burghley, remained her chief minister for the remaining forty years of his life.

The date of Elizabeth's accession and release from threat of imprisonment or death was so important to her that 'Queen Elizabeth's Day' – 17 November – was kept as a national holiday and festival until the end of her life – and astonishingly, was kept as a date of rejoicing until well into the eighteenth century, even into the reign of Queen Anne. For years, Elizabeth continued to thank the almighty for this deliverance. Within days she had gathered her attendants and lords and ladies-in-waiting, and then with a retinue of over a thousand courtiers she made her joyful way to London, to receive the unfeigned welcome of her people.

Shrewd, highly intelligent, lively yet supremely self-disciplined and diplomatic, Elizabeth undertook her duties with consummate artistry. No one has ever practised royal skills so successfully. She had the intuitive ability of an actress to know exactly how to respond to people and situations. Thus it was that when she met the lord mayor of London and acknowledged the tumultuous welcome of the huge crowds who turned out to greet her, everyone knew that here was a star performer. She knew exactly how to win their loyalty and love. Sir John Hayward, an appreciative eyewitness of Elizabeth on what would nowadays be called a walkabout, wrote:

> If ever any person had either the gift or the style to win the hearts of the people, it was this Queen. All her faculties were in motion, and every motion seemed a well-guided action; her eye was set upon one, her ear listened to another, her judgement ran upon a third, to a fourth she addressed her speech; her spirit seemed to be everywhere. Some she pitied, some she commended, some she thanked, at others she pleasantly and wittily jested, condemning no person, neglecting no office, and distributing her smiles, looks and graces so artfully that thereupon the people again redoubled the testimony of their joys, and afterwards, raising everything to the highest strain, filled the ears of all men with immoderate extolling of their princess.

As she arrived at the Tower of London, the memory of that dreadful moment when she had been taken there as the prisoner of Queen Mary filled her mind, and she uttered a public prayer before the listening crowd:

> O Lord, Almighty and Everlasting God, I give Thee most hearty thanks that Thou hast been so merciful unto me as to spare me to behold this day.

Then she turned directly to them and declared:

> Some have fallen from being princes of this land to be prisoners in this place. I am raised from being a prisoner in this place to be a prince in this land. That dejection was a work of God's justice. This advancement is a work of His mercy.

Popular and loved by the common people from these early days, there was nevertheless a deep concern among the bishops and clergy about exactly what would now take place in the churches. What exactly was the extent of Elizabeth's Protestantism? Were Catholics now in danger? And in any case, who would dare crown a heretic such as Elizabeth? And *was* she a heretic? Until she actually became queen, she had kept a wise silence.

The last Catholic Archbishop of Canterbury, Cardinal Pole, had died coincidentally and almost symbolically within twelve hours of the death of the last Catholic monarch, Queen Mary. There was, therefore, a vacancy at the head of the church. As for Nicholas Heath, the Archbishop of York, he had bluntly stated that he would refuse to crown a heretical (Protestant) queen. As for the rest of the bishops, clearly they were in a state of bemusement, lacking a leader but still adhering to Catholic beliefs and practices. After all, it was little more than two years since Archbishop Cranmer had been publicly burnt for his Protestantism.

Elizabeth publicly demonstrated her Protestantism at Christmas 1558, in the two-month period between her accession to the throne in November and her coronation in January 1559. Bishop Oglethorpe of Carlisle was to celebrate the Christmas mass in the queen's chapel at Whitehall, and Elizabeth significantly sent him sharp instructions that he was to *omit the elevation of the Host* – the most highly-charged and sacred moment in the service for Catholics, but abhorrent to Protestants who could not accept the doctrine of transubstantiation. Ogelthorpe received the queen's message but decided to ignore it. When the critical moment came and he began to elevate the bread and wine, Elizabeth broke out with loud protests and categorically ordered him to stop. The tension felt by the congregation must have been acute. Bishop Ogelthorpe, placed in an appallingly difficult situation, resolutely continued to raise the Host according to Catholic custom. As he did so, Elizabeth, livid with rage, rose from her seat and swept out of the chapel in royal fury.

Such, then, was the religious background to the coronation service which was to be held just three weeks later. Just two days after this incident at Christmas, Elizabeth issued a proclamation forbidding all preaching until further notice. Thus gagged, the bishops and clergy were in a state of ferment and none of them was prepared to crown this new queen.

Meanwhile, preparations were well in hand to stage a glittering and sumptuous state occasion. Coronations were not merely a matter of crowning and anointing, but also of showing magnificence and opulence to the crowds. Instinctively, Elizabeth knew that with the love and goodwill of the ordinary people, her hand would be immeasurably strengthened in the political and religious tussles which lay ahead. What the people adored above all were the decorations, pageants, triumphal arches, jugglers, dancers, acrobats, gorgeous dresses and ostentatious display of wealth which always went with a coronation. Queen Mary's bonfires of human flesh at Smithfield needed to be forgotten.

Elizabeth's joyful procession from the Tower to Westminster was an occasion to remember. There must have been many in the crowds who had witnessed the procession of Anne Boleyn, Elizabeth's mother, just twenty-five years before, who would have remembered that Anne was pregnant at the time with the child they were now welcoming as their queen. Elizabeth was told during her progress through the streets of London that one old man was seen to be weeping. 'I warrant you, it is for gladness!' she replied.

It became virtually impossible for the royal party to press through the people, all enthusiastically cheering and straining to get near her. The first pageant to greet her was near Fenchurch Street. A small boy, perched on a scaffold, leaned out towards her to recite a welcome. Elizabeth immediately ordered her chariot to stop, so that she could listen to the words:

O peerless Sovereign Queen! Behold, what this thy town
Hath thee presented with, at thy First Entrance here!
Behold! with how rich hope, she leadeth thee to thy Crown!
Behold, with what two gifts, she comforteth thy cheer!
The First is Blessing Tongues! which many a 'Welcome!' say,
Which pray, thou may'st do well! why praise thee to the sky!
Which wish to thee long life! which bless this happy day!
Which to thy Kingdom 'Heapes!' (Hips!), all that in tongues can
    lie.
The Second is True Hearts! which love thee from their root!
Whose Suit is Triumph now, and ruleth all the game,
Which Faithfulness has won, and all untruth driven out;
Which skip for joy, whenas they hear thy happy name!

Welcome, therefore, O Queen! as much as heart can think,
Welcome again, O Queen! as much as tongue can tell,
Welcome to joyous Tongues, and Hearts that will not shrink!
'GOD, thee preserve!' we pray; and wish thee ever well!

As the child finished, the crowds 'gave a great shout' and Elizabeth thanked them all. A contemporary account describes how 'the Queen Majesty's countenance, during the time that the child spake, besides a perpetual attentiveness in her face, a marvellous change in look, as the child's words touched either her person, or the people's tongues and hearts.' It was a memorable start to a lifetime's performance before her people.

At the end of Gracechurch Street was a symbolic representation of the union of York and Lancaster, with figures of Henry VII and Elizabeth of York, displayed with red and white roses and 'loud noises of music'. Then at the little conduit in Cheapside 'Time' and 'Truth' appeared before the queen. 'Who is yonder old man with the beard?' she asked, and when her attendant Sir John Parot told her it was 'Time', she was heard to reply, 'It is Time that hath brought me here!' 'Truth' then presented her with a Bible, which she held up in both hands, kissed, and clasped to her heart, thanking the city and 'promising to be a diligent reader thereof.' She was also pleased to accept a purse of crimson satin, richly wrought with gold, containing a thousand marks in gold. Her promise was heartfelt: 'I will be as good unto you as ever Queen was to her people! No will in me can lack! Neither, do I trust, shall there lack any power! And persuade yourselves that, for the safety and quietness of you all, I will not spare, if need be, to shed my blood: God thank you all!'

Elizabeth had come into her own at last. She relished every moment: accepting a spray of rosemary from an old woman; listening to yet more poems recited by children; making extempore speeches of thanks; and showing 'merry countenance to such as stood afar off, and most tender and gentle language to those that stood nigh.' Queen Elizabeth's procession through London marked the high-point of medieval and Tudor coronation merry-making. Never again would the capital experience quite the same spontaneous jollity, or enjoy quite such unfettered rapport with a sovereign.

Having captured the hearts of her people, Elizabeth must have felt strengthened as she entered Westminster Abbey the following day to assume regal power. Despite her popularity among her subjects, the tensions of religious controversy were still high, and many must have wondered what form of service would be chosen. Would it be Catholic or Protestant? Would it be in Latin or in English? Would the Host be elevated? And if it were, what would Elizabeth's reaction be? And in any case, who among the bishops would finally agree to crown her?

In fact, it was Owen Oglethorpe, Bishop of Carlisle, who had refused to obey the queen at that Christmas mass who broke ranks from the bench of bishops and reluctantly assented to the task of crowning Elizabeth. Much pressure was borne upon him to officiate at the forthcoming coronation and in agreeing to do so perhaps he felt that he owed some sort of gesture to the queen to atone for his disobedience. At all events, he borrowed the robes of the Bishop of London (Elizabeth had already put him in prison) and prepared to crown the 'heretic' queen.

Even so, it was a tussle of wills. Elizabeth demanded that the service should be in English. Oglethorpe refused point-blank. After what must have been a sharp exchange of views, a compromise was arrived at: after all, Elizabeth was still vulnerable and needed to be crowned and anointed, while Oglethorpe was still a practising Catholic and needed to retain credibility among his fellow churchmen. It was decided that the service should follow the medieval Latin rubric of the *Liber Regalis* but that the Epistle and Gospel should be read in English as well. It was the tentative beginning of Elizabeth's reforming compromises.

Having settled this, a further question arose. Who would assist Oglethorpe? Traditionally the sovereign was supported by the Bishops of Durham and Bath, but of course they were among those who were refusing to take part in the coronation. The matter was relatively easily solved by allowing the Earls of Shrewsbury and Pembroke to assume that duty. And then, at the centre of proceedings, the figure to step forward and hold an English Bible aloft for Elizabeth to make her coronation oath was none other than her newly-appointed Secretary, William Cecil – no ecclesiast, but a symbol of Elizabeth's practical grasp of political power. And when the moment came in the coronation service for the homage, it was the temporal peers who first knelt and kissed the queen: the bishops, for the first time, came second.

And finally, the most significant moment in the service, from the Protestant point of view, came during mass, when Oglethorpe was again insisting on elevating the Host. This time, Elizabeth was prepared for it. A coronation was hardly the moment to shout out her disapproval as she had done before, so with a deliberate preplanned move, she rose and withdrew from the service into a private curtained-off area – St Edward's Chapel – until that part of the service was over. Thus both queen and bishop emerged with honour intact and at the end of the day Elizabeth could claim to be 'Defender of the True, Ancient, Catholic Faith', while not actually having been present at a crucial part of the ritual.

Coded gestures and coded language were intrinsic to Elizabeth's coronation. Even when the Garter King of Arms proclaimed her titles, there was a curious mystification of language:

> . . . the most high and mighty princess, our dread sovereign, lady Elizabeth, by the grace of God, queen of England, France, Ireland, Defender of the true, ancient, and catholic faith, most worthy empress from the Orcade Isles to the Mountains Pyrenee. . . .

It has been conjectured that all this high-flown circumlocution meant that Elizabeth would protect all those who were renouncing the pope's authority, from the Calvinists in the north of Scotland to the reformers in the south of France. But who could pin a precise meaning to such an elaborately ambiguous proclamation?

Those who came for the spectacle were not disappointed. The torch-lit abbey was hung with rich tapestries; the music was impressive; the queen herself wore 'a mantle of crimson velvet, furred with ermine, with a cordon of silk and gold, with buttons and tassels of the same; a train and surcoat of the same velvet, the train and skirt furred with ermine; a cap of maintenance, striped with passaments of gold lace, and a tassel of gold to the same.' Everything was done with grand and punctilious ceremony, and although, later, Elizabeth confided to her ladies-in-waiting that the anointing oil 'was grease and smelled ill', she must have felt immense satisfaction at the end of the day.

Perhaps the most curious circumstance of all, however, was the fact that Elizabeth had consulted her personal astrologer – Dr John Dee – to determine the most auspicious date on which her coronation should take place. Dee had a formidable reputation as a wizard and soothsayer and he had been one of the original fellows of Trinity College, Cambridge, founded by her father,

Henry VIII, in the last year of his reign. He was an engagingly eccentric character, who had been imprisoned by Queen Mary, who thought he was trying to kill her by magic. Elizabeth, however, good Protestant as she was, consulted him on several occasions during her reign, even visiting him twice at his home in Mortlake. Dee dutifully studied his astrological charts for the new queen and triumphantly came up with 15 January as the best date for her coronation. He predicted that if Elizabeth were to be crowned on this very day, her reign would surely be glorious and prosperous.

JAMES I AND ANNE OF DENMARK

Reigned 1603–25, crowned 25 July 1603, aged 37

A Poor Man Arriving at the Land of Promise

James never knew what it was like not to be king. Of course, he wouldn't have remembered his first coronation, as King James VI of Scotland, as he was aged only thirteen months at the time.

The circumstances of that coronation, on 29 July 1567, were fraught with tension. Five days earlier his mother, Mary, Queen of Scots, had been forced to abdicate, or have her throat cut. The Scottish and Calvinist lords were only too pleased to have a baby as their king – it meant that power was freely available to anyone who could grab it. So it was that the infant James was proclaimed King James VI of Scotland in the Church of the Holy Rood, just outside Stirling Castle. The ceremony was held according to Protestant rites in the 'mother tongue' (Scots) and the baby was not anointed, as this was felt to be too 'Jewish'.

James was thirty-seven when Elizabeth I died: a king well used to authority in his own country, but not at all accustomed to the sophistication of the court in London. He had marvelled at the sumptuous country houses he had stayed in as he travelled south with his retinue – even the fact that they were not fortified against marauding clansmen was a source of surprise to him. And when he reached William Cecil's beautiful home at Theobalds, in Essex, he was so impressed with it that shortly afterwards he begged Cecil to let him have it for himself. (Cecil was given the royal residence of Hatfield House in exchange.)

Arriving at Waltham, James and his retinue were met by one of the sheriffs attended by sixty servants. From there they were brought to Stamford Hill and given a formal welcome by the lord mayor and aldermen 'in velvet and gold chains' and five hundred citizens 'richly apparelled'. William Shakespeare and eight other actors were members of this procession, each wearing 4½ yards of scarlet cloth, given them to make into cloaks. The new king was then escorted into London, and ushered into the royal residence at Whitehall.

James must have been overjoyed by his good luck, perhaps remembering that when he had given Anne her coronation in Scotland he had been so poor that he had had to write to the Earl of Mar, begging him to lend him a pair of silk stockings, and he had had to borrow spoons from Anne's courtiers for the coronation feast afterwards. Living in England was to be a much-welcome change of lifestyle for the new king and queen.

Planning the coronation was going to be difficult, however, because the bubonic plague was raging fiercely in London. More than 33,500 deaths were recorded in the metropolitan area alone. One in three of the parishioners of St Giles in Cripplegate were to die, and there were no fewer than 2,879 burials. Against this background, it was impossible to organise street festivals, and it was found advisable to cancel the traditional procession from the Tower of London to Westminster altogether. James actually forbade people to gather in the streets to celebrate the occasion.

It was a very muted occasion on 25 July – appropriately chosen because it was St James's Day – when James and Anne went by boat from Whitehall to the privy stairs of Westminster Palace and then walked into Westminster Abbey for their English coronation. Both of them had been crowned before, in Scotland, but this was a much more elaborate ceremony, with Elizabeth's trusted Archbishop of Canterbury, John Whitgift, ready to crown them, and Launcelot Andrewes, Dean of Westminster, helping to open the royal garments for the anointing, holding 'the oyle in a little goulden ladell'.

Both James and Anne were wearing robes of crimson velvet. Anne wore a coronet of gold with her fair, long hair loosely flowing down to her waist. When the king seated himself on the sacred Stone of Scone, all those Scotsmen present were delighted that at last the union of the crowns of England and Scotland had come about.

James's coronation was the first at which the coronation service was held entirely in English, following the practice of the Anglican reformed church. Furthermore, in marked contrast to Elizabeth I's coronation, *all* the bishops were present. It must have given James immense satisfaction to hear the sermon, which was preached on the text: 'Let every soul be subject unto the higher powers. For there is no power but of God: the powers that be are ordained of God.' (Romans xiii: 1). This was exactly the kind of text that a believer in the Divine Right of Kings would appreciate. Theologically, it was a good start for him.

James was crowned with only one crown, though he put on an 'Imperial Crown' afterwards – probably the small crown which Elizabeth had used. Then, according to ancient ritual, he was invested with the Ring, the Sceptre with Cross, and the Sceptre with Dove. Almost everything followed the former Latin version of the coronation service: but it was noted that after the formula 'laws which the King promised to observe' were added the significant extra disclaimer words: 'agreeable to the King's prerogative'. In other words, James was preparing to do as he liked.

Everything went according to the preordained plan, except for one major and unlooked-for event, which created much scandal at the time. Anne refused to take the Anglican sacrament. It was said 'she had changed her Lutheran religion once before' for the Presbyterian forms of Scotland, but that was hardly excuse enough. It was whispered that secretly, her real loyalty lay with the Church of Rome! *A Catholic Queen!* Whatever the reason, Anne of Denmark sat stubbornly on her throne when the moment came to take Holy Communion. Fortunately, she was merely a consort and not a queen regnant as Mary had been. And at least she had consented to be present at the coronation, unlike her successor, Henrietta Maria. The last monarch or consort who failed to partake of the bread and wine had been King John in 1199. Tongues clacked. However, it was comforting that the king himself had signified his staunchly-held Protestant stance by taking communion.

Despite the plague and the ban on public demonstrations, Westminster Hall still witnessed the traditional banquet afterwards, with the lord mayor of London acting as chief butler. Little did anyone know, but the next major event to take place there would be just over two years later, when Guy Fawkes and his fellow-conspirators would be put on trial for trying to assassinate the king.

Somewhat insensitively, the traditional triumphal progress from the Tower to Westminster, which had always taken place on the day preceding a coronation, but which had had to be abandoned because of the plague, was held belatedly the following year – on 15 March, 1604. Such a delay robbed the occasion of all real significance, and was a pathetic shadow of the spontaneous jollifications which had marked all the Tudor coronations. Much effort had gone into preparations for the event in the previous July, and perhaps it seemed a pity not to use the decorations and pageants which had been made but then set aside. Nevertheless, the affair had a hollow ring.

Thomas Dekker, the playwright and producer of court entertainments, wrote some elaborate verses for this event, in which he calls London by the name of 'Troynovant' or 'New Troy'. The statement that 'London is no longer a city' is so fancifully elusive that he felt bound to explain himself in a footnote: arguing that London on that happy day was no longer a city because 'during these triumphs she puts off her formal habit of trade and commerce, treading even thrift underfoot, but now becomes a reveller and a courtier.' His verses capture the stiff and eccentric artificiality of the new king's reign – though this was hardly the effect he intended. The verses are worth repeating, because they record for the first time the arrival of the 'newly born . . . fair Unicorn' which now adorned the royal coat of arms. (The Tudors had boasted the Welsh dragon.)

> Troynovant is now no more a city;
> O great pity! is't not a pity?
> > And yet her towers on tiptoe stand,
> > like pageants built on faerie land,
> > > and her marble arms

like to magick charms,
bind thousands fast unto her,
that for her wealth and beauty daily woo her,
yet for all this, is't not a pity?
Troynovant is now no more a city.

Troynovant is now a summer arbour,
or the next therein doth harbour
the Eagle, of all birds, that fly
the sovereign, for his piercing eye.
If you wisely mark,
'tis beside a park,
where runs (being newly born)
with the fierce Lion, the fair Unicorn;
or else it is a wedding hall,
where four great kingdoms hold a festival.

Troynovant is now a bridal chamber,
whose roof is gold, floor is of amber,
by virtue of that holy light
that burns in Hymen's hand, more bright
than the silver moon,
or the torch of noon.
Hark, what the echoes say!
Britain till now ne'er kept a holiday!
For Jove dwells here; and 'tis no pity,
if Troynovant be now no more a city.

To our minds, the name 'Troynovant' may seem theatrical and rather silly, but perhaps it was no stranger than the title that King of Great Britain James now gave himself.

'Great Britain' is now so established a term that it takes something of an effort to remember that it had to be invented. At one time it was as new and as strange as Troynovant, and as James invented it himself, without consent of parliament, the new name took a little getting used to.

Thus the ill-fated House of Stuart arrived, and now that he was crowned, James spoke of himself as having been 'like a poor man wandering about forty years in a wilderness and barren soil and now arrived at the land of promise'.

CHARLES I

Reigned 1625–49, crowned 2 February 1626, aged 25
(Also crowned in Edinburgh as King of Scots, 18 June 1633)

A Day of Disasters, While the Queen Refuses to be Crowned

Charles I chose Thursday 2 February, as the date of his coronation because it was Candlemas Day, the Feast of the Purification of the Virgin Mary. He thought it would be a pretty compliment to pay to the sixteen-year-old wife he had just married, whose name was also Mary – or more properly Henrietta Maria, Princess of France. Unfortunately, however, there was a major drawback to these arrangements : Henrietta Maria utterly refused to attend. She made her position perfectly plain. She was a Catholic, and therefore it was quite unthinkable for her to be crowned in a Protestant church, according to Protestant rites, and become a Protestant queen in a Protestant country. She *would* not be crowned. She smashed window-panes with bare fists to make her point.

Even when the marriage between Charles and Henrietta Maria had first been proposed, the pope had been most unwilling to give his consent. He certainly did not wish a royal Catholic princess to compromise herself by marrying the heretic king of England, and finally gave his permission only on the condition that 'the Queen of England should have the control of her children until they were thirteen years of age.' Henrietta, therefore, was totally convinced that it would be morally indefensible for her to attend her husband's coronation, despite all the pressure he tried to bring upon her.

Thus it was that Charles walked alone to be crowned in Westminster Abbey, while Henrietta Maria, with her frivolous French ladies-in-waiting, took a room in one of the palace gate-houses at Whitehall from where she could watch the procession. Rumour had it that she was laughing and 'frisking and dancing' as the king and his courtiers passed by. The unpopularity she earned for herself by this action was to remain with her until she died.

However, quite apart from the absence of the queen, everything else seemed to go wrong at this coronation. For a start, the traditional state progress through London was again omitted, as it had been at James I's coronation. On that previous occasion it had been the plague which had been responsible, but this time, although it was said that the plague again was the reason, the real reason was a fear of Puritan demonstrations. In any case, a procession featuring an unpopular queen may well have tempted the crowds to hiss and boo, while a procession without the queen would have been just as embarrassing. To omit the state progress altogether was probably the most tactful way of handling the awkward situation.

The coronation day itself was crammed with mishaps; and in an age of supersition and omen-watching, these various minor disasters were mulled over in later days, and found to be pregnant with doom-laden significance. To begin with, no red or purple velvet could be found to make the king's robes, and so the tiny monarch – he was only 4ft 7in tall – came to his coronation exquisitively dressed in white satin. 'Baby Charles', as his father used to call him, must have presented a startling sight among the rest of his court. Unfortunately, white was considered to be an unlucky colour, symbolic of a sacrificial victim, and ever afterwards he was given the ominous nick-name 'The White King'. This was especially to be remembered twenty-three years later, as snow fell on his coffin while it was being taken to Windsor for its midnight burial.

Superstition-mongers were given rich food for thought when it became known that the left wing of the dove on King Edward's Sceptre had broken off – 'from what casualty, God alone knew,' remarked John Oldmixon, an eighteenth-century historian. Somehow this wing had snapped off and Charles had asked his goldsmith, a Mr Acton, to mend it. Unfortunately, the repair was done so badly that it left a nasty scar. The king was so annoyed by this that he ordered the poor man to do it again properly. Somewhat scared by the king's temper, Acton secretly decided to cast a completely new dove to fix on to the sceptre – 'whereat his Majesty was well contented as making no discovery thereof.' But as Dean Stanley, the famous nineteenth-century Dean of Westminster later remarked, 'It was the first infringement on the old Regalia.'

On the coronation day itself, just as he entered Westminster Abbey, Charles slipped and almost fell. His friend 'Steenie', the

Duke of Buckingham, managed to catch him. Rumour has it that the king remarked, 'I have as much need to help you as you to assist me,' and of course once again ominous significance was later found to lie in this trivial incident. Further embarrassment came during the service itself, when a precious stone fell out of the Coronation Ring. Then, for some reason or other there was a bemused silence when the time came for those present to declare their allegiance and accept Charles as their monarch. The situation had to be rescued by the Earl of Arundel, who boldly stepped forward and told everyone to shout out 'God save King Charles.' Following this, the sermon was considered to be curiously chosen: 'Be thou faithful, and I will give thee a crown of glory.' Naturally enough, this also acquired a meaningful significance in later years.

On top of all this, there was even some speculation as to whether George Abbot, the Archbishop of Canterbury, was still properly qualified to crown the king, as he had arguably become 'uncanonical' by having accidentally killed one of the king's game-keepers with a crossbow, while out hunting a few years previously. James I had protected him and allowed him to continue in office after a period of 'self-mortification'. Nevertheless, a cloud of 'irregularity' still hung about him.

Finally, perhaps the most immediately terrifying moment, even for those of a non-superstitious frame of mind, happened just as the coronation service was coming to an end. To everyone's astonishment, there was an earthquake. It shook London violently, and Richard Baxter, the celebrated religious writer, aged ten at the time, said that he remembered it well, 'being a boy at school at the time, and having leave to play. It was about two o'clock in the afternoon, and did affright the boys and all in the neighbourhood.' Certainly, everyone had cause to remember this extraordinary coronation.

With the tension resulting from all these untoward events there is little wonder that Charles gave way to a painful outburst of sobbing as he left the building. But even then, no one could know that this was to be the last English coronation at which the ancient regalia of the kingdom would be used. Oliver Cromwell and the Parliamentarians broke virtually everything up, selling the precious jewels piece by piece, and melting down the gold.

Luckily, an inventory of the regalia was drawn up in 1649, so at

Inventory of Regalia Drawn Up in 1649, Before Its Destruction During the Commonwealth

The Kings Crowne

	£	s	d

The Imperiall Crowne of massy gold weighing 7lb 6oz,
enriched with 19 Saphires, 37 Rubies Ballass, 21
small Rubies, 2 Emrods, 28 Diamonds, 168 Pearles.
The gold (6oz being abated for the Stones) valued
at £280; the Saphires at £198; the Ballass Rubies
at £149; the small Rubies at £16; the emralds at £5;
the Diamonds at £288; the pearls at £174: amounts in all to   **1,110   00   00**

The Queenes Crowne

The Queenes Crowne of massy gold weighing 3lb 10oz,
enriched with 20 Saphires, 22 Rubies Ballass, 83 Pearles.
The gold (5oz being abated for the weight of the stones)
ye gold valued at 40 per pound, the Saphires at £120,
the Rubies ballass at £40, the pearls at £41 10s which in
all amounts to   **338   03   04**

A Small Crowne found in an Iron Chest formerly in
the Lord Cottingtons charge enrich't with Diamonds,
Rubies, Saphires, Emrods and perles the gold
Weighing 25oz (whereof 3oz being abated for the weight
of the Stones) is valued at £3 6s 8d per oz   **73   16   08**

The Diamonds, Rubies, Saphires, Emrods and pearles are
valued at   **355   00   00**

lb	oz		£	s	d
1	5½	The Globe weighing 1lb 5oz at £3 6s 8d per ounce valued at	57	10	00
	7	2 Coronation Braceletts weighing 7oz (whereof one ounce is to be deducted for the weight of the Stones and Pearles) at £3 6s 8d per ounce comes to	20	00	00
		Three Rubies Ballass sett in each of the Braceletts valued at	06	00	00
		12 Pearles	10	00	00
1	6	Two Scepters weighing 18oz at £3 6s 8d per ounce valued at	60	00	00

lb	oz		£	s	d
1	5	A long Rodd of silver gilt poz. 1lb 5oz valued at			
		5s 4d per oz	4	10	08
	10½	2 Offering peeces, and a Say of gold poz. 10oz			
		and ½ valued at £3 12s per oz	37	00	00

A note added to this list states that since the inventory was taken,
the crowns had been, according to the order of Parliament, 'totallie
Broken and defaced'. The inventory continues, listing 'that part of the
Regalia which are now removed from Westminster to the Tower
Jewell house':

	£	s	d
Queene Ediths Crowne formerly thought to be of			
Massy gould but upon triall found to be of Silver gilt			
Enriched with Garnetts, foule pearle, Saphires and			
some odd stones poz. 50 Ounces ½ valued at	16	00	00
King Alfreds Crowne of gould wyerworke sett with			
slight stones, and 2 little bells poz. 79 Ounces ½ at			
£3 per Ounce	248	00	00
A gould plate dish Enamelld sett with slight stones			
weighing 23 Ounces ½ valued at £3 6s per Ounce	77	11	00
One large glass Cupp wrought in figures and sett			
in gould with some stones and perles formerly Calld			
an Aggat Cupp pos. 68oz. ½ valued at £2 10s per Ounce	102	15	00
A dove of gould sett with stones and perle poz.			
8 Ounces ½ in a box sett with studds of silver gilt			
valued at	26	00	00
The gould and stones belonging to a Coller of Crimson			
Taffaty wrought with gould and stones sett in plates of			
silver Enamelld wanting 5 weighing 7 Ounces ½ valued			
at £2 10s per Ounce	18	00	00
	489	11	00

After this total, there follows another list of seven further items:

	£	s	d
One staff of black and white Ivory with a dove on the			
top with binding and foote of gould valued at	4	10	00
A large staff with a dove on ye top formerly thought to			
be all gould but upon triall found to be the lower part			
wood within and silver gilt without – weighing in all			
27 Ounces valued at	35	00	00
One small staff with a floure de luce on the topp			
formerly thought to be all of gould, but upon triall			
found to be Iron within and silver gilt without the			
silver valued at	2	10	00

	£	s	d
Two Sceptres one sett with pearles and stones the upper end gould the lower end silver, ye gould poz 23 Ounces valued at 55s per Ounce the lower end being horne and a little silver gilt valued at 12s. The other silver gilt with a dove formerly thought gould poz. 7 Ounces 3/4 at 5s 6d per Ounce	65	16	10½
One Silver spoone gilt poz. 3 Ounces valued at 5s 4d per Ounce		16	00
The gould of the Tassells of the Liver Coloured Robe weighing 4 Ounces valued at £2 per Ounce £8 (and the Coat with the Neck button of gold valued at £2) the Robe having some pearle valued at £3. In all	13	00	00

All these according to Order of Parliament are broken and defaced.

One paire of silver gilt spurres with buckles sett with 12 slight stones and Crimson silke strapps weighing 6 Ounces ¾ at 5s 4d per Ounce	1	00	00
	118	16	2½

This inventory appears in the Minute Book of the Society of Antiquaries and it is dated April 12 1748 – more than a century after the troubled times of the Commonwealth. It not entirely clear whether the items said to be in the 'Tower Jewell house' were destroyed, but in all probability most of them were. Much of the gold was melted down. As for the jewels, these were put up for sale and bought by private individuals: a big sapphire from the Imperial Crown was sold to a Mr Humfroy for £50; another sapphire from the small crown was sold to a Mr James Guinon for £60; a Rock Ruby from the small crown (probably the Black Prince's Ruby) was bought by a Mr Cooke for £15; and the most valuable stone of all – a large diamond also from the small crown – went to a Mr Massy for £200. Other sapphires, emeralds, diamonds and rubies went for prices varying between £15 and £1.

Fortunately, a number of these, including the Black Prince's Ruby, were rescued and were included in the crowns and regalia which were made anew for Charles II, when the monarchy was restored in 1660. A description of the present regalia used for post-restoration coronations and now displayed in the Tower of London is given in Part 3 (see pp. 211–222).

least we can visualise something of what was lost. But before we leave the ill-fated Charles I it should be remembered that he did enjoy a second coronation in Holyrood Abbey, Edinburgh, when he visited Scotland in 1633. John Spottiswoode, Archbishop of St Andrews, officiated. He had travelled south with James on his accession to the English throne, and had been made Archbishop of Glasgow in 1610, moving to St Andrews in 1615. But it was a brief pre-eminence, and he was eventually deposed and excommunicated by the Glasgow General Assembly. Charles was crowned in Scotland using the beautiful old Scottish crown and regalia, still to be seen in Edinburgh Castle.

The Scottish regalia is much older than the English crown jewels. The Scottish crown was used on 18 June 1633 to confirm that Charles I of England was also Charles I of Scotland; and then again, for the last time, on 1 January 1651, when the 20-year-old Charles II was *handed* the crown and sceptre by Archibald Campbell, Marquess of Argyll, at Scone. Although it was never used again, at least the Scottish regalia escaped the wrath of Oliver Cromwell.

OLIVER CROMWELL'S 'HAPPY INAUGURATION'

Ruled 1653–8, Inaugurated 26 June 1657, aged 58

'God Save the Lord Protector!'

Oliver Cromwell, described by the poet John Milton as 'our chief of men', sat on the coronation chair to be invested, not as a king – although many wished him to be – but as 'Lord Protector', a curiously honorific title especially invented for him. Only Cromwell's own will prevented him from becoming king in name. The French Ambassador wrote a graphic description of the state procession as it wound its way through the London streets celebrating Oliver's elevation to the Protectorate – 'with all the state and dignity of a sovereign, no difference, the same bowing and scraping, the same Ambassadors, the same decorations, the same trumpeting and magnificence – *comme s'il etait roi.*'

In fact there were two occasions at which Oliver Cromwell was proclaimed to be England's Lord Protector: the first, a rather muted event in December 1653, when the title was bestowed upon him giving him civil rather than military power; and the second in June 1657, when the title was confirmed at a more richly-elaborate ceremony, a quasi-coronation, during which Cromwell was invested with sword, sceptre, power for life and the right to nominate his successor.

The execution of Charles I on 30 January 1649 had plunged the country into political chaos, creating an inevitable power-vacuum at the top. The House of Lords, the House of Commons, the Church, the army, the judiciary: all sections of the community looked to an empty throne. It was not just that an unpopular king had met his fate, but that the country's ultimate source of authority had disappeared. A cynic once made the famous comment that if God did not exist, it would be necessary to invent Him. Similarly, in the desperate situation that England was in, it was patently obvious that as the king had ceased to exist, it was necessary to re-invent one, and who better than Oliver Cromwell, 'our chief of men'?

Here was the man who had been born in Huntingdon; educated at Cambridge; who had become a member of parliament resisting the arbitrary actions of the king; who had fought against the king's army with brilliant success at the Battles of Edgehill, Marston Moor and Naseby; and who had continued winning the war against royalists at the further Battles of Prestonpans, Dunbar and Worcester. No one had done more, and it was inevitable that Cromwell should become Chairman of the Council of State after Charles's execution. All the same, it was principally a military government. As Cromwell said of himself, 'I was the general of all the forces in the three nations of England, Scotland and Ireland, the authority I had in my hand being so boundless as it was.' It was now necessary to try to give that authority a rather more acceptably peaceful façade.

The ceremony to create a Lord Protector took place at Westminster Hall, as it was not to be a religious service, and so to hold it in the abbey would have been wholly inappropriate. Sensing the occasion, Cromwell took pains to dress in a conspicuously modest manner, wearing a plain suit of black velvet with a cloak. The only ornament he allowed himself was a gold band in his hat.

He was driven in his coach to the door of Westminster Hall, and having descended he walked up the hall to the Court of Chancery preceded by the Commissioners of the Great Seal, the judges and barons in their robes, and the lord mayor, aldermen and recorder of London. At that time the Court of Chancery was held at the far end of the hall, on the right of the steps leading up into the Chapel of St Stephen. A chair of state had been placed in the middle of a rich carpet, and Oliver Cromwell stood beside it, hat in hand, during the reading of 'a large writ in Parchment containing the power with which his Excellency was invested, and how he was to govern the three Nations and the Oath to be taken by him.' He then publicly signed this parchment, took the oath administered to him by Lord Lisle, sat on the chair, and put his hat on.

All that remained to be done was to receive the Great Seal of the Realm from the commissioners, and the sword and cap from the lord mayor. Cromwell then ceremoniously returned all these items; the assembly formed itself into a procession and everyone went back to the Banqueting House, with trumpets sounding and soldiers cheering. However, it was noted that the people of London looked on in a spirit of sceptical irony. An eminent barrister of the day, Bulstrode Whitelocke, was witness to this, and recorded many of the details, but unfortunately he did not specify which sword was presented to Cromwell.

During the three and a half years which followed this, Cromwell ruled as king but without the title. Etiquette at Whitehall and Hampton Court followed royal standards; if he entertained, Cromwell sat under a canopy, and was raised on a platform or dais some steps above the rest of the company. Only privileged persons were allowed to eat with him at the same table. He became 'His Highness the Lord Protector' and his wife Elizabeth (known as 'Old Joan' by servants behind her back) was to be addressed as 'Her Highness the Lady Protectress'. One of the very few differences Cromwell made was to change the uniform of the Yeomen of the Guard from scarlet and gold to grey trimmed with silver. But people grumbled that ''twas a dull colour'.

From this state of affairs it was only a step to formalising Oliver's position to make him fully royal, and so it was that on Monday 23 February 1657, one of the burgesses of London, Sir Christopher Pack, introduced a bill which would authorise the protector to assume 'the name, style, title and dignity of King'. Of course there was widespread argument and disagreement, but there was enough support for the proposal for it to be made formally in April of that year. Cromwell himself flatly refused. He refused again in May, when it was made a second time. 'I would not seek to set up that that providence hath destroyed and laid in the dust,' he declared, 'and I would not build Jericho again.' However, when Parliament pressed him a third time, Cromwell suggested a compromise: he would receive no royal title, but he would accept the power to nominate his successor; he would oversee the appointment of a new House of Lords to act as a brake on the fanatical Puritans in the House of Commons; and he agreed to receive a permanent revenue.

In June 1657 therefore, preparations were made for Oliver Cromwell's 'Happy Inauguration' in a unique ceremony which was to serve as a substitute for a genuine, royal coronation. The precious and ancient regalia had been broken up and sold, but luckily one item remained which had always played a central part in coronations since the time of Edward II – the coronation chair containing the Stone of Scone. Accordingly, this venerable chair, complete with the Stone of Destiny, was taken out of Westminster Abbey for the first and only time in its history, and was set up on 'an Ascent of two Degrees covered with carpets' at the south end of Westminster Hall. Above it was hung a rich cloth of state.

The Speaker of the House of Commons, Sir Thomas Widdrington, was provided with a table and chair close to the coronation chair; MPs were ranged on each side of the hall on tiers of benches; the judges sat on one side of the platform, and the lord mayor of London and all the aldermen sat on the other.

After everyone was seated in his place (no women, of course, were present – Cromwell's court was a conspicuously masculine affair) Cromwell made his formal entry attended by his gentlemen and escorted by the Serjeant at Arms, heralds, Commissioners of the Great Seal and of the Treasury, and the members of his council. The Earl of Warwick carried a sword of state before him and the lord mayor carried another sword belonging to the city.

When he arrived at the platform, Cromwell stood beneath the cloth of state for the unique ceremony:

> The Speaker, aided by Bulstrode Whitelocke and others, placed 'a robe of purple velvet lined with ermine' upon Oliver Cromwell's shoulders

The Speaker 'delivered to him the Bible richly gilt and bossed'

The Speaker girded him with a sword and handed him 'a sceptre of massy gold'†

The Speaker delivered a formal speech, explaining the significance of what had been presented to the Lord Protector

Oliver Cromwell took an oath of office

A clergyman, Mr Manton, offered prayer

Oliver Cromwell took his seat in the Coronation Chair, sceptre in hand

'Then the trumpets sounded and an Herald proclaimed His Highness' title'

Everyone present gave a loud shout of 'God save the Lord Protector'

Cromwell rose, walked down the length of Westminster Hall, his train held by two boys and a peer of the realm. He departed through the north doors, entered 'his rich coach' and was driven to the Palace of Whitehall with an escort of Life Guards.

Throughout this ceremony Oliver's son, Richard Cromwell, had stood near at hand, witnessing the solemn inauguration of his powerful father. As Oliver's nominated successor, Richard must have felt the eyes of the assembly on him. Little did anyone know that Oliver Cromwell's health would decline from that day, and that in just over a year Richard would be faced with the challenge of becoming the second lord protector.

However, Richard Cromwell, known as 'Idle Dick', was completely out of his depth when he succeeded his father. He simply could not cope with the job he inherited. It was remarked at the time: 'The vulture died, and out of his ashes rose a titmouse.'

† Bulstrode Whitelocke provides these details: but, tantalisingly, he does not mention where this sceptre came from.

CHARLES II

Succeeded 30 January 1649, reigned 1660–85, crowned
23 April 1661, aged 30

'Here's a Health Unto His Majesty!'

An odd coronation took place on 1 January 1651 at Scone, in
Scotland, at which Charles II was crowned King of England,
Scotland, Ireland and France. It was less than two years since
his father Charles I had been executed at Whitehall, and at the
time of this coronation Charles was still a very young man of
twenty.

The Scottish Covenanters who were offering him the crown
had no belief in bishops or many of the traditional coronation
ceremonies. Archibald Campbell, Marquess of Argyll, simply
handed him the crown and sceptre, but anointing with oil was
quite out of the question, as it was considered to be far too
superstitious.

After the coronation feast, Charles celebrated by playing a
game of golf – the Scottish game which his grandfather James I
had introduced into England. However, he knew, and everyone
knew, that to be crowned in an out-of-the-way place such as
Scone – historically important though it may once have been –
would not affect Oliver Cromwell and the powerful
Parliamentarians in Westminster in the slightest.

Though he was king in Scotland, Charles still had to win his
throne in England; so as soon as he could, later that same
year, he crossed the Scottish border, marching south with an
army of almost 17,000 soldiers. Naturally enough, Cromwell
immediately marched north to meet him, and the two armies
met at Worcester. The result was predictable. Watching the
defeat of his Scottish army from the top of Worcester
Cathedral, Charles must have felt that his royal hopes were
finally at an end. He fled to France, and for the next nine
anxious years he was a fugitive in a political wilderness.

However, his luck was to return. After the death of Oliver
Cromwell and the abdication of Richard Cromwell, there was an
almost tangible yearning in England to restore the king and to
make a new start. Thus it was that Charles rode into London on

his thirtieth birthday, 29 May 1660, to a rapturous welcome. An eyewitness to Charles's return wrote of the 'inexpressible joy: the wayes strew'd with flowers; the bells ringing, the streetes hung with tapestry, fountains running with wine . . . trumpets, music and myriads of people flocking'. At night there were fireworks and illuminations. Anyone suspected of disloyalty had his windows smashed.

In a curious way the coronation of Queen Elizabeth I – a full century before – had witnessed the same kind of jubilation. Both Charles and Elizabeth had been forced to live in poverty-stricken seclusion under threat of possible death. The people of England, too, had been forced to suffer during the previous months and years and so they also were longing for a restoration of normality. And on top of this, both Charles and Elizabeth shared the same intuitive rapport with their subjects, with an actor's instinctive skill of knowing how to respond to a situation. The coronation of Charles II, therefore, possessed a wild and spontaneous joy which has never been seen since, and only on rare occasions before.

Luckily, we have the reports of two exceptional eyewitnesses: John Evelyn and Samuel Pepys. Evelyn noted the finely-caparisoned horses, but Pepys was more interested in the attractive women. Sadly, the king's eve-of-coronation progress from the Tower of London to Whitehall was the last of such processions to take place. London was never again to enjoy the same sort of jollity that was staged for the 'Merry Monarch'.

As usual, London was decked out with tapestries and banners hanging from the windows: wine flowed from the fountains and triumphal arches were constructed at various points along the route. Entertainments included a mini-morality play in which a woman appeared dressed as 'Rebellion' in a crimson robe decorated with snakes. She brandished a bloody sword and was accompanied by 'Confusion' – a grotesque creature wearing the model of a ruined castle as a crown, and carrying two broken sceptres. The meaning was not difficult to decipher to those who remembered the wholesale destruction of castles and sacred emblems during the time of the Commonwealth. The play went along these lines:

> *Rebellion*: 'I am hell's daughter, Satan's eldest child.'
> *(Enter 'Monarchy' – a noble figure in dazzling robes)*
> *Monarchy*: 'To hell, foul fiend – shrink from this glorious light.'

Westminster Abbey was crowded to capacity the next day – St George's Day – for the coronation. Samuel Pepys managed to squeeze into the abbey before dawn, and 'with much ado, by the favour of Mr Cooper . . . did get up into a great scaffold across the North end of the Abbey, where with a great deal of patience I sat from past four till eleven before the King come in.'

Pepys's account of the event is so vivid and detailed that it is best simply to let him take over. Here is a slightly abridged version, but the words all belong to him:

A great pleasure it was to see the Abbey raised in the middle, all covered with red, and a throne (that is a chaire) and footstoole on the top of it; and all the officers of all kinds, so much as the very fidlers, in red vests. At last comes in the Dean and Prebends of Westminster, with the Bishops (many of them in cloth of gold copes,) after them the Nobility, all in their Parliament robes, which was a most magnificent sight.

Then the Duke† and the King with a scepter (carried by my Lord Sandwich) and sword and wand before him, and the crowne too. The King in his robes, bare-headed, which was very fine. And after all had placed themselves, there was a sermon and the service; and then in the Quire at the high altar, the King passed through all the ceremonies of the Coronation, which to my great grief I and most in the Abbey could not see. The crowne being put upon his head, a great shout begun, and he come forth to the throne, and there passed through more ceremonies: as taking the oath, and having things read to him by the Bishopp; and his lords (who put on their caps as soon as the King put on his crown) and bishopps come, and kneeled before him.

† i.e. the Duke of York, the king's brother and the future James II.

And three times the King at Armes went to the three open places on the scaffold, and proclaimed, that if any one could show any reason why Charles Stewart should not be King of England, that now he should come and speak.

And a Generall Pardon also was read by the Lord Chancellor, and meddalls flung up and down by my Lord Cornwallis, of silver, but I could not come by any. But so great a noise that I could make but little of the musique; and indeed, it was lost to every body.

I went out a little while before the King had done all his ceremonies, and went round the Abbey to Westminster Hall, all the way within rayles, and 10,000 people with the ground covered with blue cloth; and scaffolds all the way.

Into the Hall I got, where it was very fine with hangings and scaffolds one upon another full of brave ladies; and my wife in one little one, on the right hand. Here I staid walking up and down, and at last upon one of the side stalls I stood and saw the King come in with all the persons (but the soldiers) that were yesterday in the cavalcade; and a most pleasant sight it was to see them in their several robes.

And the King come in with his crowne on, and his sceptre in his hand, under a canopy borne up by six silver staves, carried by Barons of the Cinque Ports, and little bells at every end. And after a long time he got up to the farther end, and all set themselves down at their several tables; and that was also a brave sight: and the King's first course carried up by the Knights of the Bath.

And many fine ceremonies there was of the Heralds leading up people before him, and bowing; and my Lord of Albemarle's going to the Kitchin and eating a bit of the first dish that was to go to the King's table. But, above all, was there three Lords, Northumberland, and Suffolke, and the Duke of Ormond, coming before the courses on horse-back, and staying so all dinner-time, and at last bringing up (Dymoke) the King's Champion, all in armour on horseback, with his speare and targett carried before him.

And a herald proclaims that if any dare deny Charles Stewart to be lawful King of England, here was a Champion

Westminster Hall, at the coronation banquet of King George IV in 1821. This was by far the most spectacular coronation feast ever. The king is shown at the left, behind the table, and young Dymoke on horseback is seen at the right. This was the last time the king's champion made his traditional challenge.

(*Chapter Library, Durham*)

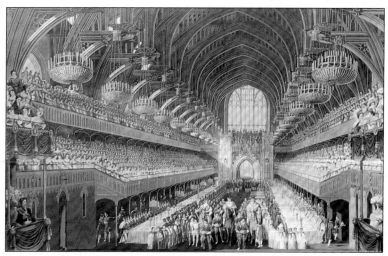

Westminster Hall looking south, as King George IV would have seen it from his banqueting table in the top picture. Here are the long tables laid out for the feast to be enjoyed by the peers. Above them are temporary balconies for the peeresses, who merely watched as the food was being eaten. Above them are the chandeliers that dripped hot wax on the peeresses' wigs and faces throughout the meal.

(*Chapter Library, Durham*)

The Regalia and Crown Jewels are permanently on view in the Tower of London. This photograph shows St Edward's Crown, used only once for the moment of crowning each new sovereign; the eagle-shaped Ampulla, containing the anointing oil; the Sovereign's Orb; the Sceptre with Cross containing the 'Star of Africa' diamond; the Jewelled Sword of State; the Sceptre with Dove; the Armills bracelets; the Spurs; and the Coronation Ring.

(Crown copyright: Historic Royal Palaces)

The Crown of State, showing the Black Prince's Ruby; underneath this is the Second Star of Africa; and set in the middle of the cross at the top is the sapphire from Edward the Confessor's ring. The Crown of State is worn on occasions such as the State Opening of Parliament. The other items are the Sovereign's Orb; the Sceptre with Cross; the Armills and the Coronation Ring.

(Crown copyright: Historic Royal Palaces)

Archbishop Dunstan crowning King Edgar in Bath Abbey, 11 May 973. Dunstan's Order of Service set the pattern for all subsequent coronations. This was the first coronation which included the practice of anointing the sovereign. At the bottom of this window the newly-crowned Edgar is shown being rowed in state on the River Dee by seven Welsh and Scottish kings.
(*Photo: Pitkin Unichrome Ltd*)

Traditionally, seven Saxon kings were crowned on or beside this ancient Coronation Stone at Kingston upon Thames, Surrey: Edward the Elder; Athelstan; Edmund I; Edred; Edwy; Edward, Saint and Martyr; and Ethelred II, 'The Unready'.
(*Photo: David Hilliam*)

Edward I captured the Stone of Scone in 1296 and ordered this Coronation Chair to be made to incorporate it. Since then, it has been used in the coronation ceremony of every English monarch. For Oliver Cromwell's 'Happy Inauguration' the Chair and Stone were temporarily taken into Westminster Hall. The Stone of Scone is now in Edinburgh Castle. (*Copyright: Dean and Chapter of Westminster*)

Below: The Liber Regalis, or 'Royal Book', in the Library of Westminster Abbey, was written and illuminated in the fourteenth century. It contains the Order of Service for coronations, and was probably used by kings and queens at their coronations from the time of Henry IV in 1399 to Elizabeth I in 1559. After Elizabeth, coronation services were no longer held in Latin. (*Copyright: Dean and Chapter of Westminster*)

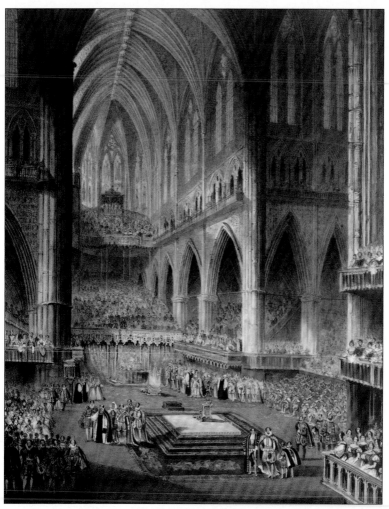

Westminster Abbey laid out in the traditional manner for Queen Victoria's coronation in 1838. The raised platform with the throne in the centre is known as the 'Theatre'. Henry III enlarged Westminster Abbey in the thirteenth century especially to accommodate a raised dais in the space between nave and transepts. King Edward's Chair, containing the Stone of Scone, is in front of the altar. Wooden balconies were specially constructed for the large number of distinguished guests at a coronation.

The moment of crowning. Elizabeth II, at her coronation on 2 June 1953, holding the Sceptre with Cross – a symbol of the Sovereign's power under the Cross – and the Sceptre with Dove, also known as the Rod of Equity and Mercy – symbolising the Sovereign's spiritual role. She is wearing the Crown of St Edward.

The Honours of Scotland are now on permanent display in Edinburgh Castle exhibited next to the Stone of Scone. The Crown, Sword and Sceptre were made in Italy in the sixteenth century and were first used as coronation regalia at the enthronement of the infant Mary Queen of Scots in Stirling Castle in 1543.

(*Crown copyright, reproduced courtesy of Historic Scotland*)

A VIEW of the GRAND FÊTE on PARKER'S PIECE, CAMBRIDGE,
To celebrate the Coronation of HER MOST GRACIOUS MAJESTY QUEEN VICTORIA, June 28th 1838.
Number of Persons seated to Dinner 15,000, required number of Spectators 25,000. — TOTAL number present 40,000.

The scene on Parker's Piece in Cambridge on the occasion of Queen Victoria's coronation, 28 June 1838. This was probably the largest two-course cooked meal ever served, as no fewer than 15,000 people were seated at table. This engraving is a copy of a lithograph made by G. Scharf, from drawings he made on the day of the feast. (*University Arms Hotel, Cambridge*) flings down his gauntlet, and all this he do three times in his going up towards the King's table. To which when he is come, the King drinks to him, and then sends him the cup which is of gold, and he drinks it off, and then rides back again with the cup in his hand.

I went from table to table to see the Bishops and all others at their dinner, and was infinitely pleased with it. And at the Lords' table, I met with William Howe, and he spoke to my Lord for me, and he did give him four rabbits and a pullet, and so Mr Creed and I got Mr Minshell to give us some bread, and so we at a stall eat it, as everybody else did what they could get.

I took a great deal of pleasure to go up and down, and look upon the ladies, and to hear the musique of all sorts, abut above all, the 24 violins.

. . . Thus did the day end with joy everywhere; and blessed be God, I have not heard of any mischance to anybody through it all, but only to Serjeant Glynne, whose horse fell upon him yesterday, and is like to kill him, which people do please themselves to see how just God is to punish the rogue at such a time as this.

Samuel Pepys ended the day's entry in his diary by remarking that he was 'sure never to see the like again in this world.' Certainly no one in 1661 had seen anything quite like it in their lifetime. Following the ascetic years of the Commonwealth, royalty had to be resurrected and visibly put together again.

After Charles had returned to England in May 1660, it was almost a year before things could be got ready for his coronation in April 1661. One of the principal problems was, of course, the matter of the crown and the royal regalia, Cromwell had destroyed them, so a new set would have to be made from scratch. A committee was formed to consider the matter, and Sir Robert Vyner, His Majesty's Goldsmith, was paid the sum of £31,978 9s 11d to provide this new set of regalia, together with all kinds of insignia for the Order of the Garter, Order of the Bath, chain and badge for the Garter King of Arms. One document which has survived lists the regalia and the cost of each item:

	£	s	d
St Edwards Crown 82 oz 5 dwt 16 gr.			
for the addition of gold and workmanship	350	–	–
For the loan of Jewels returned	500	–	–
One Crown of State, 72 gr. 1 dwt			
for the gold, jewels, and workmanship	7,870	–	–
One Sceptre with a Dove 4 oz 3 dwt 20 gr.			
for the gold, jewels and workmanship	440	–	–
One Sceptre with a Cross 32 oz 11 dwt 10 gr.			
for the gold, jewels and workmanship	1,025	–	–
One St Edwards Staff 45 oz 8 dwt 8 gr.			
for the gold and workmanship	225	6	2
One Globe with a Cross 48 oz 7 dwt 12 gr.			
for the gold jewels and workmanship	1,150	–	–
One pair of Spurs 12 oz 18 dwt			
for the gold and workmanship	63	7	6
Two Armillas (the Bracelets) 6 oz 12 dwt 22 gr.			
for the gold and workmanship	44	18	6
One Ampulla or Eglet 21 oz 8 dwt			
for the gold and workmanship	102	5	–
The Anointing Spoon 3 oz 5 dwt			
for Silver and Workmanship	2	–	–
One Chalice and Paten 61 oz 12 dwt 12 gr.			
for gold and workmanship	277	6	3
	12,050	3	5

By far the most interesting question which arises from this list concerns the huge discrepancy between the cost of the Crown of State – £7,870 – and the cost of St Edward's Crown – a mere £350. A likely, but intriguing, explanation is that the relatively paltry sum of £350 does not represent the cost of a *new* crown, but merely the cost of altering an *existing* crown.

This speculation is given extra credibility by comparing this sum of £350 with a similar bill of £305 16s 5d which James II had to pay at his coronation for repairs and small additions to St Edward's Crown. It seems hardly likely that James had to pay £305 simply for alterations to a crown whereas Charles had had to pay £350 for a brand new one. However, if we assume that Charles II's St Edward's Crown was an old one repaired for the occasion, *where did it come from?* The probable answer is that Oliver Cromwell managed to hold on to a crown, rescuing it from destruction, and keeping it for himself, although he refused to wear it or be crowned with it. Certainly, a crown, orb and sceptre were exhibited at his funeral; and it has already been noted that he was presented with a 'sceptre of massy gold' at his 'happy inauguration'.

There is a very real possibility that the present St Edward's Crown, still used for coronations and last worn by Queen Elizabeth II, is older than it seems, and that it is at least in part made from the same materials which formed the Imperial Crown of Henry VIII – parts of which can be traced back even further, to the crown belonging to Richard II.

Finally, we cannot leave the reign of Charles II without mentioning that the new regalia made for him in 1660 was the target, only eleven years later, of one of the most daring and cunning thefts ever to take place in England. It almost succeeded. However, the full story of Colonel Blood's attempt to steal the Crown Jewels is told later. (See pp. 237–241)

JAMES II AND MARY OF MODENA

Reigned 1685–8, crowned 23 April 1685, aged 51

A Tottering Crown on a Doomed King

James II was crowned in Westminster Abbey on St George's Day 1685, exactly twenty-four years to the day after the coronation of Charles II. However, although the two men were brothers, there were fundamental differences between them. Charles had been cheerful, outgoing, diplomatic and easy-minded; James, his younger brother, was morose, silent, tactless and unwilling to make compromises. More importantly for the kingdom, Charles had been a Protestant, at least on the surface; but James was openly and defiantly Catholic.

Both men were openly sexually voracious, but whereas Charles had somehow encouraged a jolly, carefree approach to his shockingly numerous affairs, making his mistresses duchesses and his illegitimate sons dukes, James's sexual adventures were much more furtive and shamefaced. In a nut-shell, he was far less popular than Charles. Even Charles himself had once joked with him, when James had been worried about his brother's lax security arrangements: 'Don't worry, Jamie,' he said. 'They'll never kill me to make you king!' But the worst had happened. Charles had died, quite suddenly, and without any legitimate children, and so James was undoubtedly his heir, Catholic or otherwise.

It says much for James's determination to be loyal to his Catholic faith that he immediately made arrangements for some special oil to be brought over from France, that was blessed by a Catholic bishop for him to be anointed with. Louis XIV helped him with this, and duly sent James some of the same holy oil of Rheims that was used by the Catholic kings of France.

James II and his queen, Mary of Modena, were first anointed and then crowned by a Catholic bishop in a secret, private coronation service before the public ceremony in Westminster Abbey. When this had been done, presumably James felt ready to go along with some sort of Protestant service, heretical though it may have been in his eyes.

Disappointingly for Londoners, James decided he would not hold the traditional coronation procession through the city from the Tower of London to Whitehall. Instead, he gave his wife Mary a glittering array of robes and regalia. In later years, poor Mary, poverty-stricken and in exile, remembered her moment of glory: 'My dress and royal mantle were covered with precious stones, and it took all the jewels that all the goldsmiths of London could procure to decorate my crown.' The royal regalia had been made anew for Charles II's coronation, but of course, as he had not been married at the time, no crown had been made for a queen. It was therefore necessary for a new one to be designed and paid for. James spent a colossal sum on Mary's rich regalia, robes and jewels, the crown alone cost over £100,000.

Two crowns, two sceptres, and a diadem or circlet to be worn before the crowning were needed for Mary's coronation. She needed two crowns: one to be crowned with, and another to be worn on her return to Westminster Hall. She was also provided with a sceptre with a cross and an ivory rod with a dove.

Fortunately, when James and Mary had to flee the country in 1688, they left all these newly-made items behind them, ready to be used, with various modifications, for future coronations. We can still see 'The Crown of Mary of Modena' among the regalia at the Tower of London, but the name is now somewhat misleading, as it was altered considerably by Queen Anne a few years later, for use as her own state crown.

Ostentatious wealth rather than jollity was the order of the day at this coronation, and at the centre of it all was Mary. James was so proud of the event that he ordered one of his courtiers, Francis Sandford, the Lancaster Herald, to write a special book about it, and its hundred and thirty-five copiously-illustrated pages leave us in no doubt that no expense was spared to make this a magnificent occasion. Another eyewitness tells us 'the jewels she had on were reckoned worth a million, which made her shine like an angel.'

Thus she arrived at Westminster Abbey, dressed in robes of purple velvet furred with ermine and with a 'huge web of pearls' shimmering over the silver brocade of her skirt. And as she walked beneath a canopy borne by sixteen Barons of the Cinque Ports, young girls went before her carrying baskets of flowers and sweet-smelling herbs to strew on the ground where she was to tread: primroses, pansies, cowslips, bluebells and violets. It was an ancient custom, prettily revived for this young queen. Following her came James himself. He too walked beneath a canopy, and it is interesting to note that the bearer of the front left-hand pole was none other than Samuel Pepys – he who had squeezed up into the scaffolding in Westminster Abbey twenty-four years earlier to see the coronation of Charles II. Now he was a mature fifty-two, older and wiser, and having completed over a quarter of a century of much-valued service to government and king.

Unfortunately, during the coronation service things started going wrong. To begin with, the crown was far too big. It had been made for Charles, whose head was generously large. The result was that when it was put on, poor James had to hold on to it constantly and seek help in preventing it from wobbling right off. It later years Mary herself remembered this, remarking that 'There was a presage that struck us and every one who observed it. They could not make the crown keep firm on the King's head; it appeared always on the point of falling, and it required some care to hold it steady.' Gossips were also quick to point out that the Royal Standard was blown off the White Tower at the Tower of

London just at the very moment that the gun announced the entry of the king and queen into the abbey. However, the most upsetting fact about James's coronation, at least to churchmen, was that the king had ordered the Archbishop of Canterbury to abbreviate the service and to leave out the communion altogether. Other parts of the ritual were also omitted, especially those parts which would be unacceptable to a zealous Roman Catholic. Obviously, as a Catholic, James was making his position clear from the very start.

Equally obviously, though in highly coded language, the Bishop of Ely tried to get the Protestant position across to the king in his sermon, pointing out the embarrassing position the church would be in, if the sovereign did not share its doctrine: he reminded the king that 'the Emperor Constantius Chlorus though not himself a Christian, had held in honour those Christians who remained true to their religion, and had treated with scorn those who sought to earn his favour by apostasy.' In other words, Don't persecute the Church of England.

These doctrinal tensions were mitigated perhaps by the impressive music, with anthems sung by two choirs: the Choir of Westminster, and the Children and Gentlemen of the Chapel Royal. Every anthem sung had been composed by a Gentle-man of the Chapel Royal, and every composer was present himself, except Henry Lawes, who had died in 1662. By now, English church music had acquired a fine and continuing tradition, and this coronation was a particularly memorable event if only for the quality of its music and the famous musicians taking part. For the record, these were the anthems:

(At the Entrance)	*I was glad*	Henry Purcell
(At the Recognition)	*Let thy hand be strengthened*	John Blow
(Before the Anointing)	*Come Holy Ghost*	William Turner
	Zadok the Priest	Henry Lawes
(After the Anointing)	*Behold, O Lord, our Defender*	John Blow
(After the Crowning)	*The King shall rejoice*	William Turner
(After the Benediction)	*Te Deum*	William Child
(At the Homage)	*God spake sometimes in visions*	John Blow
(After the Queen's Crowning)	*My heart is inditing*	Henry Purcell

One curious innovation to the service which must be recorded is the fact that the orb was used in a coronation service for the first time. Archbishop Sancroft handed the orb to the king, as well as the Sceptre with Cross and the Sceptre with Dove. No one knows why this 'extra' item was added at James's coronation. A Keeper of the Jewel House conjectured that Sancroft 'had become so thoroughly muddled in trying to adjust the Church of England Service for the Coronation to a suitable form which would be acceptable to the Roman Catholic King and Queen.' Whatever the reason, the fact remains that the presentation of an orb together with the two Sceptres has remained a feature of all coronations since that of James.

Meanwhile, in Westminster Hall, elaborate preparations had been made to provide the traditional feast with 'an Ambigu of 99 dishes of the most excellent choicest of all sorts of meats, both flesh and fish excellently well dressed and ordered all manner of ways.' There were also 'three very great chargers and fourteen large basins' containing sweetmeats and plates of blancmange, salads and jellies 'to fill up every little vacancy between the dishes . . . (and) . . . void places were left for the hot meats.' (An 'ambigu' was a medley of dishes placed on the table beforehand, thus saving time in serving. Only hot meats were carried in separately.)

James and Mary sat themselves down alone at a marble table, set apart from the rest, whereupon one hundred and seventy-five dishes were brought to them, including 'larded fawns hot, gammon and spinach, "blumange" cold in glasses, caviar and cabbage pudding, egg pies and puffins, whiting marinated, sturgeon and soused tench, asparagus and salamagundy (salad), skillets (parsnips), sheep's tongues, and udders roasted.'

As for the peers, bishops, lord mayor and aldermen, they had to make do with cockles and Bologna sausages, periwinkles and pistachio cream, pettytoes (pigs' trotters) and pigeon pie, collared veal and Dutch beef, bamboo and mangoes.

But now was the time for the final omen. As tradition demanded, the king's champion, naturally enough a Dymoke, this time a Sir Charles, grandiosely entered between the first and second courses, and three times loudly declaimed the customary challenge.

However, when he went up to kiss the king's hand the luckless champion tripped up and fell dramatically and heavily on to the floor. The poor knight was so weighed down with his unaccustomed armour that try as he might he simply could not get up again without the help of some of the other guests. If such a misfortune could happen to the king's champion, what kind of disaster would befall the king himself? Perhaps James remembered this ominous calamity as he fled from England three years later, with revolution bursting around his ears. However, he probably had other things to think about as he disappeared into the night, dumping the Great Seal of England into the Thames as he left.

WILLIAM AND MARY

William reigned 1689–1702, Mary reigned 1689–94;
crowned together 11 April 1689, William aged 38, Mary aged 26

A New Kind of Monarchy is Invented

Constitutionally, this rather unexpected coronation was easily the most important since William the Conqueror seized the throne in 1066. James II had succeeded to the throne on the death of his brother, and it was immediately obvious that he was determined to turn England back to Catholicism. He systematically filled every possible official post with Catholics. Catholic judges, Catholic army commanders, Catholic academics. It was clear that James was bulldozing his way into the reconversion of England.

However, by a previous marriage, James had had two daughters, Mary and Anne: both of them now grown up and married, but more importantly, both of them were Protestants. At the time of James II's coronation these two daughters were successively heir to the throne. Mary, the elder of the two, was married to William of Orange, Stadholder of the Netherlands who shared her Protestant convictions with militant determination. (Mary and William were in fact cousins, sharing Charles I and Henrietta Maria as their common grandparents, so they could both claim English royal blood in their veins.)

Religious matters were vitally important to the English: it was still almost within living memory that people were burnt for being Protestants, so James's reign was increasingly regarded with deep suspicion. Matters came to a head in 1688 when James's Catholic second wife, Mary of Modena, gave birth to a son, James

Stuart. It was obvious that this new son and heir would be Catholic and in all probability the whole Protestant movement in England would be lost.

Desperate situations demand desperate remedies. Thus it was that William was invited by parliament to come, with force if need be, and take over the throne of England. James tried desperately to muster an army, but his supporters drained away from him. When even his family deserted him, James and Mary fled unceremoniously into France with their baby son. For a few weeks the throne was empty – or, rather, there was an unprecedented constitutional crisis which had to be solved.

Times were tense. In the eyes of those who still supported James II, William and Mary were both usurpers, and so the Archbishop of Canterbury refused to crown them. The last occasion when an archbishop had refused to crown his monarch had been at the coronation of Elizabeth I. Then it had been a matter of religion: now it was a matter of allegiance. Archbishop Sancroft had crowned James II only 3½ years before; and as James was still very much alive and quite likely to stage a comeback, the good archbishop was reluctant to break his oath of loyalty to him, however much he disagreed with Catholicism.

Luckily for William, he had a firm ally in the person of Henry Compton, Bishop of London. Compton was a colourful figure, who had held a commission in the Horse Guards at the time of the Restoration. Later, he entered the church becoming Bishop of Oxford in 1674 and then Bishop of London in 1675. He was a vigorous Protestant and had taken a leading part in inviting William of Orange to come and take over the throne. In these troubled times he had ridden at the head of a body of volunteers and had marched into Oxford 'in a blue cloak and with a naked sword'.

Britain was still in a state of deep political crisis as William arrived to become its new king, and there were weeks of anxious debate about exactly what should happen next. It was a constitutional problem that had never presented itself before. To begin with, James hadn't actually abdicated, so in theory he was still king. Should he be formally deposed by Parliament? Or should William be asked to become regent, governing in the name of the absent James? Strictly speaking, it was Mary who was next in line to the throne. After all, she was James's elder daughter. Even more strictly speaking, it was still James's baby son – another James, who was to be known as the 'Old Pretender' by the Jacobites – who was, morally, the rightful heir to the throne: but this was tacitly ignored in the present circumstances. There was a strong argument to be made that Mary should be the next sovereign and become queen in her own right. But then what position would her husband William hold? He refused to be subjugated to the role of a mere consort. As for Mary herself, she was completely dominated by William, and was insistent that he should share the throne. As everyone knows, the constitutional impasse was finally solved in a curious compromise by which William and Mary were invited to become joint monarchs. However, when this solution had at last been arrived at, the practical niceties of holding a joint coronation had to be met. *Two* sets of regalia had to be found: thrones, crowns, sceptres, orbs, swords – it was a logistical nightmare for those who had to organise such an event.

William of Orange had landed in Brixham, Devon, in November 1688; James had fled his kingdom in December; the constitutional situation had been solved in February 1689 when William and Mary accepted the offer to reign jointly; and now, only two months later, on 11 April, the most extraordinary coronation ever to be seen in Westminster Abbey was scheduled to take place. The very haste in which everything had to be prepared was bound to affect the proceedings, but probably uppermost in Mary's mind as she got herself ready for the service was not the ceremony itself, but the fact that she was usurping her father's throne.

Her mind must have been in turmoil. Only a few days before the coronation James II landed at Kinsale in Ireland with a small army of Frenchmen. Clearly he was staging a comeback and another civil war might be imminent. What would happen to Mary then? News was coming through that he had already taken peaceable possession of the whole of Ireland, with only a few pockets of resistance. Mary had just put on her coronation robes and was preparing to take her place in the procession. Everyone was just about to set off for Westminster Abbey when a letter arrived for her. It was written by her father, King James himself – the first he had written to her since she had accepted the throne that was still rightfully his.

He told her bluntly that he had excused her treachery to him until now because he thought she was simply obeying her husband, William of Orange. But now that she was intending to have herself crowned beside him, it was perfectly obvious she was acting according to her own will. He ended by saying that 'if she were crowned while he and the Prince of Wales were living, the curse of an outraged father would light upon her, as well as of that God who has commanded duty to parents.'

Mary was stunned. She was even more taken aback when William declared that he hadn't done anything except by her advice and with her approval. The whole scene seemed to be turning into a tragic farce. Mary was overheard retorting that 'if her father regained his authority, her husband might thank himself for letting him *go as he did*.' Whatever she meant by this, her words certainly got back to James, who firmly believed, from that moment on, that Mary wished some kind of evil against him. Little wonder that in the heat of the occasion, the coronation was temporarily quite forgotten.

Mary questioned Mrs Dawson, the old midwife who had been present at the birth of her half-brother, the baby James Stuart. It was this baby's arrival which had triggered the whole sequence of events leading to James fleeing the country. Rumour had it that the infant was not really the child of the king and queen, but had in fact been smuggled into the queen's bedroom in a warming-pan. It was a preposterous and malicious rumour, but it had taken such a hold in people's minds that James had found it necessary to gather all the forty-odd people who had actually been at the birth – lords, ladies, bishops, midwives, physicians – at an extrardinary council at which they were required to swear on oath that the birth *had* taken place. It seems strange that now, just before her coronation, Mary should ask Mrs Dawson to tell her the facts yet again; and of course the trusted old midwife told her that, yes, she had delivered baby James Stuart just as she had delivered Mary herself, twenty-six years before.

All this may seem trivial and irrelevant, but it points to the chaotic state of Mary's mind. For a moment she may well have been tempted to cancel the coronation. However, things had gone too far, and she eventually pulled herself together and went on into the abbey. William had already gone ahead. The coronation which should have begun at 11.00 a.m. didn't get under way until 1.30 p.m.

And what a ceremony! It turned out to be a chapter of embarrassing moments, especially with the oddness of two monarchs being installed simultaneously. In fact there were many absentees among the bishops and nobility, for there were still many who had serious doubts about the legality of the situation. John Evelyn remarked in his diary: 'Much of the splendour of the ceremony was abated by the absence of divers who should have contributed to it. There were but five bishops and four judges; no more had taken the oaths.' However, the entire House of Commons attended – the first time that they had done so.

Throughout the service William and Mary gave oaths together in unison; they kissed the Bible together; and when the sword was offered at the altar they carried it together, presenting a somewhat absurd sight as Mary was so much bigger than her rather diminutive husband. A particularly awkward moment occurred when it was necessary for them to make the usual offertory of twenty guineas presented in a silken purse. The purse was there, but the money wasn't. The offertory basin was given to the king, but he had no money on him; then it was given to the queen, but she too was penniless. The treasurer looked to the lord chamberlain, but he had no money either. Eventually Lord Danby fished in his pocket and, to everyone's relief, produced the required amount.

The two monarchs were anointed separately, and here it became obvious that William was taking precedence, as the Bishop of London poured the oil on William's head first, and then on the queen's. And indeed, because it hadn't been possible to make a complete duplicate set of the regalia for Mary, she was not invested – as perhaps she should have been – with the sword, the spurs, or the armilla (bracelets). Nevertheless, a new orb with a cross and a new sceptre with a dove were both made specially for her. Luckily, there were already enough crowns to go round.

By the end of the ceremony, which had been so long delayed, it was late in the afternoon as the royal party left Westminster Abbey to go to Westminster Hall for the customary banquet. Meanwhile, fresh rumours and counter-rumours kept arriving, giving news of the progress of King James in Ireland. Princess Anne, sister of the newly-crowned queen, made a rather sarcastic remark to her about the worries surrounding her queenly position, whereupon Mary sharply retorted, 'A crown, sister, is not so heavy as it appears.'

Not surprisingly everyone was very much on edge during the meal, especially when the time came for Dymoke the champion to enter and make the traditional challenge. Minutes went by without any sign of him. Two hours elapsed. Eventually, at dusk, when daylight had almost completely gone, Sir Charles Dymoke made his appearance at last and issued his belated challenge 'in the name of our sovereign Lord and Lady, William and Mary'.

The gauntlet was flung, and then, in the gloom, what appeared to be a little old woman hobbled forward on crutches, picked it up, and replaced it with a lady's glove. Later, it was found to contain a letter answering the challenge and specifying a place in Hyde Park where a duel should be fought the following day. However, in the darkness, the 'old woman' had darted so swiftly out of the hall, and with such surprising agility, that no one had really been able to get a proper view of her.

Such was the surprising end to the day's events and one which was long remembered, especially by the Jacobite supporters of the exiled James, now to be obliquely referred to as 'the King over the water'. Rather disappointingly, although a well-built stranger was seen to be lurking in the appointed spot in Hyde Park the following day, the redoubtable Dymoke did not turn up to meet his challenger. Had he done so, no doubt an interesting sequel to this chapter would have ensued.

There is, however a serious sequel to this account of William and Mary's strange coronation, because this day brought about what is always referred to as Britain's 'Glorious Revolution', and this is why it can be claimed to be the most important event since the coronation of William the Conqueror. Even at the time it was heralded as such. The very next day all the members of the House of Commons met the new king and queen in the Banqueting House in Whitehall to congratulate them on this turning point in English history. It was proudly declared that 'the English should no longer date their laws and liberties from Saint Edward the Confessor's days, but from those of William and Mary'.

By accepting the throne from Parliament William and Mary were subject to the will of the people, deriving their authority entirely

300 YEARS OF ROBE-MAKING

A company founded by the Shudall family in London have been making robes for royalty since 1689. Since 1921 it has been known as Ede and Ravenscroft, famous worldwide for providing gowns, hoods, judges' and barristers' wigs and ceremonial robes for all occasions.

Probably the most important contract the firm had was to provide robes for the coronation of George IV. Its owner and director, William Webb, who had been robe maker to George III, received a new warrant from George IV less than three months after the new king's accession to make the rich garments for the most elaborate coronation ever seen.

Webb's records show that twenty-seven tailors worked for many months. 726½ yds of crimson satin and 643 yds of white silk mantua were needed for the mantles and surcoats of the Knights Grand Cross of the Bath alone. Then further mantles were needed for hundreds of others: nobles, kings of arms, heralds, pursuivants and many other officers and holders of various honours.

However, even after the robes had been made and delivered, there were other duties to attend to, as shown by a footnote to the account:

> 19 July 1821 Attendance of 20 Men at the Coronation to Robe and unrobe the Peers. Expenses for Provisions And boats to and from Westminster: £43 10s 6d

Willliam Webb's fee was £2,044 4s – a colossal sum in those days. However, it was the prestige that the firm gained that was the real reward, for it was used for the coronations of William IV in 1831 and Victoria in 1838. It is not surprising that his successor in 1901, Rosa Ede, wrote to Buckingham Palace 'soliciting the honour of making the Coronation Robes for His Majesty the King' – Edward VII. Her request was granted.

The success of Rosa Ede's work led to her receiving a signed and framed print of Queen Alexandra in her coronation robes. For the coronation of George V and Mary in 1911 the same robes were used, with slight alterations. Ede and Ravenscroft were again asked to provide the robes for George VI and Elizabeth in 1937 and Elizabeth II in 1953.

from them. As never before, Britain had now acquired a 'Constitutional Monarchy', and neither William and Mary nor any future king or queen could ever wield power without constitutional reference to parliament.

ANNE

Reigned 1702–14, crowned 23 April 1702, aged 37

The Last of the Stuarts

Fate was unkind to Anne. True, she was queen, but when she died she had suffered the misery of sixteen stillbirths, her only surviving son had died aged eleven, and she had been afflicted with gout, erysipelas, porphyria and venereal disease – not to mention obesity, which made it necessary for her to be carried everywhere for the last years of her painful life. Even at her coronation she was suffering so badly from gout that she simply could not walk to Westminster Abbey, and had to be borne in an open chair. Aged only thirty-seven, she was already a permanent invalid.

Both William and Mary had died prematurely. Mary had died first, of smallpox, after only five years on the throne, aged thirty-two. William reigned for another eight years before a riding accident which was to prove fatal. When it became evident that William was probably on his death-bed, Anne could hardly wait to hear of his death, together with the good news that she had become queen years earlier than she had expected. 'It is a fine day,' she remarked, when the Bishop of Salisbury, Dr Burnet, drove furiously from Kensington Palace to St James's Palace, desperately determined to be the first to prostrate himself at the new queen's feet.

It was quite clear, legally, that Anne was first in line to the throne, as sister-in-law to the dead king, but there were still plenty of people who were still 'Jacobites' at heart. Anne knew that feelings still ran high about the way in which her father, James II had been ousted from the throne, so she could never be quite certain of sincere loyalty from those around her. In fact King James had died only six months before, but there was still the 'warming-pan baby' – James Stuart – now aged thirteen, who was already being hailed as 'James III' by his supporters.

Although it was a Sunday when William III died, both Houses of Parliament met that morning to confirm Anne's accession, and she was pleased to accept their deputations, presented to her the same evening. She spoke with dignity, conscious of her beautiful voice – after all, her uncle, Charles II, had insisted that she was given special elocution lessons by an actress friend of his to make it even more attractive.

Anne was also conscious that she owed her very position to the members of parliament assembled before her, so she was careful to assure them that she would follow their wishes during her reign. 'As I know my heart to be entirely English,' she declared, 'I can very sincerely assure you that there is not one thing you can expect or desire of me which I shall not be ready to do for the happiness or prosperity of England.'

She was soon to realise that she was indeed in their hands when she tried, but in vain, to elevate her husband, Prince George of Denmark, to a position of king consort. No one would entertain the idea. Prince George had to be content with merely taking precedence over everyone else at her coronation, which was fixed for 23 April, the same date as her father's and also of her uncle's coronation.

People were somewhat scandalised by the speed with which Anne and her husband had moved into Kensington Palace and also the speed with which she had herself crowned – less than a fortnight after William's funeral, but these were difficult days, and she needed to legalise her position before any Jacobite rebellion could gather momentum.

So it was that on St George's Day, 1702, Queen Anne, last of the Stuarts, was carried, on account of her infirmity, by the Yeomen of the Guard to Westminster Abbey in her open chair. Her extremely long train of purple velvet flowed over the back of this chair and was carried by the Duchess of Somerset and four Ladies of the Bedchamber – one of whom was Mary Pierpoint, the future Lady Mary Wortley Montague, who later became famous for her pioneering support of the vaccination against smallpox. According to an eyewitness, Anne's finery included a dress of crimson velvet with an under-robe of 'gold tissue, very rich embroidery of jewels about it, her petticoat the same gold tissue with gold and silver lace between rows of diamonds embroidered . . . her head as well dressed with diamonds that brilled and flared'. She also wore a wig 'with long locks and puffs'.

A curious oddity in the proceedings was the presence of two gentlemen who purported to be the the the 'Dukes of Normandy and Aquitaine', wearing strange, anachronistic tabards. In everyday life these two, James Clark and Jonathan Andrews, were simply gentlemen of the Privy Chamber: but on this occasion they spendidly upheld the grandiose fiction that Queen Anne, as queen of England, still possessed vast tracts of land in France. Whether she was carried right into the abbey is not clear, but certainly the two bishops supporting her found it necessary to give her physical help during the long five-hour service, having to prop her up whenever she was standing.

The service followed the usual pattern, but by far the most significant part in it was the declaration which Anne was required to make, which made quite clear to everyone that she was indeed an upholder of the Protestant faith. Anne was now the second monarch after the Glorious Revolution, and it is clear in this declaration that the sovereign had, by now, become the mouthpiece of tenaciously anti-Catholic and anti-Jacobite ministers. In 1953, Elizabeth II merely promised to maintain 'the Protestant Reformed Religion established by law', but this vague phrase would not have been clear enough for those who drew up Queen Anne's promise in 1702. It is almost alarmingly specific.

I, Anne, by the grace of God, Queen of England, Scotland, France and Ireland, Defender of the Faith &c., do solemnly, in the presence of God, profess, testify and declare that I do believe that in the sacrament of the Lord's Supper there is not any transubstantiation of the elements of bread and wine into the body and blood of Christ, at or after the consecration thereof by any person whatsoever,

2ndly, That the invocation or adoration of the Virgin Mary, or any other saint, and the sacrifice of the mass as they are now used in the church of Rome, are superstitious and idolatrous,

3rdly, And I do solemnly, in the presence of God, profess, testify, and declare, that I do make this declaration, and every part thereof, in the plain and ordinary sense of the words read to me, as they are commonly understood by

English protestants, without any evasion, equivocation, or mental reservation whatsoever, and without any dispensation already granted me for this purpose by the pope, or any other authority or person, or without any hope of such dispensation from any person or authority whatsoever, or without thinking I am, or can be, acquitted before God or man, or absolved of this desclaration, or of any part thereof, although the pope, or any other person or power whatsoever, should dispense with or annul the same, or declare that it was null and void from the beginning.

After such a declaration, repeated aloud sentence by sentence by the new queen, who could possibly doubt the continuance of the Protestant faith in England?

The Archbishop of Canterbury, Thomas Tenison, duly crowned, anointed and blessed her, and then somewhat tactlessly prayed that she would leave 'a numerous posterity to rule these kingdoms after you by succession in all ages'. She had already given birth seventeen times and less than two years previously she had buried the only child to survive beyond an eleventh birthday – the pathetic little Duke of Gloucester. She would never again expect further children, despite the archbishop's prayers: a sadness for her and a worrying uncertainty for her realms.

No traditional jolly procession from the Tower to Westminster had taken place: those days were now in the past. However, after the coronation Anne and her husband dutifully attended the customary banquet in Westminster Hall. Despite fears to the contrary, the champion did his duty without a repetition of the embarrassment which had occurred at William and Mary's coronation.

The only cause for muttering was the fact that although the members of parliament, who had been responsible for confirming Anne as their new sovereign, were invited to the banquet, all they were expected to do was to watch the rest of the company eating it, as no places at table had been reserved for them.

As for the Jacobites, there was a discreet silence. However, the constitutional position of Scotland presented the government with something of a problem. It was now a century since James VI of Scotland had been invited to London, nominated by Elizabeth I to be king of England. In 1603 he had taken leave of his Scottish court and kingdom promising to come back – but it was fourteen years before he made his one and only return visit to his native land. Similarly, Charles I had made just one visit, to be crowned in Edinburgh as king of Scotland in 1633; and Charles II, as a young man on the run from the Parliamentarians, had been given a Covenanters' coronation at Scone. Since then, no Scottish coronation had taken place. Indeed, as a consequence of James's succession to the throne of England, the independent and separate line of Scottish kings and queens had quietly come to an end. James II never went to Scotland during his reign; neither did William or Mary.

The accession of Queen Anne brought the question that somehow the situation between the two countries ought to be legally regularised and settled. Accordingly, at the Act of Union in 1707, England and Scotland formally became one country, with a single parliament governing from London.

Scottish royalists must have been deeply saddened to realise that never again would their beautiful ancient crown be used. Thus it was, with something of a dramatic gesture, that the Scottish crown, sceptre and sword – the Honours of Scotland – were walled up in a little room in Edinburgh Castle, never to be seen again by anyone then living.

GEORGE I

Reigned 1714–27, crowned 20 October 1714, aged 54

'The Elephant' and 'The Maypole'

Despite the coronation prayers of the Archbishop Tenison, Queen Anne did *not* leave a 'numerous posterity to rule these kingdoms'. Indeed, there was no immediately obvious heir to the throne when she died, except, of course, James II's Catholic son, James Stuart, now exiled and living in France.

However, the situation had been foreseen as long ago as 1701 under William III. Recognising that it was their responsibility to find future kings and queens, and resolutely determined to ensure a Protestant succession, members of parliament had passed the Act of Settlement which passed the throne, if need be, to Sophia, Electress of Hanover, and her heirs. (The curious title

'Elector' or 'Electress' simply meant that that the position traditionally entitled the holder to 'elect' the Holy Roman Emperor.)

Sophia was in fact directly descended from James I, albeit through the female line. She was James I's grand-daughter: daughter of his 'dearest Bessie' who had married the king of Bohemia. At the time of the Act of Settlement Sophia was seventy-one, but she was still as sprightly as ever, with a reputation for sparkling intelligence, and fluency in five languages. If Sophia *had* become Queen of England – as she easily might have been – hers would have been a fascinating and memorable reign. But alas, she would have been too old to have occupied the throne for long. In fact, she missed her chance to become queen of Great Britain by less than two months – dying in June 1714.

When Queen Anne died just a few weeks later, in August, the throne was offered to Sophia's son, George Lewis, aged fifty-four, who had now become Elector of Hanover. 'Low of stature, of features coarse, of aspect dull and placid', he was totally different from his mother, and appeared to be interested only in women, hunting and food. He had divorced his wife, another Sophia, and had locked her up permanently for daring to enjoy the company of another man. As for himself, he enjoyed numerous mistresses, and planned to bring his two favourites to England with him when he became king.

George was never popular: never more than merely tolerated. In view of this, he has always been given a bad press, described in sniggering terms by almost all who met him or by later historians, who emphasised his boorishness. 'A lank gentleman with a vermilion complexion,' goes one description, adding that he had 'a shelving forehead and a receding chin, and colourless eyes, the whole enshrouded by a light ginger-coloured wig.' He did not like England, hated poets and painters, and did his best to visit his native Hanover whenever he could.

It has been calculated that at the time of his arrival there were at least fifty-seven better claimants to the throne – but a firm Protestant was what was required.

Curiosity was intense as George arrived at Greenwich on a foggy Saturday evening in September 1714. Torches and flares had to be lit so that George could see his way into Wren's new building to be greeted by the Archbishop of Canterbury in the ageing primate's somewhat rusty French. It was quickly realised that the new king could not speak English – and of course very few of his new courtiers could manage any German. So it was that throughout his reign George and his English subjects had to struggle with French or Latin to communicate with one another.

The fog had lifted by the Monday morning and all London's society swarmed into Greenwich Park to see their new king: anybody who was anybody got into their coaches, many of them drawn by six horses, and eventually 2,000 people moved off in procession to accompany George to St James's Palace.

This welcoming triumphal procession bore some resemblance to the triumphant progresses which had traditionally taken place from the Tower of London to Westminster, but this time there were no pageants or decorated arches or children declaiming verses: simple curiosity was the order of the day as King George was slowly brought in triumph to his palace. The authorities had made sure that the roads from Greenwich to London had been repaired for the occasion; the streets were cleaned, and carts and drays were cleared off the processional route. No coaches or carriages were allowed to stand by the roadside.

At Southwark the king stopped to hear the city's welcome read by the recorder, Sir Peter King, and to receive an expression of 'duty and loyalty' from the lord mayor and the corporation. Here, the procession was enlarged by the addition of various officials: a detachment of the Artillery Company, the Knights Marshal's men, the King's Kettle Drums and Trumpets, the Heralds, the Sergeant-at-Arms, the Gentleman Usher of the Black Rod, and the Yeomen of the Guard. Coming from the relatively tiny town of Hanover, George was astonished at the pomp and crowds of onlookers. Afterwards, he commented that it made him think of pictures of the Resurrection. Quickly one of his new courtiers, a Lady Cowper, responded: 'Sire, it is our political resurrection!'

George was crowned by Archbishop Tenison at Westminster Abbey just one month later. A new king, a new dynasty, and a new mood among the political grandees at Westminster. After all, now that a non-English-speaking king had arrived who was completely ignorant of what was what or who was who in his own kingdom, the power of his advisers was visibly increasing day by day. Sir Robert Walpole steadily assumed the position of a 'Prime Minister' and cabinet government became a practical necessity.

Despite the traditional pomp, therefore, this coronation signalled a very different kind of monarchy, with power draining away from court and establishing itself even more firmly than ever before in parliament and its chief ministers. George could not have understood much of what was going on around him at this coronation. The ceremonies had to be explained to him in broken French or stuttering Latin by his bishops and ministers. It was jokingly said that 'much bad language' passed between them.

More importantly, there must have been quite a number of Jacobites at the coronation ceremony, and people wondered if there would be any kind of demonstration. It was known that the day was celebrated at Oxford by awarding degrees to Jacobites, and there were Jacobite riots in Bristol. However, in Westminster Abbey itself the service passed off without overt opposition. But the mood of the occasion can be judged by Lady Cowper's commentary, noted in her diary:

> One may easily conclude this was not a Day of real Joy to the Jacobites. However, they were all there, looking as cheerful as they could, but very peevish with Everybody that spoke to them. My Lady Dorchester stood underneath me; and when the archbishop went round the Throne, demanding the consent of the People, she turned to me and said, 'Does the old Fool think that Anybody here will say no to his Question, when there are so many drawn swords?'

George was crowned alone. The fact that his ex-wife, Sophia Dorothea, was still imprisoned in Ahlden Castle in Germany for alleged unfaithfulness was a cause for much scandal, especially as he had come to England accompanied by 'all his German ministers and playfellows male and female', as Lady Mary Wortley Montagu cattily observed. His two principal mistresses were Ermengarda Melusina von Schulenburg – extremely tall and thin – who was quickly nicknamed 'The Maypole' by the gossiping English court; and Sophia von Kilmansegg – prodigiously large and fat – who became known as 'The Elephant'.

His male 'playfellows' were a couple of Turkish servants, Mustapha and Mahomet, whom he had captured in the campaign against the Turks at the relief of Vienna. Malicious rumour suggested that these were his personal procurers. Also included among George's personal entourage from Hanover were eighteen cooks and one washerwoman. George had his priorities!

Whatever he thought of his coronation, George was quite prepared to enjoy the banquet afterwards, in Westminster Hall. Silently and alone he sat for more than two hours steadily stuffing himself, while 17 bishops and 150 peers, grouped in order of precedence, solemnly watched him. Lady Dorchester, a former mistress of James II, who had made such acid comment on the Archbishop of Canterbury during the service, looked round and saw two of her old friends, Louise de Keroualle, Duchess of Portsmouth, a former mistress of Charles II, and Lady Orkney, a former mistress of William III. The piquancy of the situation amused her. 'Good God!' she exclaimed, 'Who would have thought we three whores would have met together here!' Nevertheless, the coronation passed off without incident, and some, at least, were prepared to give George the benefit of the doubt. Lady Wentworth wrote with innocent optimism: 'All hear are in great raptures of the King and say he is the Wysest and the Richis Princ in Yoarup. I hope he will prove soe.'

GEORGE II AND CAROLINE OF ANSBACH

Reigned 1727–60, crowned 11 October 1727, aged 43

Handel's Zadok the Priest *is Heard for the First Time*

Sir Robert Walpole was eating dinner at his home in Chelsea when news was brought to him that George I was dead, having suffered a stroke on his way to Hanover. Desperately eager to be the first to inform the Prince of Wales that he was now king, Sir Robert wasted no time. Just as he was, casually dressed, he leaped into the saddle and galloped so violently to Richmond that it is reported that two horses died under him from sheer over-exhaustion before he finally arrived to greet his new monarch.

Prince George had already gone to bed, but roused himself and, half-dressed, heard the good news that his father was dead: son and father had hated each other. Their relationship cannot have been improved by the fact that the Prince's mother, Sophia Dorothea, had been forced to live under house-arrest for alleged infidelity for the last thirty-two years of her life. She too was dead, having died just six months before, still a prisoner in the moated castle of Ahlden.

King at last, George II made no arrangements for his father's funeral. However, he quickly ordered Handel to write four new anthems for his coronation. It was perhaps surprising that he should have approached Handel, for arguably the task should have gone to Maurice Green, the recently-appointed organist and composer of the Chapel Royal. Also, as Handel had been a favourite of George I, it would have been quite understandable if he had been passed over. It says much for Handel's powerful reputation that he won the favour of George II.

Luckily, one of George I's final acts in England before he died had been to sign the papers giving Handel British citizenship. It was 'An Act for naturalizing *Louis Sechehaye, George Frideric Handel*, and others'. Thus it was that Handel, the newly-created Englishman, could compete on equal terms with any of his rivals for appointments in England.

Handel was not merely granted the honour of composing the four anthems, but also, except for *Zadok the Priest*, he was given the freedom to choose his own words. A later handwritten comment on a copy of these coronation anthems, possibly by George III, adds that Handel 'had but four weeks for doing this wonderful work which seems scarcely credible, as to the first *Zadok the Priest* it is probably the most perfect if possible of all His superb compositions'.

Not unnaturally, the Archbishops of Canterbury and York were somewhat alarmed that an ex-foreigner such as Handel should have been entrusted with the task of choosing biblical texts for such an important event, and offered to help Handel make acceptable decisions. However, Handel was adamantly independent. 'I have read my Bible very well,' he growled, 'and shall choose for myself.'

In the event, the four anthems he produced were *Let thy Hand be Strengthened*, to be performed during the Recognition; *Zadok the Priest* for the Anointing; *The King Shall Rejoice*, for the crowning of the king; and *My Heart is Inditing*, for the crowning of the queen. It is worth recording the texts Handel chose, and noting how appropriate they were for these points in the coronation service:

(For the Recognition)	Let thy hand be strengthened and thy right hand be exalted.
	Let justice and judgement be the preparation of thy seat;
	Let mercy and truth go before thy face! Alleluja.
(For the Anointing)	Zadok the Priest and Nathan the Prophet, anointed Solomon King.
(words chosen by Archbishop	And all the people rejoiced, and said: God save the King!
Dunstan for Edgar's Coronation in 973)	Long live the King! God Save the King! Amen. Alleluja.
	May the King live for ever!
(For the crowning of the king)	The King shall rejoice in thy strength, O Lord.
	Exceeding glad shall he be of thy salvation.
	Glory and (great) worship hast thou laid upon him.
	Thou hast presented him with the blessing of goodness
	And hast set a crown of pure gold upon his head.
	Alleluja.
(For the crowning of the queen)	My heart is inditing of a good matter;
	I speak of the things which I have made unto the King.
	King's daughters were among thy honourable women.
	Upon thy right hand did stand the Queen in vesture of gold.
	Kings shall be thy nursing fathers, and Queens thy nursing mothers.

Many musical critics have commented upon the gentle and warm music which Handel wrote for Queen Caroline, *My Heart is Inditing*. Caroline was not only a powerful character but also a sensitive patron of the arts. Handel's music was a graceful personal tribute to her.

Rumours that Handel had written music of quite extraordinary quality found expression in London and provincial newspapers. Even the rehearsals were newsworthy items. *Parker's Penny Post* of 4 October, just one week before the coronation, buzzed with excitement:

> Mr Hendle (*sic*) has composed the Musick for the Abbey at the Coronation, and the Italian Voices, with above a Hundred of the best Musicians will perform; and the Whole is allowed by those Judges in Musick who have already heard it, to exceed any Thing heretofore of the same Kind: It will be rehearsed this Week, but the Time will be kept private, lest the Crowd of People should be an Obstruction to the Performers.

Handel was obviously enjoying the financial freedom to engage a huge orchestra. *Read's Weekly Journal* reported:

> Yesterday there was a Rehearsal of Musick that is to be performed at their Majesties Coronation in Westminster Abbey, where was present the greatest Concourse of People that has been known.

And the *Norwich Gazette* spelled out the orchestral requirements:

> Yesterday there was a Rehearsal of the Coronation Anthem in Westminster-Abbey, set to Musick by the famous Mr Hendall: There being 40 voices, and about 160 Violins, Trumpets, Hautboys, Kettle-Drums, Bass's proportionable; besides an Organ, which was erected behind the Altar: And both the Musick and the Performers, were the Admiration of all the Audience.

It was, of course, *Zadok the Priest* in particular which enraptured everyone who heard it. It has been said that 'even today, at every coronation, the central part of Zadok is, quite simply, awe-inspiring'. Music critics down the centuries have struggled to find words for this 'blaze of sound' – the 'supreme example of ceremonial music' – with its 'inspired opening crescendo and breathtaking entry of the seven-part chorus with trumpets' – 'that shattering choral entry' – 'the greatest public ceremonial music of its kind ever composed.' Handel was already famous for his operas and oratorios, but now the splendour of these Coronation Anthems added dramatically to his reputation. He had yet to write *Messiah*.

The coronation of George II and Caroline did have a few awkward moments, even in parts of the music. The Archbishop himself made some acid comments in his copy of the Order of Service, noting that the anthem *I was glad* 'was omitted and no Anthem at all Sung . . . by the Negligence of the Choir of Westminster.' Nevertheless, the overall effect of this ceremony for the second Hanoverian monarch was one of hitherto unparalleled magnificence.

George II and Caroline had waited literally half their lives for this coronation, for they had both been twenty-two when George I, somewhat unexpectedly, came to the English throne. George II was a relatively small man, and it was generally accepted that his wife Caroline, built on ampler proportions and mother of his nine children, was the dominant personality: people giggled at the doggerel verse chanted behind his back:

> You may strut, dapper George, but 'twill all be in vain,
> We know 'tis Queen Caroline that reign.

A close observer of the court at the time, Lord Hervey, wrote that 'As soon as ever the prince became king, the whole world began to find out that her will is the sole spring on which every movement in the court turns'. And it is in the gossipy memoirs of Lord Hervey that we read this somewhat malicious eye-witness account of the details of George and Caroline's coronation:

The coronation of George II was performed with all the pomp and magnificence that could be contrived; the present King differing so much from the last, that all the pageantry and splendour, badges and trapping of royalty, were as pleasing to the son as they were irksome to the father.

The dress of the Queen on this occasion was as fine as the accumulated riches of the city and suburbs could make it; for besides her own jewels (which were a great number, and very valuable), she had on her head and on her shoulders, all the pearls she could borrow of the ladies of quality at one end of the town, and on her petticoat all the diamonds she could hire of the Jews and jewellers at the other; so that the appearance of her finery was a mixture of magnificence and meanness, not unlike the *éclat* of royalty in many other particulars when it comes to be really examined, and the sources traced to what money hires or flattery lends.

Certainly the event was planned with precision. Mantles of viscountesses were to trail a yard and a quarter on the ground, but those of mere baronesses were allowed to trail only a yard. Similarly, it was ordained that petticoats were to be 'cloth of silver, or any other white stuff, either laced or embroidered'. And the etiquette over pearls on coronets was severely strict; jewellers were told not to raise them on spikes, or answer 'to their perils'.

Peers had to arrive at the House of Lords by 8.00 a.m.; George and Caroline arrived at 9.00 a.m.; and then at noon precisely the procession of church dignitaries and lords accompanied the royal couple from Westminster Hall to Westminster Abbey, walking on a blue carpet with handmaids scattering sweet-smelling herbs before them.

After the coronation itself was over, the party returned to Westminster Hall for the traditional banquet. The king's champion, dressed in white armour and riding a white charger, entered with a flourish to demand whether anyone contested the king's title, but despite the known existence of the Jacobite 'King over the water' – the Old Pretender – no one took up the challenge. Finally, once the challenge had been successfully completed, the peers of the realm were ready to gorge themselves with several hours of eating and drinking in the main body of Westminster Hall. The unlucky peeresses, however, had to sit in specially-made tiered balconies running along each side of the hall. Sitting on these hard wooden seats with their 'laced or embroidered' petticoats well out of sight, all they could do was to look on with patience as their menfolk gluttonised.

CORONATION MUSIC AND MUSICIANS

One of the supreme musical events at any crowning came at George II's coronation in 1727 when Handel's *Zadok the Priest* was heard for the first time.

Another great coronation anthem is Sir Hubert Parry's *I was glad*, commissioned for the entrance of Edward VII and Alexandra in 1902. Sir Frederick Bridge, director of Music for the Coronation, wanted a new processional anthem. It was completed swiftly, and like *Zadok*, it made such an impression that it became a regular part of all subsequent coronations.

By the coronation of George VI and Elizabeth in 1937, the BBC had emerged as a new and powerful commissioning body. In March, two months before the coronation, the BBC commissioned 'a symphonic march for Coronation Week', and offered forty guineas to William Walton, 'the one person of the younger generation of composers most able to do this,' as the writer of a memorandum observed. The result was the splendidly majestic *Crown Imperial* that was played for the entry of Queen Mary.

Fifteen years later Walton was asked, by the Arts Council, for a march for the coronation of Elizabeth II. Entitled *Orb and Sceptre*, and dedicated to the new queen, it was first heard in Westminster Abbey on Coronation Day. Sir William McKie, the Abbey Organist and Director of Music for the service, had also asked Walton to compose a new *Te Deum*.

One of the most popular pieces of music written for an English coronation was Elgar's *Coronation Ode*, written for Edward VII's coronation, with the tune taken from *Pomp and Circumstance, March No. 1*. It is better known as *Land of Hope and Glory*. Elgar recognised the huge potential of this theme, writing to Dora Penny (the Dorabella of the *Enigma Variations*): 'I've got a tune that will knock 'em - knock 'em flat!' Elgar's friend, Jaeger (*Nimrod*) was horrified to think that he could contemplate putting words to the melody – he thought it would be 'quite impossible' and 'downright vulgar'. The words, written by A.C. Benson, are known and sung throughout the world.

Many English composers were chosen for the coronation of Elizabeth II. Though Elgar and Purcell were not represented, the list included Byrd, Gibbons, Handel, Parry, Wesley, Walton, and Vaughan Williams.

GEORGE III AND CHARLOTTE OF MECKLENBURG-STRELITZ

Reigned 1760–1820, crowned 22 September 1761, aged 23

A Mysterious 'Mr Brown' Attends the Coronation

George III was a fresh-faced youngster of twenty-three when he married seventeen-year-old Charlotte Sophia of Mecklenburg-Strelitz on 8 September 1761. Just a fortnight later the young newly-weds were crowned king and queen, not merely of Great Britain and Ireland but also of Britain's increasingly numerous overseas possessions – including the thirteen American colonies.

His was to be the second longest reign of all – sixty years – beaten only by Queen Victoria in the following century, and it is a great pity that our final memories of him are that of a senile, mentally-afflicted old man, who in his last years had to be locked in a padded room in Windsor Castle. Everyone remembers 'Mad King George', but this is hardly fair to a conscientious young monarch who for many years tried his best to do what he considered right during some very difficult circumstances.

The reason why he was so young at his coronation was that his father, Prince Frederick, had come to an untimely early death, having suffered complications after being hit on the chest by a cricket ball.

At the time of his coronation, George had only just met his new wife. She had arrived from the tiny and obscure Duchy of Mecklenburg-Strelitz earlier in the month and within twenty-four hours had married George – whom she had never met before – in a wedding-dress which had been chosen for her to wear.

Of course, it was George's duty to marry. 'Be a King!' his mother, the Dowager Princess Augusta had told him. And so, if that entailed marrying a foreign princess whom he had never even seen, then marry her he would: he was determined to do his duty. In fact, he was still madly in love with one of the ladies about court, Sarah Lennox, but this liaison had to be abandoned, as Lady Sarah was a mere commoner. Nevertheless, during the marriage service to Charlotte, people looking closely at George noticed that when a prayer was said containing the words 'Abraham and Sarah', George blushed bright scarlet on hearing her name. But whatever his feelings, from that moment on George stuck devotedly and faithfully to his little German bride, and they were eventually to have fifteen healthy children.

Now, a fortnight after their wedding, Westminster Abbey was crowded to capacity for their coronation. Quite apart from all the lords and ladies in the seats on the floor of the abbey, other guests could be accommodated in special rooms, oddly called 'nunneries', which were constructed high up in scaffolding between the pillars each taking up to twelve guests. Someone must have been making a huge profit from these, for no less than fifty guineas was being asked for the privilege of occupying a nunnery and having a good view of the coronation down below.

William Hickey, a schoolboy aged eleven, had the good fortune to be present in one of these nunneries with his father and friends. Young as he was, he was able to note the events with a wickedly precocious eye for detail. Apparently his family had started off at midnight in three carriages to reach the abbey, but even in 1761 traffic-jams were part and parcel of London life:

. . . at the end of Pall Mall the different lines of carriages, nearly filling the street, our progress was consequently tedious, yet the time was beguiled by the grandeur of the scene, such a multitude of carriages, with servants behind carrying flambeaux, made a blaze of light equal to day, and had a fine effect.

Opposite the Horse Guards we were stopped exactly an hour without moving onward a single inch. As we approached near the Abbey, the difficulties increased, from mistakes of the coachmen, some of whom were going to the hall, others to to the abbey, and getting into the wrong ranks. This created much confusion and running against each other, whereby glasses and panels were demolished without number, the noise of which accompanied by the screeches of the terrified ladies, was at times truly terrific.

William and his family managed to get into their nunnery at last, and after a hot meal they settled down to wait several hours for the ceremony to begin. It wasn't until one o'clock the following afternoon that George and Charlotte entered Westminster Abbey, and William noted with satisfaction that he 'had a capital view of the whole ceremony'. He continues:

> Their Majesties . . . being crowned, the Archbishop of Canterbury (Thomas Secker) mounted the pulpit to deliver the sermon, and as many thousands were out of the possibility of hearing a single syllable, they took that opportunity to eat their meal when the general clattering of knives, forks, plates, and glasses that ensued, produced a most ridiculous effect, and a universal burst of laughter followed.

This was not the only thing to go wrong at this coronation, which seemed to produce one embarrassment after another. Even before the day itself there had been difficulties when the workmen putting up the decorations and stands went on strike, and during the service itself and the banquet which followed, arrangements seem have been little short of chaotic.

Lord Effingham, the deputy earl marshal, totally forgot the Sword of State and the canopy. Gallantly, the lord mayor lent his own sword, but the difficulty in producing a hastily-constructed canopy at the last moment delayed the start of the procession so much that from then on everything was much later than anticipated. Even worse, the whole service was so under-rehearsed that there were several long pauses while the participants wondered what to do next.

George was in some doubt whether he should remove his crown while taking Holy Communion, and asked Archbishop Secker what he should do. The archbishop was nonplusssed, and asked the bishop of Rochester, but he did not know either. George took the matter into his own hands, took off the crown, and laid it down while he took the bread and wine. The gesture was seen with rapture: 'How happy in this day of greatest worldly pomp he should remember his duty to the King of Kings,' wrote old Lady Montagu afterwards. However, it put Charlotte into a quandary, because when she tried to get *her* crown off, she found it was stuck in her hair, and simply would not come off, however hard she tugged. George told her not to worry, kindly telling her that it was not important for her to do the same.

Another unfortunate incident occurred when the largest jewel fell out of the crown. Naturally enough, this was interpreted as a portentous omen. Later, the fortune-tellers were able to realise, in hindsight, that of course it foretold the loss of America! Further embarrassment came when Bishop Drummond of Salisbury got so muddled that he spoke of the extraordinary number of years the king had already sat on the throne. In the end the coronation service lasted a full six hours.

All the same, despite these difficulties and the laughter as people ate their way through the sermon, it was noted that the king's dignified behaviour was exemplary, and the music throughout was excellent, including *Zadok the Priest* now being heard for the second time at a coronation.

Owing to the delayed start, the return procession for the banquet in Westminster Hall did not take place until nightfall, so that when the guests arrived there they had to fumble about in almost total darkness to find their places. Apart from the lack of chairs-of-state for the king and queen, nothing at all had been provided for the lord mayor and aldermen of London; nor for the Knights of the Bath; nor for the barons of the Cinque Ports. All three groups began to argue furiously with Lord Talbot, the high steward, demanding proper places as were their due.

The aldermen were the most vociferous and 'by dint of many hard words, and not a few bullying threats' forced Talbot to give them places which were in fact far above their proper rank. The Knights of the Bath, on the other hand, were rather more docile, and had to accept a private dinner by themselves in the Court of Requests. But the poor barons of the Cinque Ports came off worst. Lord Talbot completely lost his temper with them, shouting 'If you come to me as Lord Steward, I tell you it is impossible; if as Lord Talbot, I am a match for any of you!' Whether they did get a dinner or not in the end is not recorded.

Then the lights came on. It had been planned as a surprise – and surprise it was. Thomas Gray, the poet, was there, and gives this description:

The instant the Queen's canopy entered, fire was given to all the lustres at once by trains of prepared flax that reached from one end to the other. To me it seemed an interval of not half a minute before the whole was in a blaze of splendour. It is true that for that half minute it rained fire upon the heads of all the spectators, the flax falling in large flakes; and the ladies, Queen and all, were in no small terror, but no mischief ensued. It was out as soon as it fell, and the most magnificent spectacle I even beheld remained. The King bowing to the Lords as he passed, with the crown on his head, and the sceptre and orb in his hands, took his place with great majesty and grace. So did the Queen with her crown, sceptre and rod. Then supper was served in gold plates.

All seemed to be well at last. But there were still some surprises to come. Horace Walpole, who was also present, tells that 'The Champion acted his part admirably, and dashed down his gauntlet with proud defiance.' However, he was accompanied by three others on horseback, including the luckless Lord Talbot. At his entry, the proceedings moved into high comedy. Apparently Lord Talbot, knowing that proper etiquette demanded that he should never turn his back on royalty, spent many hours practising and training his horse to walk backwards. He hoped he would make a deep impression by virtue of this equestrian skill. However, when the time came for his entry, his horse had been so well trained that nothing on earth could stop it from *entering* the hall backwards, rump-first towards their majesties. The assembled lords and ladies collapsed with uncontrolled, hysterical laughter – and clapped with loud applause as the wretched Lord Talbot made his exit! 'A terrible indecorum,' as one onlooker remarked afterwards.

Meanwhile more indecorum was in evidence along the tiered galleries. It was the custom for the ladies present to be installed in the wooden upper gallery running the length of each side of the hall. Perched up above, they did not actually take part in the banquet, but were graciously allowed to watch their husbands and men-friends gorging at tables beneath them. They had been in their places six tedious hours before the king and queen had even arrived. Desperately hungry and frustrated at the long hours of waiting, they began to form ropes of handkerchiefs tied together, so that they could haul up chicken-legs, bottles of wine, or other tit-bits which their gallant spouses passed up to them.

THE CORONATION ROBES

The principal robes used at a coronation are the *Supertunica*, the *Pallium Regale* or Imperial Mantle, the Stole, the Girdle and the *Colobium Sindonis*.

The oldest and most magnificent, the Imperial Mantle, made for George IV's coronation, is made of gold thread, and is embroidered with roses, thistles, shamrocks, fleur-de-lys.

The *Supertunica* was made for George V's coronation in 1911, and was designed to resemble the robe worn by a Roman Consul. Like the Imperial Mantle, it is made of gold thread. Their combined weight is 23 lb; Prinny almost fainted under the strain of wearing the mantle over all the other robes.

The Girdle and the Stole were made by the Worshipful Company of Girdlers as a gift for Elizabeth II. The Stole is beautifully decorated with the emblems of Ceylon, India, New Zealand, Australia, Canada, Ireland and Britain.

The *Colobium Sindonis* is a plain white linen garment that harks back to the Byzantine emperors, who, at the time of their anointing, would remove their royal robes and offer themselves at the altar dressed as a peasant. Its stark simplicity makes a striking contrast to the magnificence of the other robes.

After the Restoration in 1660 it was the custom to make new robes for each coronation, but since 1901 the *Supertunica* and the Imperial Mantle have been reused. Future monarchs will undoubtedly make use of the Stole and Girdle.

Since its foundation in 1872 the Royal School of Needlework has embroidered robes for all subsequent coronations. A ledger entry in 1952 records an item that Ede and Ravenscroft was to supply for the forthcoming coronation. It was for

making and supplying Imperial State Robe for the coronation of Her Majesty Queen Elizabeth II being a six yard train in best quality hand made purple silk velvet, trimmed with best quality Canadian ermine 5" on top and underside and fully lined with pure silk English Satin complete with Ermine cape and all being tailed in ermine in the traditional manner and including embroidery by the Royal School of Needlework.

The splendour of the finished article worn by the queen will live in the nation's memory for a long time.

George and Charlotte emerged from all this with good grace. 'The King's whole behaviour at the coronation was justly admired and commended by every one, and, particularly, his manner of ascending and seating himself on the throne after his coronation,' wrote one of the bishops who had been present. However, George must have been upset by all the various mishaps, and made a justifiable complaint to Lord Effingham, the deputy earl marshal, whose original negligence over the sword and canopy had caused such havoc with the timing. Effingham's reply was a masterpiece of indiscretion: 'It is true, sir, that there has been some neglect,' he admitted, 'but I have taken care that the *next* coronation shall be regulated in the exactest manner possible.'

Finally, there is an intriguing tailpiece to this coronation. After it was over, it was rumoured in London that a very special visitor had been witness to the event in Westminster Abbey – none other than the King over the Water, Charles Stuart, the Jacobite Young Pretender himself, attending the ceremony under the name of 'Mr Brown'.

This was probably completely untrue, but like many a gossipy tale, it went the rounds for years, even complete with a conversation which is supposed to have taken place when a Jacobite supporter whispered in his ear: 'Your Royal Highness is the last of all mortals whom I should expect to see here.' Reportedly, Bonnie Prince Charlie replied: 'It was curiosity that led me, but I assure you that the person who is the cause of all this pomp and magnificence is the man I envy least.'

Did the Young Pretender come to London for the coronation, as he is alleged to have come, incognito, on previous occasions? It would not have been entirely beyond the bounds of possibility. He would have been forty at the time, and would have had to have made the journey from Rome, where he was living in permanent exile. No one will ever know the truth. However, if Bonnie Prince Charlie really did see the third Hanoverian King George settling himself on the throne with such dignity, surely his fading hopes of a Stuart return to power were extinguished for ever.

GEORGE IV

Reigned 1820–30, crowned 19 July 1821, aged 59

'Like Some Gorgeous Bird of the East'

'Prinny', as everyone called the prince regent, had begun his regency, deputising for his mentally sick father, as long ago as 1810 – eleven years before his eventual coronation. In a sense, therefore, he was king in all but name. In those eleven years he had been able to plan for himself the most gorgeously elaborate and costly coronation ever witnessed in England.

The whole affair was staged on such a grand scale that inevitably many eyewitnesses put pen to paper afterwards to record what was to prove, perhaps, the apotheosis of Prinny's preposterous egomania. Even before preparations began, he ordered that a gigantic book should be compiled by the Garter King at Arms to mark down all the details. After all, he himself had designed the weirdly-extravagant costumes worn by all the lords and officers of state who took part, and so naturally he wanted posterity to enjoy the occasion long after the event itself. The prologue to this book provides something of the mood of this coronation:

TO THE MOST HIGH, MOST MIGHTY AND MOST EXCELLENT MONARCH GEORGE THE FOURTH, BY THE GRACE OF GOD OF THE UNITED KINGDOM OF GREAT BRITAIN AND IRELAND, KING, DEFENDER OF THE FAITH, KING OF HANOVER, DUKE OF BRUNSWICK AND OF LUNEBURGH,

Sire,

With all humility I presume to lay before Your Most August Majesty an Historical Record of Your Majesty's Sacred Coronation, in the completion of which I have laboured with the proudest anxiety to fulfil Your Majesty's Royal Commands.

Supported by Your Majesty's Government in the discharge of this honourable and gratifying Duty, I have endeavoured to offer both to the present Age and to Posterity a Memorial of this most Royal and Dignified Solemnity, illustrated by

Representations of the Superb Habiliments which your
Majesty, not less regardful of the Posterity of Your People
than of the Splendour of Your Throne, was pleased to enjoin
should be worn upon the occasion, thereby affording
employment to Thousands of Your Industrious and loyal
subjects, and rendering the solemn Ceremony the most
magnificent which this Country ever beheld.

That your Most Sacred Majesty may long continue to reign
in the Hearts of a brave, affectionate and loyal People, is the
earnest prayer of,

Sire,

YOUR MAJESTY'S

Favoured and devoted Subject and Servant,

GEORGE NAYLER, Garter

Unfortunately Nayler died before he could complete this book,
and it was not until 1839 that it was finally published – a splendid
tome consisting of 134 pages of text and 45 coloured plates,
showing not only the 'Superb Habiliments' but also many aspects
of the occasion. At the time of its publication it was called 'the
finest book in the world.'

Prinny's lifestyle was extraordinary and extravagant in every
way. He had enjoyed a huge number of mistresses in his earlier
days; his gluttonous love of food and drink was proverbial; and
his exotic taste in art and architecture had already produced
England's most flamboyant building – the Royal Pavilion in
Brighton. Not content with his magnificent palace, known as
Carlton House (later destroyed), he bullied parliament to provide
vast sums of money to enlarge Buckingham House into a new
'Buckingham Palace'; and he razed London streets in order to
construct a special 'Regent Street', leading up to a new 'Regent's
Park'. London simply would not have been the same without his
ruthless building programmes.

As well as all of this, Prinny enjoyed – or perhaps it would be
truer to say endured – *two wives*! The first was a 'secret' marriage
(although it was a widely-open secret) to Mrs Maria Fitzherbert, an
actress, whom he had married as long ago as 1785. The problem
with this marriage was that she was a Catholic, and of course for
a member of the royal family such a liaison was not merely
imprudent, but positively illegal. Nevertheless, at the time of his

coronation, Prinny and Maria had already passed their silver wedding anniversary. However, by then Maria had been discarded and was living in penury in France.

His second wife was his cousin, Caroline of Brunswick, whom he had married ten years later, in 1795. But the problem with *this* marriage was that the pair of them hated each other and had separated almost immediately. In the eyes of Prinny Caroline was coarse and ill-mannered, and they both recognised that they had no interests in common. From the start, therefore, Caroline had lived apart from Prinny in a house on Hampstead Heath, reputedly enjoying a large clientèle of men-friends and frequently travelling abroad, where she lived riotously and scandalously. In Italy she became a laughing-stock, on one memorable occasion even dancing topless.

This was the background to George IV's coronation. Behind the scenes, as elaborate preparations were being made, the event was fraught with tensions. Prinny knew that he was unpopular, and in fact waited seventeen months after his father's death before he dared make his planned extravagant appearance in public. At last he chose the date, Thursday 19 July 1821, taking the wise precaution of recruiting numbers of prize-fighters to act as ushers and door-keepers.

The 'Superb Habiliments' which Prinny had designed for all the nobles and state functionaries were odd to say the least, mostly quite anachronistic. For example, the Privy Councillors who were not peers had to wear an Elizabethan costume of white and blue satin with trunk hose. Sir Walter Scott, who was there as an honoured guest, wrote that 'separately so gay a garb had an odd effect on the persons of elderly or ill-made men', but he generously added that 'when the whole was thrown into one general body, all these discrepancies disappeared.'

Naturally enough, the most gorgeously-apparelled figure was that of Prinny himself – now His Most August Majesty King George the Fourth. Seven supporters, eldest sons of peers, were needed to uphold the nine yards of his heavy and magnificent train of crimson velvet, decorated with golden stars. Beneath the train he wore a tight-fitting white satin suit in sixteenth-century style, with a neo-classical mantle of blue velvet, embroidered in gold and lined with ermine. On his head he flaunted a black Spanish hat decked with white ostrich feathers and a heron's plume. Curls of his wig fell coquettishly over his forehead.

Just two days before the coronation an official announcement had been made that full court dress was to be worn by everyone who had a ticket for the abbey or the banquet in Westminster Hall. This unexpected edict created panic everywhere, as ladies rushed to their dressmakers in desperation to beg them to create the necessary clothes. As for the menfolk, the scrabble to obtain anything remotely resembling an official costume became almost hilarious. Military uniforms or clerical garments were pressed into incongruous service and swords were buckled on without proper regard for the correct side to wear them.

As the guests arrived, the excited crowds of onlookers were alternately cheering and hissing, according to how their fancy took them. Luckily for the king, his fears that he might be booed or even pelted with garbage proved to be groundless. He was greeted with tremendous enthusiasm as he entered Westminster Hall for the preliminary rituals before the coronation itself. The painter Benjamin Haydon was present to see the king's entry and wrote a memorable description:

> Something rustles, and a being buried in satin, feathers and diamonds rolls gracefully into his seat. The room rises with a sort of feathered, silken thunder. Plumes wave, eyes sparkle, glasses are out, mouths smile and one man becomes the prime object of attraction to thousands. The way in which the King bowed was really royal. As he looked towards the peeresses and foreign ambassadors, he showed like some gorgeous bird of the East.

However, the crowds outside were waiting for the most controversial event of the day. Word had got round that Caroline, Prinny's discarded wife, and now indisputably his queen, was fully intending to take part in the coronation ceremony, even though Prinny himself was emphatically forbidding her to do so.

Caroline had been abroad when she first heard that Prinny was king, and had immediately written to the prime minister to ask what arrangements were being made for her coronation. Although she had received no reply, she made her way to England and was greeted by a royal salute from Dover Castle, receiving a rapturous welcome from flag-waving crowds shouting 'God save Queen Caroline'. All the way to London she was treated 'like a fairy princess returning to fight an ogre'. Everywhere she went, she was regarded as victim of her husband's spite. But George was adamant: he forbade anyone even to mention her name, and positively insisted that the churches should *not* include 'our most gracious Queen Caroline' in their prayers.

The crowds were agog as Caroline made her appearance. She was in court dress, wearing much jewellery and a long violet velvet robe lined with ermine. On her head was a great crown of diamonds. She was driven from her residence in South Audley Street in her carriage, accompanied by her friends Lord and Lady Hood and Lady Anne Hamilton, and all along her route – by Birdcage Walk and Prince's Street to Dean's Yard, the soldiers presented arms and there were deafening shouts of 'Long live the Queen!'

At last, arriving at Westminster Abbey, she tried to find a way in, but door after door was closed in her face. Eventually, leaning on Lord Hood's arm, she found an entrance by Poets' Corner, only to be greeted by a nervous young man who told her, 'It is my duty to announce to your Majesty that there is no place in the Abbey prepared for your Majesty.' Rumour has it that the young man asked her for an entrance-ticket, and that Lord Hood tried to bluster his way in, offering to lend Caroline his own ticket. 'Did you ever hear of a queen being asked for a ticket before? This is your Queen! Am I to understand that you prevent me from entering the Abbey?' Caroline replied, but the doorkeeper was resolute, managing to stutter out the same sentence: 'It is my duty to announce to your Majesty . . . .' At this, Caroline gave in. Her courage failed her and she turned away. Embarrassingly, the crowds turned against her as she got back into her carriage and hissed and booed as she fled back home. She immediately wrote to the archbishop, Charles Manners Sutton, requesting that she should be crowned a few days later, while the abbey was still arranged for a coronation, thus avoiding unnecessary extra expense. But this was never done: within three weeks she was dead, dying painfully of a bowel obstruction.

Somewhat surprisingly, only one crown was used at the coronation – an entirely new Imperial Crown specially made for the occasion. Apparently, St Edward's Crown was not used at all.

According to Dean Stanley, the coronation oath was somehow forgotten – a vitally important omission, which had to be rectified by asking the king to make his signature at the foot of the oath as printed in the service book. However, these unusual aspects passed almost unnoticed in the general atmosphere of over-the-top magnificence. The king's costume was so cumbersome that he could hardly walk and indeed during the coronation service he had to be revived with smelling-salts. He became so hot that he had to use handkerchief after handkerchief to mop his brow, afterwards handing each of them to the ever-suffering archbishop. At last, after five hours of pomp, the ceremony was over, and it was time for the participants to move on to the banquet in Westminster Hall.

Sixty years had passed since the coronation of George III in 1760, and in the meantime Westminster Hall had been partitioned into a number of rooms which were used by the Court of King's Bench. A special Act of Parliament had to be passed to enable these to be swept away to make way for two tiers of galleries. These were intended for the lady guests so that they could watch (not, of course, partake in) the elaborate banquet following the ceremony in the abbey. Twenty-eight chandeliers were brought in to enhance the brilliance of the scene, suspended from the medieval angels in the roof. by golden chains. Each chandelier contained sixty wax lights in brass sockets and glass saucers. They must have provided an impressive and beautiful sight – but there were distinct disadvantages.

This was the biggest coronation banquet ever seen in Westminster Hall – a climax to hundreds of years of such feastings – and it was to be the last. The next sovereign, William IV, saw no point in holding any kind of celebration, and it was thought inappropriate for the nineteen-year-old Queen Victoria when she came to be crowned. So, in all its rich splendour, George IV's banquet was to be the *finale* to this ancient tradition.

Sadly, this was the last coronation when the king's champion threw down his gauntlet. This was to be the last of the long series of challenges which had begun in Winchester at the coronation of William the Conqueror's wife, Queen Matilda. The Reverend John Dymoke, 'Lord of the Manor and Barony of Scrivelsby, in the County of Lincoln', had written to King George IV to beg that the

honour of assuming the role of champion should be given yet
again to a Dymoke – 'whereof the memory of Man runneth not to
the contrary.' However, as a country parson, he felt he fell below
the task, so he was making the request on behalf of his son, not
yet twenty-one. Permission granted, the young man rode a piebald
horse borrowed from a circus, and entered the banqueting hall in
full armour, escorted by the Duke of Wellington and Lord Howard.
The challenge was given three times, and the doughty Dymoke
was cheered to the rafters.

The banquet itself was on a gargantuan scale: the statistics are
almost horrendous. An eyewitness lists: '7,442 lbs of beef –
7,133 lbs of veal – 2,474 lbs of mutton – 20 quarters of house-
lamb – 20 legs of house-lamb – 5 saddles of lamb – 55 quarters
of grass lamb – 160 lamb's sweetbreads – 389 cow-heels – 400
calves' feet – 250 lbs of suet – 160 geese – 720 pullets and
capons – 1,610 chickens – 520 fowls for stock – 1,730 lbs of
bacon – 550 lbs of lard – 912 lbs of butter – 84 hundred of eggs.'
This was just for starters, however, for there were also plates of
fish, shellfish, venison, pastries, creams and jellies, and of course
hundreds of bottles of wine, port, sherry, champagne, and 100
gallons of iced punch.

All this was for three hundred and twelve *male* guests. As we
have seen, the ladies were crowded into two tiers of wooden
galleries which had been constructed to run each side, along the
entire length of the hall. Here they were expected to sit and wait
and watch for hours as their menfolk gourmandised below.

The ladies must have been famished – but this was not the sum
total of their discomfort. As time went by, 2,000 candles in the
chandeliers above them began to sputter and drizzle hot wax
onto their beautiful coiffures and silken dresses. An observer
pointed out that 'the wretched tenants of a slave ship were never
more closely packed together. If a lovely female dared to raise her
look to discover from what quarter the unwelcome visitation
came, she was certain of receiving an additional patch upon her
cheeks.' For hours the poor peeresses suffered hunger and hot
wax. It was not until about 8.30 p.m. that the king finally rose to
go back to his home at Carlton House.

It was then whispered to the king that an ugly mob was
gathering along the return route, hoping to jeer at him and pelt
his carriage. He was warned that it would be highly inadvisable to

use the roads which he was expected to take. Luckily, Lord de Ros, who had been educated at Westminster, knew the district well, and he offered to take the king by a twisting back-route through what were still fields and country lanes around Tothill Fields and Chelsea. Thus, after a very rough night-ride along dark, unlit paths, His August Majesty, who was 'horribly nervous and kept continually calling to the officers of the escort to keep well up to the carriage windows', made his way back to the safety of Carlton House. It was a sad anti-climax to a most extraordinary day.

WILLIAM IV AND ADELAIDE OF SAXE-MEININGEN

Reigned 1830–7, crowned 8 September 1831, aged 66

A King Wanting to Abolish His Coronation

When George IV died, he had no surviving legitimate children. Tragically, his only legitimate child, Charlotte, had died in childbirth, aged twenty-one, just two years before he came to the throne. The crown therefore passed to his younger brother, William, the third son of George III. A greater contrast between two brothers could hardly be imagined.

Whereas George had been passionately – almost exclusively – interested in architecture and the arts, William had spent most of his life at sea, and had joined his first ship as a midshipman, aged just thirteen. He had been given no privileges, and ate, drank, swore, gambled and whored, just like many a rough-and-tumble teenager in the navy.

All his life he had hated airs and graces, and when he came out of naval service he lived quietly and privately with Mrs Dorothy Jordan, a successful actress, fathering their ten illegitimate children.

However, as it became more and more obvious that he might be king, duty demanded that he should find himself a proper wife. Accordingly he sent out proposal after proposal to various prospective brides from the royal houses of Europe, each proposal being turned down as soon as it had been received. At last his patience was rewarded by an acceptance. It was to be the

25-year-old Princess Adelaide from the small German Duchy of Saxe-Meiningen. They were married in 1818 and at fifty-two, William was exactly twice her age. Sadly, when William and Adelaide became king and queen twelve years later there were no surviving children, as their two little girls had died in infancy.

Such was the background to the coronation of William IV and Adelaide at Westminster Abbey on 8 September 1831, more than fourteen months after their accession to the throne. In those intervening months, William, who loathed any kind of pomp or ceremony, had strenuously tried his best not to have any coronation at all. In the end, he went through with an extremely low-key event. Partly, of course, it was a reaction against the enormous ostentation and extravagance of his brother's coronation, which had taken place only ten years before, and to that extent it was a popular move. Indeed he was a relatively popular monarch after the shameless exhibitionism of George IV. All the same, it was a pity that with William's cut-price coronation many of the ancient customs were lost for ever.

There was no procession through the streets beforehand. There was no banquet in Westminster Hall and therefore no Dymoke to throw down the gauntlet. In the coronation service itself William was keen to cut out any unnecessary ceremony or expense as well. There was no ceremonial walk to the abbey; the sword was not buckled on him, as had always been the custom; and even the number of musicians was strictly limited.

William also abandoned the medieval custom in which the sovereign was solemnly placed on a throne by the great officers of state in Westminster Hall immediately before the coronation. It was a symbolic act representing the choosing of the sovereign by the secular lords. This had been followed by a message sent to the archbishop within the abbey, asking him to bless the new sovereign. On receiving this request, the clergy of Westminster then went in procession from the abbey to Westminster Hall carrying the coronation regalia needed for the ceremony. The sovereign was then escorted back to the abbey, where the archbishop asked the people present to confirm the choice of the lords. And with this Recognition the archbishop was empowered to go ahead with hallowing, investing and crowning the new king or queen.

Symbolically, this old ceremony demonstrated the three 'Estates' within the realm: the Church (or Lords Spiritual), the Officers of State (or Lords Temporal), and the People of the Realm. The theory was that a king needed a holy investment of authority by the church – but the church itself needed to be given direction by the lords, concerning who should rightfully be crowned and anointed. However, before the ceremony could legitimately proceed, the people of the realm had to give their assent. It was a nicely-balanced set of authorities uniting together to hand over the ultimate authority to the person who was universally accepted as the rightful monarch. For many, this ancient ritual was a meaningful and moving act. But for William, the whole business of a coronation was 'a pointless piece of flummery'.

However, perhaps the most astonishing moment came when William was due to be anointed. When his outer robe was removed, he revealed himself to be wearing the full-dress uniform of an Admiral of the Fleet! This was so tightly-buttoned that the Archbishop of Canterbury, William Howley, in a state of consternation, was faced with the embarrassing problem of having to anoint a fully-clad admiral on the breast, the shoulders, or even the elbows. Quite what was done in the circumstances is best left to the imagination.

Parliament had voted £243,000 for George IV's coronation, but William's cost a mere £37,000. The only new pieces of jewellery that he allowed to be made were two special coronation rings. The king's ring was a ruby St George's Cross laid upon a background of sapphires surrounded by diamonds: the queen consort's ring was a large plain ruby surrounded by diamonds. These rings have become a part of the regalia, and have been used by all sovereigns and their consorts ever since, with the exception of Queen Victoria.

Money was not a commodity which William IV liked to fling about unnecessarily. When the moment came in the coronation service for him to put his oblation into the gold basin, he whispered apologetically to the archbishop: 'I haven't got anything: I'll send it to you tomorrow!'

VICTORIA

Reigned 1837–1901, crowned 28 June 1838, aged 19

'I Will be Good!'

After her two eccentric uncles, George IV and William IV, the accession of a teenage girl was something of a novelty. Queen Victoria is so often remembered as a glum-looking, dumpy old woman that it is sometimes forgotten that she was a slim and vivacious youngster at the time of her coronation. She was, however, always determined to maintain impeccable standards of decorum.

Victoria was only ten when she realised that she was next in line to the throne, and her famous promise, 'I will be good', was constantly remembered with rapture by her subjects in later years. A book entitled *The Queen's Resolve*, published at her Diamond Jubilee instantly sold over 200,000 copies.

Apparently, her governess, Baroness Lehzen, had deliberately slipped an extra piece of paper, a genealogical table, into the young Princess Victoria's history book one day, hoping to alert her to the facts of her position as heir to the throne. 'I am nearer to the throne than I thought,' Victoria remarked, when she had read it. Then, when the full implication had sunk in, she raised her finger and said: 'I will be good. I understand now why you urged me so much to learn Latin.' Even after her accession, Victoria wrote to Baroness Lehzen regularly every month for many years, until the old lady died, and when the baroness reminded her of this promise, Victoria wrote in the margin of her letter: 'I cried much on learning it.'

Victoria was crowned by William Howley, Archbishop of Canterbury, who had baptised her when he had been bishop of London. He had been at the deathbed of William IV at Windsor on 20 June 1837, and had immediately galloped to Kensington Palace in the early morning darkness, accompanied by the lord chamberlain.

The princess was asleep when they arrived, and they waited until six o'clock before they roused her. Quickly, she put on her slippers and a shawl over her cotton dressing-gown, and came downstairs to meet them. They announced to the young princess, then aged eighteen, that she was now queen. She seized the opportunities of her independence with speed, and immediately banned her mother, the Duchess of Kent, from her bedroom and slept alone. Indeed, she even demanded that the duchess should not see her, except by appointment. Such was the 'queen's resolve'.

A year later at her coronation, the old archbishop must have felt emotional as he conducted the service, for Dean Stanley remembered his 'tremulous voice asking for the Recognition'. In many respects, however, Victoria's coronation was oddly marred by a series of mishaps. She arrived half an hour late, having driven from Buckingham Palace dressed in a robe of crimson velvet. Her attendant ladies were quite at sixes and sevens trying to cope with her train, twelve yards long, as well as their own. Then, after she had been conducted to King Edward's chair, one of her attendants, the octogenarian Lord Rolle, having to walk backwards, stumbled over and rolled down the steps to the throne. A contemporary writer described how 'the large infirm old man was held up by two peers, and had nearly reached the royal footstool when he slipped through the hands of his supporters, and rolled over and over down the steps, lying at the bottom coiled up in his robes.' Everyone nearby rushed forward to help, including the queen herself, and the sight of the queen's sudden and natural concern was spontaneously applauded by the lords and ladies surrounding her, who had witnessed the affair.[†]

Then there were problems over the presentation of the orb, and after that the bishop of Bath and Wells clumsily turned two pages of the service order together. Victoria told him to go back and start that section again. However, the worst incident of all happened when the Archbishop of Canterbury tried to put the ruby coronation ring on her finger. Victoria's fingers were so tiny that a new and special coronation ring had been made for her. Now, fingers can be counted in two ways: either starting with the thumb or else starting with the index finger, and unfortunately the jeweller wrongly assumed that he should start with the index

---

[†] The moment was captured by John Martin in his painting of the coronation, now in Tate Britain, London. Martin (1789–1854) was not an official court painter, and was best known for his apocalyptic works.

finger, thus making a ring to fit Victoria's little finger, whereas he should have been making one to fit the third finger. The good archbishop insisted on ramming this tiny ring on to Victoria's middle finger, thus causing the poor girl agony. In fact she spent two hours later that day trying to get it off.

No other king or queen has written more lengthily or more vividly about their coronation than Queen Victoria – she wrote voluminously throughout her long life. Therefore, as no description of this ceremony can outdo her own, the following paragraphs are taken from her own *Journal*, dated on the coronation day itself:

At 10 I got into the State Coach with the Duchess of Sutherland and Lord Albemarle and we began our Progress. . . . It was a fine day, and the crowds of people exceeded what I have ever seen; many as there were the day I went to the City, it was nothing, nothing to the multitudes, the millions of my loyal subjects, who were assembled *in every spot* to witness the Procession. Their good humour and excessive loyalty was beyond everything, and I really cannot say *how* proud I feel to be the Queen of a Nation. . . .

. . . I reached the Abbey amid deafening cheers at a little after half-past eleven; I first went into a robing-room quite close to the entrance, where I found my eight train-bearers. . . . All dressed alike and beautifully in white satin and silver tissue with wreaths of silver corn-ears in front, and a small one of pink roses round the plait behind, and pink roses in the trimming of the dresses.

After putting on my mantle, and the young ladies having properly got hold of it, I left the robing-room and the Procession began. . . . The sight was splendid; the bank of Peeresses quite beautiful all in their robes, and the Peers on the other side, My young train-bearers were always near me, and helped me whenever I wanted anything. The Bishop of Durham stood on the side near me, but he was, as Lord Melbourne told me, remarkably *maladroit*, and never could tell me what was to take place.

At the beginning of the Anthem, where I've made a mark, I retired to St Edward's Chapel, a dark small place immediatey behind the Altar, with my ladies and train-bearers – took off my crimson robe and kirtle, and put on the supertunica of cloth of gold, also in the shape of a kirtle, which was put over a singular sort of little gown of linen trimmed with lace; I also took off my circlet of diamonds and then proceeded bare-headed into the Abbey; I was then seated upon St Edward's chair, where the Dalmatic robe was clasped round me by the Lord Great Chamberlain. Then followed all the various things; and last (of those things) the Crown being placed on my head – which was, I must own, a most beautiful impressive moment; *all* the Peers and Peeresses put on their coronets at the same instant.

My excellent Lord Melbourne, who stood very close to me throughout the whole ceremony, was *completely* overcome at this moment, and very much affected; he gave me *such* a kind, and I may say *fatherly* look. The shouts, which were very great, the drums, the trumpets, the firing of the guns, all at the same instant, rendered the spectacle most imposing.

. . . When my good Lord Melbourne knelt down and kissed my hand, he pressed my hand and I grasped his with all my heart, at which he looked up with his eyes filled with tears and seemed much touched, as he was, I observed, throughout the whole ceremony. . . .

As the procession was being formed, Victoria was shocked by the state of St Edward's Chapel.

I then again descended from the Throne and repaired . . . to St Edward's Chapel, as it is called; but which, as Lord Melbourne said, was more *un*like a Chapel than anything he had ever seen; for what was *called* an *Altar* was covered with sandwiches, bottles of wine, etc., etc. The Archbishop came in and *ought* to have delivered the Orb to me, but I had already got it, and he (as usual) was confused and puzzled and knew nothing, and – went away. There we waited some minutes; Lord Melbourne took a glass of wine, for he seemed completely tired; the Procession being formed, I replaced my Crown (which I had taken off for a few minutes), took the Orb in my left hand and the Sceptre in my right, and thus *Loaded* proceeded through the Abbey, which resounded with cheers, to the first Robing-room.

. . . At about half-past four I re-entered my carriage, the Crown on my head, and the Sceptre and Orb in my hands, and we proceeded the same way as we came – the crowds if possible having increased. The enthusiasm, affection and loyalty were really touching, and I shall ever remember this day as the *Proudest* of my life! I came home at a little after six, really *not* feeling tired.

Later, back in Buckingham Palace after dinner, Victoria records that Lord Melbourne 'turned round to me with the tears in his eyes, and said *so* kindly: "And you did it beautifully – every part of it, with so much taste: it's a thing that you can't give a person advice upon; it must be left to a person."'

There were, of course, countless services and celebrations throughout the country on Queen Victoria's coronation day. Probably the most remarkable event to mark the occasion was the gigantic feast on Parker's Piece in Cambridge. This almost certainly holds the record as the largest outdoor sit-down meal ever served in England. The citizens of Cambridge decided to hold this huge feast at the very time of her coronation, and they prepared a two-course cooked meal for no fewer than 15,000 of the poorer inhabitants and the Sunday School children of the town. A large orchestra played in the centre, raised up on a special platform adorned with flags and flowers, with the Royal Standard flying above them. Then, in a circular promenade around this, strolled the ladies and gentlemen whose generosity had paid for all these celebrations. Three circles of tables came next, to seat 2,762 Sunday School children; and finally, radiating like spokes from a wheel were 60 other tables, seating no fewer than 12,720 adults. Serving this multitude were 351 stewards, 547 carvers, 441 waiters, 297 beer-waiters and 41 tapsters.

The statistics are staggering. For the first course there were 7,029 joints of beef, mutton, pork, veal and bacon (it was reckoned that about 1 lb of meat was needed per person). Then there were 72 lb of mustard; 144 lb of salt; 125 gallons of pickles; and 4,500 2 lb loaves. For the dessert, 1,608 plum puddings were provided, each of about 6½ lb. To make these, the cooks used 10 sacks of the finest flour, 2,470 lb of raisins, 825 lb of suet, 360 gallons of milk and 3,300 eggs. 14,000 yards of calico were needed to cover the tables and an extra 1,247 yards were used to make the plum-pudding bags. Finally, 99 barrels of ale were needed to toast the new young queen and 100 lb of tobacco and 6 lb of snuff were distributed.

Sports and fireworks ended the day, and a Mr and Mrs Green ascended in a hot-air balloon, landing at Fulbourn, four miles away (they are in the top right corner of the picture in the plate section). It is well worth visiting the University Arms Hotel in Cambridge, which adjoins the large open space known as Parker's Piece, to see a modern version of this lithograph, painted by the artist, Sarah Janson, as a large mural in the entrance hall.

EDWARD VII AND ALEXANDRA OF DENMARK

Reigned 1901–10, crowned 9 August 1902, aged 60

The King's Fortune-Teller Advises Him on the Best Date for the Coronation

Victoria's long reign must have seemed interminable to Edward VII. He was fifty-nine when at last he came to the throne; not the oldest – William IV had been sixty-six when he was crowned – but as Edward knew from birth that he was the heir apparent, his long period of waiting must have been particularly frustrating. Moreover, he had been forever waiting in the wings, as Queen Victoria never allowed him the slightest part in running the affairs of state.

In 1902 more than sixty years had elapsed since the last coronation, and much had happened during that time. For one thing, Victoria had become the 'grandmother of Europe', as so many of her children had married into the royal houses on the continent. Therefore it was necessary to invite an enormous number of foreign guests to the coronation. Furthermore, as England had now become the focal point of an ever-expanding empire, it was necessary to include representatives from every one of these countries, especially India.

Edward came to the throne in a world vastly different from that of his mother in 1837 – it was now the high noon of British influence in the world. He adored pomp and circumstance, and burst from the chrysalis of an attendant prince into the regal splendour of his reign with superb aplomb, relishing every detail of ostentatious protocol and magnificent ceremony.

Taking the name of Edward was perhaps a surprise to those around him, for he had aways been known as 'Bertie' by his family and more formally, Albert Edward. It was, perhaps a deliberate distancing of himself from his formidable parents when he announced that although he did not undervalue the name of Albert, nevertheless there could be only one Albert, 'who by universal consent is, I think deservedly, known by the name of Albert the Good.' Edward was clearly determined to be his own man.

Thus it was that preparations went ahead for a coronation which was to herald in a new monarch, a new century, and an entirely new, revitalised royal lifestyle. Vast numbers of royal and foreign guests had attended Queen Victoria's funeral in January 1901, and of course they were naturally expecting to be invited to take part in the coronation festivities of the new reign. As no coronation had been organised for so long, the whole process had to be reconsidered: records had to be searched; hereditary claims investigated; proper precedents had to be established.

One of the new features of the arrangements was that many Indian princes were to be invited – and it was difficult to find proper accommodation and decide their relative importance, for they were rich and powerful potentates, and needed to be treated as such. Some of these great personages were suitably accommodating. The Maharajah of Bikanir, the Maharajah of Gwalior, the Maharajah of Kolapore and the Maharajah Sir Pratap Singh all professed themselves willing to adopt a European lifestyle, except of course in the matter of eating beef. However, the Maharajah of Jaipur announced his intention of bringing an entourage of 200 attendants and insisted on living strictly according to Hindu custom.

Accordingly, a house had to be found for the maharajah and his enormous retinue, not too far from Buckingham Palace (this was important to him), and, moreover, it had to have proper accommodation for a cow! A further stipulation was that as a strict Hindu he would not touch water that had passed through a metal pipe. Poor Percy Armytage, who was in charge of the Indian princes, was at his wits' end until he disovered a large house at Campden Hill, with a paddock and a well. Even then, the maharajah sprang two more awkward demands upon his hosts. Firstly, in the matter of the cow, it had to be a shorthorn and above all it had to be pure white. And then, at the last moment he declared his intention of bringing a large God with him. Not only that, but the God had to have its own large room, and very special food would have to be prepared for it, in a separate kitchen. Sir Percy Armytage managed all this as a matter of routine, privately wondering what happened to all the God's special food, so ceremoniously laid out in front of it. He came to the conclusion that perhaps this daily banquet was a perk of the priestly attendant in charge of it.

Luckily, most guests were much easier to deal with, and everyone was looking forward to a coronation of magnificent splendour, scheduled to take place on 26 June. Strangely enough, one of the Indian princes, the Maharajah of Kolapore, did in fact have grave reservations about this date, because his private astrologer, having undertaken special ceremonies, had advised the prince not to go to England for he predicted that the coronation would not take place as planned. It was an uncanny prophecy.

Early in June, just as the guests were beginning to arrive in England, Edward developed appendicitis. Perhaps this was partly due to his gargantuan appetite, which he had indulged over a lifetime. His 48 inch chest *and* waist earned him the well-deserved nick-name 'Tum Tum'. His huge breakfasts, larger lunches, and prodigious dinners (rarely consisting of less than twelve courses, one of which was invariably grilled oysters) were legendary. Queen Alexandra herself confessed that she thought his gluttony was 'just terrible', but she could never do anything to persuade him to change his habits.

However, Edward's condition steadily worsened during the run-up to the planned coronation. Banquet after banquet was being arranged for the innumerable royal guests; London was packed with visitors; decorations were everywhere; grandstands were erected along the route of the procession. Of course, right up to the last minute, the public was quite unaware of the king's condition and Edward himself tried his best to make light of his illness, refusing even to contemplate postponing the coronation.

However, on 23 June his doctors told him bluntly that he now had peritonitis, and that this would kill him unless he had an immediate operation. Even then, at the last moment, the king argued furiously that the coronation should take place, exploding with anger when Francis Laking, his physician, told him that the coronation simply had to be postponed. 'Laking, I will stand no more of this,' he roared, 'I am suffering the most awful mental agony that any man can endure. Leave the room at once!'

Laking, no doubt with considerable apprehension, told the king that in these circumstances obedience was impossible, and with careful diplomacy managed to persuade Edward of the wisdom of both undergoing the necessary operation and the consequent postponement of the coronation. Thus it was that on 24 June, just two days before the date planned for the coronation, King Edward underwent a forty-minute operation which at the time was considered to be extremely dangerous, and indeed life-threatening. Luckily, the surgeon, Frederick Treves, a great friend of Thomas Hardy, succeeded triumphantly and the king was soon well on the way to recovery. One of his first acts was to confer baronetcies upon Laking and Treves, thanking them both for saving his life.

He was, however, still uncrowned, and many of the foreign guests, greatly disappointed, had to return to their various countries. The Indian Princes, who had put themselves to considerable trouble to come, were mollified when they were told that they were welcome to stay on until the coronation could take place, later on. That the coronation *would* take place was never in any doubt, but *when* was a different matter. The day chosen was 9 August, but the manner in which this was decided was one of the strangest features of the event.

Throughout his life Edward had been remarkably superstitious. His valet, for example, was forbidden to turn his mattress on Fridays; and he had a horror of sitting down with thirteen at table (once, he was relieved to find that a thirteenth guest was pregnant, and so in fact there were fourteen after all!†) Once when he was ill earlier in his life he had consulted a well-known

---

† There were 15 in fact! The pregnant guest, his niece Margaret of Prussia, was expecting twins (see John Van der Kiste, *Queen Victoria's Children*, pp. 140–1).

clairvoyant, 'Cheiro' ('Count' Louis Hamon), who had told him that he would live to be sixty-nine. Now, during the king's serious illness, and remembering the former prophecy, Queen Alexandra herself brought Cheiro to Buckingham Palace to see the king again.

Cheiro reassured the king that he would recover from his appendicitis and that he *would* live to be sixty-nine, and when Edward asked him to pick the most auspicious date for the coronation, Cheiro selected 9 August.

After the successful operation, the uncrowned Edward and Alexandra took the opportunity to take a convalescent cruise in *Victoria and Albert*, and when they returned it was noted that the king was not only bronzed and fit, with six inches less round the waist, but he also looked much younger and was far less irritable. Clearly, he was in better physical shape than he had been for many years.

The drama of the king's illness and the consequent delay served only to heighten the rapturous mood of the people when the Coronation Day came at last. As always, crowds thronged the streets, and were rewarded by seeing their new monarch drawn through the streets in the gilded coach that had been made for the coronation of George III, drawn by eight cream Hanoverian horses. Everyone knew that the British Empire covered a fifth of the earth's surface. Now, the great king-emperor had come into his rightful inheritance. The importance and magnificence of the occasion was to make this coronation one of the most spectacular ever seen – but without the extreme theatricality and near-farce which accompanied that of George IV.

The coronation ceremony in Westminster Abbey was accompanied by music chosen from English composers from the sixteenth to the twentieth century: Merbecke and Tallis, Purcell, Handel (a naturalised Englishman), Samuel Wesley, Sir Arthur Sullivan, Sir John Stainer, and Sir Charles Stanford. And it was with a superb sense of occasion that Edward and Alexandra entered the abbey to the sound of Hubert Parry's great anthem *I was glad when they said unto me* – specially written for that moment, and now heard for the first time.

Owing to the king's recent illness, several changes were made in the ceremony, shortening it in order to save Edward from unnecessary fatigue. One of the chief differences was that he was crowned with the Imperial State Crown instead of St Edward's Crown. This was somewhat unusual, considering the fact that Edward was known for his strict adherence to details of dress and decoration. Apparently, it had been his intention to be crowned with St Edward's Crown and then to change to the Imperial State Crown afterwards. In fact, St Edward's Crown was present throughout the ceremony, but in the event it was the lighter Imperial State Crown, suitably altered to fit the king's head and with added pearls and diamonds, which was used. Perhaps the confusion and frailty of the archbishop led to the 'wrong' crown being used. Edward also changed the colour of the Caps of Estate (or Caps of Maintenance) for all the crowns, from crimson to purple; a change which has remained ever since.

As for Queen Alexandra, she was crowned with a new crown, specially made for the occasion. It had been seventy-one years since a king had been crowned together with his queen: the last time was at the coronation of King William IV and Queen Adelaide in 1831. Now, in 1902, the great Koh-i-noor diamond, the 'Mountain of Light' was used in a crown for the first time. It had been presented in 1849 by the East India Company to Queen Victoria, who had worn it set in a brooch or bracelet.

The major worry, however, throughout the service was the state of health of the 81-year-old Archbishop of Canterbury, Frederick Temple: physically, the whole affair was almost beyond him. His hands were trembling so much that Edward himself had to guide them as the archbishop placed the crown on his head – and even then, he put the crown on back to front. Then, after reciting the formula of the homage, the archbishop was so overcome with emotion that he added 'God bless you, Sir,' and struggled desperately to rise to his feet to kiss the king's cheek. He simply couldn't manage it, and the newly-crowned king had to help him up while the bishop of Winchester held on to him firmly to prevent him falling over again. In fact, just after the blessing, the archbishop did eventually collapse to the ground, but he brushed aside the bishops rushing to his aid, crying, 'Go away, it's not my head, it's my legs!' He was clearly in a very feeble state, and died only weeks later.

Owing to the archbishop's weakness, Queen Alexandra was crowned by the Archbishop of York, an unusual departure from precedent, but sensible in the circumstances. There were interesting differences in the two crownings: Edward had been crowned seated, but Alexandra was crowned as she knelt on a faldstool. Also, Edward had been annointed on his head, breast and hands, but Alexandra was annointed on the head only. One of the four duchesses holding up the canopy over the queen noticed 'the shaking hand of the Archbishop as, from the spoon which held the sacred oil, he anointed her forehead. I held my breath as a trickle escaped and ran down her nose. With a truly royal composure she kept her hands clasped in prayer; only a look of anguish betrayed concern as her eyes met mine and seemed to ask "Is the damage great?"'

However, despite these minor problems, the coronation of Edward and Alexandra passed off with dignity. Edward was deeply moved as his son, the future George V, came to swear allegiance to him. Departing from custom, after George had pledged his allegiance, the king kissed him in return. The new king must have reflected that he had nearly failed to make it to the throne, and that it would, in all probability, not be so long before the next coronation would occur. Two more future English kings were present, watching from a special box in the abbey, both wearing kilts – the future Edward VIII, then aged eight, and the future George VI, then aged six.

The crowds cheered wildly as King Edward VII and Queen Alexandra left the abbey and processed back to Buckingham Palace. Queen Victoria, although she had become almost a sacred icon during her final years, had been remote and invisible to the people, living virtually in seclusion at Osborne House on the Isle of Wight. Now, with a popular and vigorous king on the throne, together with two generations of successors, the future of the monarchy seemed unassailable.

Fewer foreign guests were present than had been expected for the coronation planned in June, so there was more of an 'English' feel about it, and the poor of London were delighted to be given a special £30,000 banquet. As for the fortunate white shorthorn cow, which had enjoyed the attention of the Maharajah of Jaipur, it was to live in the lap of luxury for the rest of its life, for the good maharajah insisted on presenting it to Lord Fitzhardinge, on the explicit promise that it should live at Berkeley Castle until it died a natural death.

GEORGE V AND MARY OF TECK

Reigned 1910–36, crowned 22 June 1911, aged 46
Also given a coronation ceremony at a Durbar in Delhi,
12 December 1911

Westminster and Delhi: King and Emperor

There is a famous photograph taken at the end of the nineteenth century showing four generations of the royal family: the reigning monarch, Queen Victoria; her son, the future King Edward VII; her grandson, the future King George V; and her great-grandson, the future King Edward VIII. The photograph is an epitome of the ethos of solid respectability and unassailable royal continuity which existed at that time. From the final decades of the nineteenth century until the First World War British influence throughout the world was at its zenith – so much so that when George V succeeded to the throne, he knew that his subjects numbered more than a quarter of the total population of the planet.

However, for the first twenty-six years of his life George had not expected to be king at all. He was merely a second son. Nevertheless, when his elder brother 'Eddie' unexpectedly died of pneumonia in 1892, George had to adjust to the thought that sooner or later, after the death of his grandmother and his father, he would eventually inherit the throne. As he was still unmarried, a wife – a future queen – was an urgent necessity. Queen Victoria swiftly came to the rescue. As Eddie was dead, George should marry Eddie's fiancée, Princess May of Teck. And as no one ever dared to disagree with Queen Victoria, the wedding duly took place eighteen months later.

Princess May of Teck, was the daughter of Francis, Duke of Teck, and Princess Mary of Cambridge, a granddaughter of King George III. Princess May (as she was then known) was born in the same room in Kensington Palace where Queen Victoria had been born. She had always been a member of the English royal family – albeit a minor royal who would never have been particularly remembered if she had not been swept to the forefront of public affairs by her engagements. Her background, however, was impeccably regal, and so when George came to the throne as

George V she proved herself to be a splendid support to him – quintessentially and archetypally a queen. The pair of them presented an image of unquestioned respectability and rectitude: conventional, traditional, somewhat old-fashioned, not necessarily bad qualities in a dignified head of state and his consort.

However, by 1911, when the pair were crowned by Randall Thomas Davidson, Archbishop of Canterbury, the modern world was beginning to develop. Louis Blériot had already flown across the channel in 1909, and the world of cars, newspapers and telephones was speeding up everyone's pace of life. This was the first coronation at which 'cinematograph operators' were allowed to photograph the regalia passing through the cloisters of Westminster Abbey; as a result, there were more pictures and accounts of this coronation than ever before.

Despite the advent of the car, peers who still owned state coaches were requested to bring them out of mothballs for this coronation. Of course, all these needed to be renovated and polished up for the occasion and many had to be brought up to London specially by train. However, horses were also required, and these poor animals, brought up from their quiet country paddocks to practise pulling coaches in the busy London streets, caused momentary traffic chaos in the run-up to the coronation.

However, when the day came, the organisation was impeccable. Fifty thousand troops under the command of Lord Kitchener lined the route taken by the procession and hundreds of military contingents marched through the streets: from India, east and west Africa, Malaya and Ceylon, the East Indies and West Indies, and from many other parts of the world under British rule. As the proclamation of the Union of South Africa had taken place in 1910 there were now four dominions to be represented. It was a massive display of Empire, eliciting an acid remark from the socialist leader Keir Hardie: 'with its pomp and show, the make-believe, the glorification of militarism and all its mockeries of the solemnity of religion, is an affront to all that is true, and self-respecting in our national life.'

This view was not shared by the majority. Certainly, for the new king and queen this coronation was a solemn act of dedication, closely following the ancient rubric as laid down in the fourteenth-century *Liber Regalis*, even by then centuries old, and by now the accompanying pomp and ceremony gathered about it had become incredibly elaborate.

The procession entering the abbey was headed by the Chaplains in Ordinary, the Domestic Chaplains, the Prebendaries of Westminster, the Heralds and the officers of the Orders of Knighthood. Following these came the standards of South Africa, New Zealand, Australia, Canada and India, each carried by a former Governor-General. Now came the standard of England, carried by a gentleman with a formidable family history – a Mr Frank Dymoke! No longer required to mount a charger or throw down a gauntlet at a post-coronation banquet, Mr Dymoke continued his family's involvement, though in a new and different manner.

After Mr Dymoke came the standards of Wales, Scotland and Ireland; then the standard of the Union, carried by the Duke of Wellington, and the Royal standard, carried by Lord Lansdowne. The king's regalia came next: St Edward's staff; the sceptre with the cross; the two golden spurs; the sword of temporal justice, carried by Lord Kitchener; the sword of spiritual justice carried by Lord Roberts; the sword of mercy (*Curtana*), carried by the Duke of Beaufort; the orb; the sceptre with the dove; St Edward's crown. Then, immediately in front of the king came the Bishops of London, Ripon and Winchester, carrying the paten, the Bible and the chalice.

After all these secular and religious emblems came King George V himself, in all regal splendour, wearing a crimson robe of state borne by eight young pages. He was flanked by twenty Gentlemen-at-arms; following him were various high officers of the household; and finally at the end of the whole procession came twenty Yeomen of the Guard.

George V was essentially a man of simplicity: unemotional, not particularly articulate, straightforward and direct. His biographer, Harold Nicolson, commented that 'He was not a man who was able or accustomed to express, at least in writing, the emotions which he felt most deeply. The written word was not his language.' Nevertheless, it is worth setting down George's own account of the day, as he recorded it in his diary. In its 'almost disconcertingly restrained' language and abrupt sentences It displays much of the king's character:

Thursday 22 June. Our Coronation Day. Buckingham Palace. It was overcast & cloudy with some showers & a strongish cool breeze, but better for the people than great heat. Today was indeed a great & memorable day in our lives & one we can never forget, but it brought back to me many sad memories of 9 years ago, when the beloved Parents were crowned. May & I left B.P. in the Coronation coach at 10.30 with 8 cream-coloured horses. There were over 50,000 troops lining the streets under the command of Lord Kitchener. There were hundreds of thousands of people who gave us a magnificent reception. The Service in the Abbey was most beautiful, but it was a terrible ordeal. It was grand, yet simple & most dignified and went without a hitch. I nearly broke down when dear David (*the future King Edward VIII, later Duke of Windsor*) came to do homage to me, as it reminded me so much when I did the same thing to beloved Papa, he did it so well. Darling May looked lovely & it was indeed a comfort to me to have her by my side, as she has been ever to me during these last eighteen years. We left Westminster Abbey at 2.15 (having arrived there before 11.00) with our Crowns on and sceptres in our hands. This time we drove by the Mall, St James' Street & Piccadilly, crowds enormous & decorations very pretty. On reaching B.P. just before 3.00 May & I went out on the balcony to show ourselves to the people. Downey photographed us in our robes with Crowns on. Had some lunch with our guests here. Worked all the afternoon with Bigge & others answering telegrams & letters of which I have had hundreds. Such a large crowd collected in front of the Palace that I went out on the balcony again. Our guests dined with us at 8.30. May & I showed ourselves again to the people. Wrote & read. Rather tired. Bed at 11.45. Beautiful illuminations everywhere.

The prosaic matter-of-factness about this almost hides George's laconic admission that he 'nearly broke down' during the ceremony at the moment when his eldest son David, heir to the throne had come to kiss him formally in the act of homage. Just as David was moving away from him, George had impulsively pulled him back and had kissed him in return. It was a simple act of fatherly emotion, all the more remarkable as George was never one to show feelings in public. Years later, as Duke of Windsor, David wrote of that moment: 'When my father kissed my cheeks, his emotion was great, as was mine.'

The day after the coronation the new king and queen drove in an open carriage through the streets of London to receive a tumultuous welcome from the cheering crowds – a reception somewhat reminiscent of the great medieval processions from the Tower. The popularity of King George and Queen Mary was self-evident. 'A wonderful drive,' the king wrote in his diary, 'a sight which I am sure could never be seen in any other country in the world.'

However, immediately after celebrating this coronation George V was determined that another country should be given the chance to witness what would in effect be his *second* coronation. He persuaded the government to agree to let him go to India. As emperor he positively owed the Indian sub-continent a duty to display himself there. He wrote to Lord Morley, the Secretary of State for India: '. . . I am convinced that if it were possible for me, accompanied by the Queen, to . . . hold a Coronation Durbar at Delhi, where we should meet all the Princes, officials and vast numbers of the People, the greatest benefits would accrue to the Country at large. I also trust and I believe, that if the proposed visit could be made known some time before, it would tend to allay unrest and, I am sorry to say, seditious spirit, which unfortunately exists in some parts of India.' Despite cabinet misgivings over costs and the difficulties of organising such an event, preparations duly went ahead. In retrospect, it can be argued that this 'Durbar' (an old Persian word meaning a prince's court) represented the apotheosis of the British Empire.

There were very unusual problems to be solved. For example, there was an awkwardness over the crown. It was pointed out that constitutionally the crown could never be allowed out of the country. The only way to get round this difficulty would be to have a new crown specially made for the occasion – and probably for future Durbars – though no one knew at the time that this unique Durbar would be the last. Eventually, a superb crown, the Imperial Crown of India, containing four gigantic sapphires, four rubies, nine emeralds and more than 6,000 diamonds, was ready to go with the king to India. Made by Garrards, the Crown Jewellers, it cost £60,000, and after some embarrassing dispute this cost was borne by the people of India. It had been supposed that the 135 ruling Indian Princes themselves would have donated sufficient stones, but the viceroy drew the line at having to beg them. 'I really do think it should have been considered where the crown was to come from,' he wrote.

Then came the problem over who should crown the king. Surely it would not be the Archbishop of Canterbury – in a country which hardly acknowledged the claims of Christianity. Should the king crown himself, as Napoleon had crowned himself emperor? But George V was no Napoleon, and such an act would certainly have smacked of self-aggrandisement. Eventually, an ingenious but simple solution was arrived at – the king would arrive *already wearing his crown*. Thus an embarrassing potential disaster was neatly side-stepped.

At last the day arrived and the king-emperor, a 'semi-divine' figure, accepted homage from India's richest and most powerful princes under a golden-domed pavilion. The scene was set in the centre of a huge amphitheatre, watched by thousands. Everywhere there were exotic decorations, with emblematic lotus flowers, king cobras and Tudor crowns jostling in incongruity. Attendants bore peacock fans, yak-tails and gilded maces. Turbaned sons of maharajahs formed an impressive entourage as the king and queen moved towards the marble dais covered with cloth-of-gold, on which awaited gleaming solid silver thrones.

Once the king-emperor and queen-empress were seated on their thrones, the Indian princes, each in his own distinctive and colourful costume, advanced towards the dais to be presented and bearing astonishing gifts. The Nizam of Hyderabad, for example, gave a ruby necklace in which each ruby was as big as a pigeon's egg and His Highness of Panna presented an umbrella carved out of a single piece of emerald.

In his speech, King George decreed that India's capital city would transfer from Calcutta to Delhi – New Delhi – and to launch this new seat of government he laid its foundation stone. Sir Edwin Lutyens had designed the buildings which would soon be built there, worthy of the English Raj.

The whole affair was unique. No other king or queen enjoyed a Durbar. Victoria, the original empress, was too old and forever in perpetual mourning when she officially became empress of India on 1 January 1877 – a title devised for her by her favourite Prime Minister, Benjamin Disraeli. Edward VII had been too preoccupied with the delicacies of European alliances to manage a visit to India. Edward VIII was never crowned, as he was much too busy with Mrs Simpson.

Finally, the problems of the Second World War made it impossible for George VI to go to India or hold a Durbar. In any case, on the stroke of midnight 15 August 1947, he ceased to be its emperor as India won its independence.

GEORGE VI AND ELIZABETH BOWES-LYON

Reigned 1936–52, crowned 12 May 1937, aged 41

'I Never Wanted This to Happen!'

Like so many kings, including his own father, George VI never expected to succeed to the throne: he was a second son. When George V died, his eldest son David, Prince of Wales, became King Edward VIII, but only for 325 days. However, as everyone knows, David was besotted with an American woman (no one in English society at that time would have called her a 'lady') – Mrs Wallis Simpson. The Prime Minister, Stanley Baldwin, quite bluntly told the king: 'in the choice of a queen, the voice of the people must be heard,' and made it clear that the king could have either the throne or Wallis Simpson, but not both. The problem was that Mrs Simpson was a divorcee – she had already divorced one husband and was just about to be divorced a second time in order to marry her third husband, the king.

In those days the whole affair seemed unthinkable. To marry a doubly-divorced American was considered completely unacceptable. In any case, the unspoken thought in many people's minds was that at forty she was unlikely to bear any children. Other unspoken thoughts centred on Edward himself, who frequently horrified his courtiers and ministers by his sloppy and casual approach to royal duties: documents went unread; appointments were abandoned; there was tactless interference in foreign affairs. Once, visiting Germany with Wallis in 1937 (after his abdication), he notoriously gave the Nazi salute when he met

Hitler. Naturally, the Führer was much impressed with him, and thought that Wallis would have made a good queen.

Edward VIII's decision to abdicate seemed cataclysmic in 1936, but time has shown that his younger brother, Prince Albert, Duke of York, – known to his family as Bertie, who became George VI – proved to be a man of tenacious integrity, devoting himself unswervingly to the duties of kingship he desperately did not want. The abdication of Edward VIII came with unnerving suddenness. Bertie is known to have told his cousin, Lord Louis Mountbatten: 'Dickie, this is absolutely terrible. I never wanted this to happen; I'm quite unprepared for it. David has been trained for this all his life. I've never even seen a State paper. I'm only a Naval Officer, it's the only thing I know about.'

It was true, Bertie had been completely overshadowed by his elder brother. Furthermore, he had the great misfortune to have an appalling stammer, which made it difficult for him to take on public engagements which involved speaking. This was so embarrassing that at the time of Edward's abdication many people privately considered Bertie not to be up to the job of being king. Indeed, there is speculation that at the centre of the crisis there was a serious discussion concerning the possibility of passing over both Bertie and his brother the Duke of Gloucester, and offering the throne to the youngest brother – the Duke of Kent, who already had a son. Bertie, of course, had two young daughters, but it was felt that perhaps the prospect of eventually inheriting the throne would be too heavy a burden for any woman.

Robert Lacey, in his book *Majesty* notes that there was a curious and inexplicable period between Saturday 5 December and Monday 7 December when Bertie was completely left out of the urgent discussions being conducted between King Edward VIII and the Prime Minister. This 'strange hiatus' when Bertie was virtually ignored was tantamount to a 'crisis within a crisis', but as Lacey remarks, 'The facts . . . are not fully known, and never will be.'

In May 1937, at the time of the coronation of George VI and Elizabeth, these tensions and complications were successfully hidden from the public at large – as indeed the whole Wallis Simpson affair had been tacitly ignored by the British press for months – even years – before the final crisis. Nowadays it would be inconceivable for such an important matter to be concealed, but this is simply a measure of how different the world was in the 1930s.

The coronation of George VI and Elizabeth took place just five months after Edward VIII signed his 'Instrument of Abdication', renouncing the throne for 'the woman I love'. The actual date chosen was 12 May, the same date on which Edward VIII would have been crowned. Everything went ahead as normal: the same venue; the same archbishop; the same regalia; the same throne; the same ritual. The only change was in the person being crowned, and of course there was a queen consort to be crowned as well.

George's wife, Elizabeth, had come from an old Scottish family. Lady Elizabeth Bowes-Lyon, as she was at the time of their wedding in 1923, was the youngest daughter of the 14th Earl of Strathmore and Kinghorne. As Bertie had not the faintest thought at that time of becoming king, he had been able to fall in love quite naturally with a commoner – even an earl's daughter is a 'commoner' in the eyes of royalty. Somewhat surprisingly, Elizabeth was the first commoner to become queen since Catherine Parr became Henry VIII's sixth wife in 1543. Despite an initial reluctance on Elizabeth's part (Bertie had to propose three times before she accepted him), their eventual marriage was happy and successful. They had settled into the semi-public-semi-private lifestyle of minor royals when they were propelled into positions which horrified them all. At the time of their coronation Princess Elizabeth was aged eleven, and Princess Margaret Rose was aged six.

Bertie was concerned that nothing should go wrong at the coronation service, taking great precautions to rehearse the complicated ritual, even having the crowns specially marked so that they should not be put on the wrong way round. The Imperial State Crown, which was becoming rather worn out, was remade and the gems were reset. As for Elizabeth, she had an entirely new crown made for the occasion, based on a circlet which had been worn by Queen Victoria. The legendary diamond, the Koh-i-Noor ('Mountain of Light'), was set in the front cross-patee. This magical stone was once owned by the Mogul Emperors of India, and for a while belonged to Mumtaz Mahal, the queen in whose memory the Taj Mahal was built.

Everything went reasonably well at rehearsal, despite an alarming moment when it was thought that the orb had been lost. People scurried everywhere looking for it, until it was discovered that six-year-old Princess Margaret was playing with it on the floor. On the coronation day itself Bertie confessed later that he 'could eat no breakfast & had a sinking feeling inside'. Nevertheless, he need not have worried. London and the whole country went wild with its newly-focused, but nevertheless, unfeigned loyalty. The new king and queen, with the two princesses, Elizabeth and Margaret Rose, presented an image of a perfect 'royal family', photogenic and wholesome – a complete contrast with the military dictators on the continent. Hitler himself tacitly recognised the difference when he called Elizabeth 'the most dangerous woman in Europe.'

And so the golden coronation coach of George III was once more wheeled out of the Royal Mews for another grand event ('one of the most uncomfortable rides I have ever had in my life', wrote George VI afterwards) and all the panoply of a coronation procession was brought out into the streets of the capital. People throughout the country felt themselves to be eyewitnesses to the occasion, for even if they were not able to be present personally, film of the event was brought to cinemas all over the country, thanks to forty newsreel cameramen in Westminster Abbey, all in full evening dress.

Not only was the service broadcast almost in its entirety on radio, but also the coronation processsion was shown as the first major outside broadcast by the BBC's new television service. Freddie Grisewood, the commentator, described the scenes to no fewer than 50,000 viewers, and George and Elizabeth were briefed beforehand exactly where they should wave.

This, then, was the first 'modern' coronation, inasmuch as the mass media were crowding in upon the scene as never before. Luckily, the minor mishaps were not at all apparent at the time. Archbishop Cosmo Gordon Lang, had made it almost impossible for George to read the oath, clumsily holding his thumb over the vital words as he held up the service book; one of the clergy had fainted, and at one time George was pinned to the ground by one of the bishops, who was treading on his robe. 'I had to tell him to get off it pretty sharply!' recorded George in his diary.

However, what was apparent was the solemnity and sincerity

THE STONE RETURNED TO SCOTLAND AFTER 700 YEARS

Ever since Edward I stole the Stone of Scone in 1296 the Scots felt bitter at their loss. They were mollified somewhat when James VI of Scotland became James I of England and was crowned over the stone in 1603. However, the stone remained in Westminster where English kings were crowned.

Then on Christmas Day 1950, the nation was told that the stone was missing! A wooden bar holding it in place had been wrenched away and marks on the abbey floor showed the route where it had been dragged out to freedom.

The Dean of Westminster spoke emotionally on the radio saying that he would go to the ends of the earth to find the stone. Press attention was intense. A Dutch psychic, Peter Hurkos, came to London to discover it. Meanwhile, police manned all roads to Scotland. Hurkos told the police that he felt that the stone was now in Glasgow, that it had been taken by students, and would be back in Westminster in weeks. At the same time, police were following up a lead given them by Archdeacon Marriott who had found a man with a Scottish accent among the abbey tombs on the evening before the theft. The man had told the archdeacon he came from Forgandenny.

Detectives searched the registers of Glasgow University and discovered that there was a student from Forgandenny at the university, and that he had recently borrowed books from the library on Westminster Abbey. They shadowed him and discovered his companions, but they were reluctant to make any arrests until the stone had been found. However, on 11 April 1951 three men left the stone at Arbroath Abbey. After it had been declared genuine the stone was returned to Westminster and hidden underground, as it was considered inadvisable to put it on display immediately. One of the first acts of the new queen, Elizabeth II, was to restore the stone to its old resting place under St Edward's Chair on 26 February 1952.

However, in 1996, seven centuries after it was seized by Edward I, the Stone of Scone was taken to Edinburgh. It was carried in procession along the Royal Mile, to be displayed in the castle with the Honours of Scotland. Among the people watching that historic event were three of the students who had stolen the stone forty-six years earlier.

of both king and queen at this service as they were beginning their unwanted and unlooked-for life of royal duties. Ramsay Macdonald even felt that they seemed to be in a state of religious trance. Certainly each of them was deeply conscious of the sacred nature of the coronation ceremony. Their resolution would soon be put to the test, for although no one could imagine it on that day in 1937, only two years later the Second World War would be upon them, and the 'Abdication Crisis' would be seen as a relatively trivial irrelevance as Hitler's bombs dropped on Westminster Abbey, the Houses of Parliament, and Buckingham Palace.

ELIZABETH II

Reigned 1952–, crowned 2 June 1953, aged 27

The Queen Insists the Coronation Must be Televised

The coronation of Queen Elizabeth II was the fifty-third to take place in Westminster Abbey. Forty reigning monarchs and most – but not all – of their consorts had previously been crowned there since that day in early January 1066 when Harold, last of the Saxon Kings, became the first sovereign to be crowned in Edward the Confessor's newly-built abbey. Even then, the coronation service itself was old, dating back – largely in the form that we know it today – to that impressive service in Bath Abbey, when Archbishop Dunstan had crowned Edgar the Peaceful on 11 May AD 973.

By 1952, when Queen Elizabeth acceded to the throne on the death of her father, the weight of tradition and complexity of custom had become almost indescribable. One thing was certain: Elizabeth was fully conscious of the duties and responsibilities that she was bound to undertake. Since she was ten, when her uncle David had abdicated, Elizabeth knew what her future would be. At the time of the abdication, her younger sister, Princess Margaret, aged six, had suddenly realised it too. 'Does that mean that you'll have to be the next queen?' she asked. 'Yes, some day,' was the reply. 'Poor you!' exclaimed Margaret. It was an astonishingly perceptive response for a six-year-old.

Throughout her childhood, then, and into her teens, when she had trained in vehicle maintenance in the ATS (Auxiliary Territorial Services) as 'Second Subaltern Elizabeth Windsor', during the final months of World War Two, Princess Elizabeth had always been aware of what was in store for her. This awareness had been shared with her future subjects on the occasion of her twenty-first birthday. On a visit to South Africa, she took the opportunity to make a broadcast in the form of an act of self-dedication to the work which she knew she would have to undertake. 'I declare before you all,' she said, 'that my whole life, whether it be long or short, shall be devoted to your service and the service of our great Imperial Commonwealth to which we all belong.' The call to duty came with unexpected suddenness, for in February 1952, Elizabeth and her husband Philip were urgently summoned back to England from Kenya, where they were on safari. King George VI had died in his sleep, and Elizabeth returned to Great Britain as its queen.

Transition from one monarch to another always involves an enormous amount of work and planning behind the scenes. In 1952 new designs for all the royal insignia had to be prepared and approved; a new coinage had to be minted; new stamps had to be issued; new letter-boxes had to be manufactured; uniforms, letter-heads, titles, prayers – indeed anything and everything connected with royalty had to be changed. As there was now a queen instead of a king, even the National Anthem became 'God Save the Queen' – and older people singing these words were strangely reminded of the long reign of Victoria. All the media hype in those early months of the new queen's reign was to herald in a 'New Elizabethan Age'.

Crucially, the main task for the immediate future was to plan a coronation. It would be an enormous task, as all state occasions are, but especially so for this event, as Britain had changed so much during the first half of the century. By far the most influential innovation then beginning to play a central role in people's lives throughout the country was television.

However, the unanimous opinion of all the queen's advisers was that under no circumstances should the coronation be televised. The Archbishop felt that it would turn a sacred service into a public spectacle; the Earl Marshal and other advisers thought that it would destroy the mystique of the monarchy;

Winston Churchill thought that it would destroy the solemnity of the occasion, and also that it would put too much strain on her. It says much for the Queen's foresight and common sense that she ignored all these objections and insisted that television cameras should be brought in and that the service should be televised 'live' and in full, except only for the part in which she would be taking holy communion.

Britain by now was becoming a fast-paced, modern, sophisticated society, where split-second timing was necessary and formal occasions had to be rehearsed with utmost precision. Elizabeth herself, with the exemplary conscientiousness which has always been the feature of her reign, was determined that absolutely nothing should go wrong – and a spin-off of her decision to televise the whole event meant that everything had to be rehearsed again and again, both inside and outside the abbey, in the run-up to the June coronation. The coronation would be seen by millions of people throughout the world. No previous coronation had ever had to be planned with such meticulous attention to detail. The man in charge of organising the whole event – the Duke of Norfolk acting in his office of Earl Marshal – worked tirelessly for months to orchestrate an event of unprecedented magnitude.

Models of central London and Westminster Abbey were constructed, so that the procession along the route could be plotted with care, and a huge chart of the abbey was made, using colour-coded pins for everyone taking part. In this way the best positions could be worked out. After all, the last time there had been a coronation of a married queen was that of Queen Anne in 1702, so that everything in 1953 had to be worked out afresh – and the need to accommodate television cameras certainly brought a new dimension into every aspect of the affair.

For weeks beforehand those who were most closely involved with the service regularly came to the abbey to practise their movements and actions. On one memorable occasion, Archbishop Geoffrey Fisher, trying to show the maids of honour how to walk down the stairs leading from the throne, picked up his cassock, tripped, and rolled over and over three or four times down the steps. He joined in the laughter – but it was an accident that no one could afford to make on the day itself.

As for the queen herself, she was particularly concerned about the part of the service which involved moving down those same steps, wearing the heavy Crown of St Edward, and carrying the sceptres. She insisted on wearing the traditional St Edward's Crown, despite suggestions that she should wear the lighter State Crown, as Queen Victoria had done. Nevertheless, she too came to the abbey to watch the Duchess of Norfolk take her place as queen, uniquely being 'crowned' with St Edward's Crown. Later, the duchess spoke about the experience: 'The crown itself was very heavy, and one had to make sure that it fitted absolutely right. It feels like falling off the whole time, so you have to tell whoever's putting it on to put it on a little bit forward or a little bit back.' The queen went to the abbey a second time, and practised wearing the crown herself. Nothing, absolutely nothing, was left to chance.

The coronation of Elizabeth II in 1953 has been described many times and, being the first to be recorded on film, it was the only coronation that had been watched by millions. At the climax of the ceremony there was a slight stirring in one of the balconies containing members of the royal family. It was realised that young Prince Charles, then aged four and a half, was being brought in to watch that crucial moment when the Crown of St Edward was placed on his mother's head. He stood between his grandmother, Queen Elizabeth, the Queen Mother, and his aunt, Princess Margaret. Young as he was, he must have had some awareness of the importance of that moment.

Afterwards, the Prime Minister, Winston Churchill, summed up the nation's feelings: 'We have had a day which the oldest are proud to have lived to see and which the youngest will remember all their lives.'

And the queen then spoke:

Throughout this memorable day I have been uplifted and sustained by the knowledge that your thoughts and prayers were with me. I have been aware all the time that my peoples, spread far and wide throughout every continent and ocean in the world were united to support me in the task to which I have now been dedicated with such solemnity.

The ceremonies you have seen today are ancient and some of their origins are veiled in the mists of the past. But their spirit and their meaning shine through the ages, never perhaps, more brightly than now.

I have in sincerity pledged myself to your service, as so many of you are pledged to mine. Throughout all my life and with all my heart I shall strive to be worthy of your trust.

Thus the day of the fifty-third coronation in Westminster Abbey came to an end, and Elizabeth's long reign began.

3
THE CROWN JEWELS

The crown jewels are by no means as old as the monarchy itself. Oliver Cromwell and the Parliamentarians ruthlessly destroyed almost all the ancient regalia immediately after Charles I was beheaded in 1649. Only the eagle-shaped ampulla and the anointing spoon survived. The Crown Jewels are permanently on public display in the Tower of London. At the mention of a coronation most people think immediately of crown, orb and sceptre, but there are many other items which comprise the regalia – for example the eagle-shaped Ampulla (a vessel for containing the anointing oil) and the golden Anointing Spoon.

When the monarchy was restored and Charles II returned to England in 1660 it was necessary to make an entirely new set of items for his coronation. Luckily, some of the jewels from the broken-up older regalia were returned and re-set in the new crown, orb and sceptre. It may even be possible that some of the melted-down gold was rescued and incorporated into the new 'St Edward's Crown.'

Over the following centuries extra items have had to be added to the regalia, as circumstances demanded – for example, as Charles II was unmarried when he was crowned, no crown was needed at that time for a queen. However, since then it has been necessary to provide extra items for various consort queens. The joint monarchy of William and Mary, crowned together in 1689, meant that everything needed to be provided in duplicate – even the throne.

A number of new acquisitions, such as the Koh-i-Noor diamond, presented to Queen Victoria in 1849, have been added into the regalia from time to time. The result of this is that the crowns, orbs and sceptres have never been fixed. There have always been changes and modifications.

A final point to remember is that the symbolism of the coronation service is richly embodied in a number of other royal items. As well as the crown, orb and sceptre, there is also a fine assemblage of swords, spurs, bracelets, various rings, and robes.

The full effect may be visually overwhelming, but each and every item is filled with significance. The priceless jewels are not merely an ostentatious display of wealth, but tangible symbols of our constitutional monarchy. Monarchs do not own these bejewelled objects, neither do they claim unlimited power by being invested with them. The regalia can be seen to remind everyone in this realm – prime ministers and judges, field marshalls and archbishops, ordinary men and women, and even monarchs themselves – that the essence of authority is infinitely more important than any single person who, for a brief period in history, is entrusted with it. To emphasise this, at the State Opening of Parliament, the State Crown itself is carried, alone, in its own carriage, to Westminster.

CROWNS

St Edward's Crown

This is the largest, heaviest and most important crown, used once by each monarch at the actual moment of coronation. Even then, it is worn only briefly. The crown we see today, known as St Edward's crown, was made for the coronation of Charles II in 1661, to replace the ancient St Edward's crown destroyed by Oliver Cromwell and the Parliamentarians. Although its name reminds us of the older crown, it does not date back to the time of Edward the Confessor, although it is quite possible that some of the gold of the previous, ancient crown was kept or rescued and now forms the basis of the lower half of the new crown.

St Edward's crown is instantly recognisable by the generously bowed golden arches, dipping in the middle. Rising from the centre of this dip, at the intersection of the arches, is a *monde*, or orb, surmounted by a golden Maltese cross, from which hang two drop-shaped silver pearls. The frame, *monde*, and cross are all of solid gold, and the whole crown is set with about 440 precious and semi-precious stones.

For the monarch who is to wear this enormous crown, the main problem is its weight – over 71oz 14 dwt (2.04kg). Queen Victoria, did *not* wear it, instead she had a new, light-weight state crown specially made for her own coronation. Again, at the coronation of Elizabeth II there were suggestions beforehand that it would be advisable for her to be crowned by the more manageable state crown.

Tradition is tradition, however, and Queen Elizabeth II firmly decided that it was essential that St Edward's crown should be used for her coronation in 1953. Nevertheless, the prospect gave her some concern, especially the moment when she would have to descend from the throne while still wearing it. The thought that it might wobble or even fall off was so worrying that she spent some time privately practising how to wear it.

Priceless though St Edward's crown is, it does not contain the most valuable or historic jewels in the royal collection. When Queen Victoria ordered the new Imperial State crown to be made for her coronation, some of the more famous jewels were removed from St Edward's crown and reset in the new state crown – and there they remain.

From every point of view, therefore, the present imperial state crown, worn by the sovereign on important occasions such as the State Opening of Parliament, is by far the most interesting item in the whole collection.

The Imperial State Crown

This is the crown which is most easily recognised, and which is worn by the sovereign on major state occasions such as the State Opening of Parliament. As explained in the introduction to this section, the royal crowns have been constantly changed and modified from monarch to monarch, in a series of what are known as 'manifestations' – i.e. shapes or forms. The present Imperial State Crown is about the tenth manifestation since the time of King Charles II, when virtually everything had to be made anew for his coronation in 1661.

Queen Victoria, as a petite young monarch aged only nineteen at the time of her coronation in 1838, found it wise not to wear St Edward's Crown, because of the sheer weight. Instead, she had a new State Crown specially made, and in this process many of the most precious stones were transferred from St Edward's Crown to this new State Crown. Even since then, the State Crown has been altered twice: it was remade for George VI in 1937; and altered again in 1953 for Queen Elizabeth II, when the arches were reduced in height. Queen Elizabeth had this crown remodelled to fit her head exactly, soon after her accession.

During the coronation service, the monarch is crowned with St Edward's Crown and then takes Holy Communion, after which he or she withdraws to St Edward's Chapel, where preparations are made for the final procession out of the abbey. At this point in the service, St Edward's Crown is exchanged for the Imperial State Crown. St Edward's Crown is never worn again until the next monarch succeeds to the throne and is crowned with it. As for the Imperial State Crown, this is the crown which is worn on all subsequent state occasions throughout the reign.

Owing to the changes made by Queen Victoria, the Imperial State Crown contains a collection of some of the most extraordinary jewels in the world. Quite apart from its 2,868 diamonds, 17 sapphires, 11 emeralds, 5 rubies and 273 pearls, there are in particular five items of exceptional interest:

> the sapphire from a ring which belonged to King Edward the Confessor
> the Black Prince's Ruby
> the great piece of diamond known as the Second Star of Africa
> the Stuart Sapphire
> four large drop pearls known as Queen Elizabeth's earrings, said to have been worn by Queen Elizabeth I.

The stories linked to each of these items are so fascinating that no description of the regalia can be complete without an account of them.

The Sapphire from King Edward the Confessor's Ring

On top of the intersection of the arches of the Imperial State Crown is an orb, or *monde*, and on top of this is a cross-patée. Set in the centre of this cross, at the very topmost part of the crown is the legendary sapphire which is believed to have belonged to St Edward himself. If so, it is older than the Tower of London in which it is kept.

Edward the Confessor wore this sapphire in a ring, about which a famous medieval legend was told. According to this story, the Confessor was on the way to the dedication of a chapel of St John the Evangelist when he was accosted by a beggar who begged him for alms. The king had no gold or silver with him, so after a moment's silence he drew from his hand a precious ring which he gave to the beggar, who thereupon vanished. Little did the Confessor know, but the beggar was really St John the Evangelist in disguise.

Shortly afterwards two English pilgrims travelling in Syria found themselves lost until they chanced upon an old man 'white and hoary' who befriended them and guided them to an inn. When they told the old man where they came from and described the saintly king who ruled in England, the old man was delighted. He announced that he was John the Evangelist and gave them the ring to carry back to the king. He also told them that in six months the Confessor would die and join him in paradise. On their return to England, the pilgrims found the king, who naturally enough acknowledged the ring, and duly prepared to go to heaven.

This legend became widespread in the Middle Ages and is depicted in many places, including a stained-glass window at St Lawrence's church in Ludlow, where the pilgrims came from, and in the St John window at York Minster.

Edward the Confessor was buried wearing this holy ring, but it did not remain with him for long. It was probably removed when the saint's body was put into its new shrine in 1163, when the king was formally canonised.

The sapphire's subsequent history is obscure, but it is thought that Henry VIII included it in the Crown Jewels.

The Black Prince's Ruby

This magnificent blood-red stone, set in the middle of a cross-patée, appears dramatically in the central position at the front of the Imperial State Crown. Strictly speaking it is not a ruby, but a 'balas' or 'spinel' – old names for this semi-precious stone. Its history is startlingly blood-curdling.

No one knows the earliest history of this great balas ruby. Undoubtedly, it is of eastern origin, with an ancient gold setting at its back. What is known, however, is that in the fourteenth century it belonged to the king of Granada – probably the greatest gem in the western world. So famous was it that the neighbouring king of Castille, Don Pedro the Cruel, slaughtered the hapless king of Granada in cold blood and carried the ruby off with the rest of his jewels.

Shortly afterwards, in 1367, Pedro the Cruel needed military help against his enemies in northern Spain, so Edward the Black Prince, son of Edward III, obligingly fought and won the Battle of Najera for him. It was said of the Black Prince that he never fought a battle which he did not win, and Pedro was so delighted that he rewarded the prince by giving him the famous ruby. Probably he had a bad conscience about it. Much of the subsequent history of the Black Prince's Ruby, as it came to be called, is fully documented, and it has stayed in the royal collection ever since.

The Black Prince wore it sewn on to the velvet cap under his coronet. He bequeathed it to his son, who became Richard II. Two reigns later, Henry V boldly wore it on the front of his coroneted helmet as he fought at the Battle of Agincourt. Indeed during that battle the ruby was almost broken or lost as Henry personally fought with the duc d'Alençon, who had challenged him to mortal combat. After the battle it was discovered that a piece of the king's helmet had broken off, having received a hefty blow, only narrowly missing the ruby.

There is a story, probably untrue, that Richard III wore the ruby at the Battle of Bosworth. However, what is certain is that at the time of the sale of the Crown Jewels after Charles I was beheaded in 1649, one item on offer was 'one large ballas ruby wraped in paper value £4'. Quite what happened to it no one can be certain, but luckily it was returned and set in the State Crown for the coronation of Charles II in 1661.

The last adventure to befall the Black Prince's Ruby occurred when it fell victim to Colonel Blood's attempt to steal the Crown Jewels in 1671. Luckily, Colonel Blood was unsuccessful, and the Black Prince's Ruby has been worn in the place of honour in the front of the State Crown of every English monarch from Charles II to the present day.

The Second Star of Africa

Set in the front of the Imperial State Crown, just below the Black Prince's Ruby, is a part of the enormous diamond found in South Africa in 1905. The entire uncut diamond weighed 3,106 carats (1.33 lb) and was named the Cullinan Diamond, after Sir Thomas Major Cullinan, chairman of the Premier Diamond Mine, Johannesburg. It is the largest diamond ever discovered – three times the size of its nearest rival.

The Cullinan Diamond was bought by the Transvaal Government and presented to Edward VII on his sixty-sixth birthday in 1907, with the request that it might become one of the brightest jewels in the British Crown. Obviously, there was a great security risk in sending this precious object to England, and a heavily guarded ship was sent to South Africa, ostensibly to bring it back.

In actual fact, the package which the ship's captain locked up in his cabin's safe was a fake, and the real Cullinan Diamond was sent to London by parcel post! However, when it arrived, the problem was that it was so big that it could not be used just as found. The king, therefore, decided that it should be split – a task guaranteed to test the nerve of anyone brave enough to undertake it. Eventually, the firm of Messrs Asscher, of Amsterdam, was asked to split it, and Mr J. Asscher himself braced himself for the task.

At the first blow, the steel cleaving knife broke in two. Poor Mr Asscher screwed up courage to try again, and at the second blow he was so wound up that he fainted. On regaining consciousness he learned to his great relief that he had succeeded in dividing the stone into two pieces. Subsequently, the pieces were cut again into four and a number of smaller pieces.

The largest piece, which is pear-shaped and weighs 530 carats, is now known as the 'Star of Africa' and is set in the head of the Royal Sceptre. The second largest piece, a square of 317 carats, is known as the 'Second Star of Africa' and it is this which is set in the Imperial State Crown.

The other pieces, the Third and Fourth Stars of Africa, were set in Queen Mary's Crown by Messrs Garrard, the Royal Jewellers, in such a fashion that they could, if desired, be removed and worn separately. Other smaller pieces were set in various brooches and rings, much treasured by Queen Mary. Apparently, all these various cleavings of the Cullinan Diamond are still referred to by the present royal family as 'Granny's chips'.

The Stuart Sapphire

The early history of this stone is obscure. It is thought that it was worn in the mitre of George Neville, brother of Warwick the Kingmaker and Archbishop of York from 1465 to 1476. After his death Edward IV seized it and had it set in his State Crown.

Like the Black Prince's Ruby, it managed somehow to survive the Commonwealth destruction, and was set in Charles II's new State Crown in 1661. The story after this is intriguing, for when James II fled to France at the end of 1688 he took this sapphire with him, and apparently he used to carry it about with him in his pocket, while he lived out his permanent exile. Perhaps he liked to have it about him as a keepsake of happier times.

On the death of James II in 1701 it passed to his son, James Stuart – the Old Pretender – and when he died in 1766 it passed his younger son, Henry, brother of Bonnie Prince Charlie. By then, Henry had become a cardinal living in Rome, and had given up any royal ambition, though staunch Jacobites still thought of him as 'Henry IX'. Cardinal Stuart must have had nostalgic thoughts as he wore this Stuart Sapphire in his mitre – the second mitre to contain this beautiful gem.

On Henry's death, the last of the Stuart line died out and it was believed that the Stuart Sapphire was directly bequeathed to George, Prince of Wales, later to become King George IV. More detailed research, however, has revealed that Cardinal Stuart actually sold the sapphire, not long before his death, to a Venetian merchant, a Mr Arenberg, who in turn sold it to an agent acting on behalf of the Prince Regent.

Prinny gave the sapphire to his daughter, Princess Charlotte, who died in childbirth in 1817, and on her sad and unexpected death he asked for it to be returned to him, as it was considered to be a Crown Jewel. Prinny gave it to one of his mistresses – Lady Conyngham – who is alleged to have worn it in her headdress as she danced at a royal ball.

How the sapphire was recovered from Lady Conyngham is not known, but fortunately, it returned once more to the Crown

Jewels and was set in Queen Victoria's new Imperial State Crown for her coronation in 1838, mounted in the place of honour, just below the Black Prince's Ruby. (Victoria was crowned with this State Crown, not the traditional St Edward's Crown.)

The Stuart Sapphire remained at the front of the State Crown for the coronation of Edward VII in 1902, and it would have stayed there still, but for the discovery of the Cullinan Diamond in 1905. The presentation of this new gem to Edward in 1907, asking that 'it might become one of the brightest jewels in the British Crown' meant that the Stuart Sapphire was then moved to the *back* of the Imperial State Crown, where it is still mounted, and the 'Second Star of Africa' took its place.

It's a pity that the Stuart Sapphire is not so easily seen now, in its present position, but it is well worth looking at both the front and the back of the Imperial State Crown, in order to enjoy the sight of this much-travelled jewel.

Queen Elizabeth's Earrings

Just below the intersection of the arches on the Imperial State Crown hang four large drop-shaped pearls, known as 'Queen Elizabeth's Earrings', said to have been worn by Queen Elizabeth I. Despite this romantic name, it is not known for certain whether she did wear them. Certainly she owned a set of seven famous drop pearls, and it is more than likely that the four pearls hanging in the State Crown did belong to that set.

A set of pearls were given by Pope Clement VII to Catherine de Medici, on her marriage to Henry II of France. In turn, Catherine gave them as a wedding present to her daughter-in-law, Mary Stuart, later Mary Queen of Scots, when Mary married Louis, the dauphin of France. Many years later, when Mary was prisoner in Lochleven Castle, she was forced to give up all her jewels to the Regent Murray which were bought by Elizabeth I for £12,000. The pearls may well have been a part of that collection.

On Elizabeth I's death, most of her jewels went to James I, whose daughter was *also* called Elizabeth – and there is a strong possibility that the 'Queen Elizabeth' referred to was in fact this relatively forgotten princess. James's daughter Elizabeth, his 'dear Bessie', was married to the King of Bohemia, and so was often referred to in England as 'Elizabeth of Bohemia' – but of course when she was on the continent she was referred to as 'Elizabeth of England' (she was to become the great-grandmother of George I, and it was through her that the Hanoverians could claim the English throne on the death of Queen Anne).

In the National Portrait Gallery in London there is a picture of Elizabeth of Bohemia, painted in 1642 showing her wearing four pearl earrings looking remarkably like the ones which are now set in the Imperial State Crown. So, are these really the pearls we see today? And does the name 'Queen Elizabeth' really refer to James I's 'dear Bessie'? We shall never know. What we do know, however, is that 'dear Bessie' returned to England with her nephew, Charles II, at the restoration of the monarchy. She died two years later, and so her jewels must have passed back into the royal collection with her death. Queen Victoria had the pearls set in the Imperial State Crown at the beginning of her reign, and they have remained there ever since.

The Imperial Indian Crown

The Imperial Crown of India rests in a solitary position in its own separate display-case in the Tower of London. In a way, this is appropriate, for it is a reminder of a part of British history which is never likely to be re-enacted. It was specially made by the Court Jewellers, Messrs Garrard, for the Durbar of George V, at which he was acclaimed emperor of India in 1911.

The Imperial Indian Crown contains more than 6,000 diamonds, together with emeralds, sapphires and rubies. Much discreet controversy surrounded its manufacture when George V insisted on going to India to be crowned as its emperor. When it was pointed out to him that St Edward's Crown and the Imperial State Crown could not leave the country, it was obvious that a new crown would have to be made. The first problem was who would pay for it? Eventually the cost, £60,000, was met by the India Office. A second problem arose over how the king should be crowned, and by whom? Obviously, it would be inappropriate for the Archbishop of Canterbury to crown the king at a Christian service in India. The king suggested that he might crown himself, but this idea was rejected, as it would create a difficult precedent.

Eventually, it was decided that the king would appear with the crown already on his head. Afterwards, George wrote in his diary: 'Rather tired after the wearing the Crown for 3½ hours, it hurt my head, as it is pretty heavy.' It was to be the first, last and only time the Imperial Indian Crown was ever worn.

The Crown of Mary of Modena

This crown was originally made for Mary, consort of James II, for their coronation in 1685. It was worn in the next reign by Mary II, who used it as her state crown. It was greatly altered a few years later by Queen Anne, who wore it as her state crown when she came to the throne in 1702. George I also wore it as his state crown, but when George II came to the throne it was used by his consort, Queen Caroline. It is sometimes known as the 'queen consort's crown' but it has not been worn since the mid-eighteenth century. The last queen to wear it was Queen Charlotte, consort to George III.

The Crown of Queen Mary
(Consort of King George V)

This crown, as its name implies, was made for Queen Mary, consort of George V, who wore it at her coronation in 1911. It contains more than 2,200 diamonds and originally it also contained the Koh-i-Noor diamond as well as the third and fourth stones of the Cullinan diamond (the Third and Fourth Stars of Africa). The jewels in royal crowns have always been changed and moved from one crown to another, and this was no exception. The two stones of the Cullinan Diamond were set in such a fashion that they could be removed if desired and worn as separate brooches. The famous Koh-i-Noor diamond was originally set in the Maltese cross at the top, but this was removed in 1937 so that it could be reset in a new crown for the coronation of Queen Elizabeth, consort to George VI. The arches in the Crown of Queen Mary are detachable, so that the crown can also be worn as a circlet. Queen Mary wore it in this fashion when she attended the coronation of her son, George VI, in 1937.

THE STORY OF THE
KOH-I-NOOR DIAMOND

The early history of this extraordinary jewel is shrouded in legend. Hindu mythology tells how it belonged to Kama, King of Anga, 3,000 years ago. The first European to see it was the great French traveller, Jean Baptiste Tavernier, in 1665 when it was in the possession of the Mogul Emperor of India, Aurangzebe, who had it set in the eye of a peacock in his famous Peacock Throne at Delhi. Tavernier described how even then the great diamond was regarded with intense wonder and admiration, as it was already one of the most famous gems of the east. Aurangzebe had inherited it from his father, Shah Jehan, builder of the Taj Mahal.

When the powerful King of Persia, Nadir Shah, invaded India and conquered the Mogul Emperor, Muhammad Shah, in 1739, he hoped to capture the Koh-i-Noor, but, according to tradition, he found that it had completely disappeared. His attendants looked everywhere, but clearly it had been hidden very successfully.

Nadir Shah resorted to guile and cunning. The defeated Muhammad Shah was still being allowed to live in some degree of luxury, even to the extent of keeping a large assortment of wives. Some of these were quite happy to share their female charms with the conquering Persians, and one particularly indiscreet young wife let out the great secret – the Koh-i-Noor diamond was now being kept permanently hidden in Muhammad Shah's turban.

Nadir Shah was delighted. At last he knew where it was, but he decided that mere murder or brute force would not be appropriate. Instead, he prepared a great banquet and invited Muhammad as his special guest of honour. During the course of this meal, Nadir Shah made a complimentary speech, extolling the virtues of his guest, swore eternal friendship, and suggested that as a token of their undying alliance they should exchange turbans. Poor Muhammad had no option but to comply. He realised clearly that his conqueror had outwitted him, and it was now probably a choice between losing his turban – and its precious contents – or his head!

Nadir Shah travelled back to Persia with the Koh-i-Noor. However, some time later one of his bodyguards, Ahmed Shah, murdered him, seized the jewel and escaped with it into Afghanistan, where he eventually became ruler and founder of the Durrani dynasty. Four Afghanistani rulers later, Ahmed's descendant Shuja Shah was deposed and fled to Lahore in the neighbouring Indian state of Punjab, taking his most prized possession, the Koh-i-Noor diamond, with him. Arriving at Lahore, Shuja found asylum with the Maharajah Runjeet Singh, the 'Lion of the Punjab', who promised shelter and assistance, but only on condition that Shuja would give him the Koh-i-Noor diamond. Accordingly, it changed hands yet again. Runjeet delighted in the acquisition and wore it conspicuously – sometimes, in a fit of ostentation, even decorating his horse with it. However, pride came before defeat.

After wars with the British forces in the 1840s, Runjeet Singh was forced from power. In 1849 his eleven-year-old son, Duleep Singh, signed away his rights to some of the richest land in India, as well as the Koh-i-Noor diamond. 'Poor little fellow,' wrote Lord Dalhousie, the Governor-General. 'He does not care two pence about it himself – he will have a good and regular stipend all his life and will die in his bed like a gentleman; which under other circumstances, he certainly would not have done.'

The handsome little Maharajah, Duleep Singh, was taken into British care and brought to England, where he lived in comfort. Queen Victoria was greatly taken with him: 'Poor boy, I feel so much for him,' she had said when she first met him; and not only did she commission her favourite painter, Franz Winterhalter, to paint his portrait, but also she painted him herself in watercolours. Later, she became godmother to Duleep's elder son.

The Koh-i-Noor, by this time, was in the royal jewel collection, and Queen Victoria was pleased to wear it on occasions of major importance, such as the opening of the Great Exhibition in 1851, where she arranged for it to be put on public exhibition.

Unfortunately, however magnificent it was, the Koh-i-Noor had been damaged by unskilful cutting, and so it was to be properly cut, under the assiduous eye of the Prince Consort. The 83-year-old Duke of Wellington, victor at Waterloo, was given the honour of cutting the first facet, personally starting the grinding machinery. He arrived at Garrard's, the crown jeweller, at 25 Haymarket, in the summer of 1852, mounted upon his white charger. He died only a few weeks afterwards, so this must have been one of his last royal duties.

The Crown of Queen Elizabeth the
Queen Mother (Consort of King George VI)

This was the last British royal crown to be made, and is unique in that it is made of platinum rather than gold or silver. As Consort to George VI, Queen Elizabeth used to wear this crown in circlet form as she accompanied the king on State Openings of Parliament. Later, in 1953, she wore it as a circlet at the coronation of her daughter, Elizabeth II. The London crowds and millions of TV viewers had the opportunity to see this beautiful crown in April 2002, as it rested on the Queen Mother's coffin at her lying-in-state and funeral.

It contains about 2,800 diamonds, most of which were taken from a circlet which had belonged to Queen Victoria. However, by far the most interesting jewel in this crown is the famous Koh-i-Noor diamond, which is set in the central front, within a glittering Maltese cross.

The Koh-i-Noor diamond was given to Queen Victoria in 1849, who wore it in a brooch or bracelet, but on her death it was mounted first in the crown of Queen Alexandra, and then it was again reset in the new crown of Queen Mary, where it was positioned in the Maltese cross at the very top.

Koh-i-Noor means 'Mountain of Light', and a part of the mystique that surrounds it is that it will bring bad luck to any man who wears it. Thus, in England, only Queens Victoria, Alexandra, Mary and Elizabeth have worn it in their crowns.

The Crown of George, Prince of Wales

This crown was made for George, Prince of Wales, the future George V, for the coronation of his father, Edward VII, in 1902. It was also worn by Edward, Prince of Wales, the future Edward VIII, for the coronation of his father George V in 1911.

Somewhat surprisingly, on his abdication Edward VIII, or the Duke of Windsor as he became, took this crown with him to France and kept it with him until he died. Crowns are not normally allowed out of the country, and it is not clear how or when the ex-king managed to effect this permanent loan. Crown jewels, after all, belong to the nation, and not to a specific person. The crown must have given the duke many nostalgic memories as he contemplated it during his lifelong, self-imposed exile. It was returned to Britain and placed in the Jewel House after he died in 1972.

Queen Victoria's Small Diamond Crown

This exquisite little crown was made for Queen Victoria in 1870, using diamonds taken from one of her necklaces. It was her personal possession and she loved wearing it, as it was so light and easy on her head. She complained that the Imperial State Crown was too heavy for her, but this crown, weighing under 6 oz and less than 4 inches in diameter, was just right for her. Small though it is, it contains about 1,300 diamonds. She was fifty-one when it was made, about halfway through her long reign. During the last three decades of the century she frequently wore it on top of her widow's cap, even on occasions such as the State Opening of Parliament. There are so many portraits and photographs of her with this crown that it has become her best-remembered image. Indeed, when she died, it was placed on her coffin. Although Queen Alexandra wore it on several occasions, it has never been worn at a coronation. King George VI added it to the regalia kept in the Tower of London in 1937.

ORBS

The Sovereign's Orb

'What am I to do with it?' asked Queen Victoria, at her alarmingly under-rehearsed coronation. 'Your Majesty is to carry it, if you please, in your hand.' replied Lord John Thynne. 'Am I?' she exclaimed; 'it is very heavy!'

In fact the orb is a golden ball, with a 6 inch diameter and weighing just over 42 oz. It is encrusted with over 600 precious stones – rubies, sapphires and emeralds, set in clusters of diamonds, and with bands of pearls. It is surmounted with a large amethyst, upon which is a cross, in the middle of which is another sapphire. It was made by Sir Robert Vyner, the court jeweller, for the coronation of Charles II in 1661, replacing an earlier orb which was lost during the Commonwealth.

The orb symbolises the domination of the Christian religion over the world, and it is delivered to the sovereign only briefly during the coronation service. It is then delivered a second time, together with the Crown of State, in St Edward's Chapel, for the sovereign to carry in procession out of Westminster Abbey.

In earlier times the orb was also carried symbolically at important occasions such as the State Opening of Parliament, but nowadays the orb is used only at coronations.

The orb has twice been temporarily 'lost'. (See pages 204 and 239.)

Queen Mary's Orb

An orb is given only to a reigning sovereign: not to consort queens. However, when William and Mary came to the throne as joint monarchs in 1689 it was necessary to make a second orb for Mary to use. Hence the regalia contains this smaller orb, similar to the sovereign's, but less richly jewelled. It has never been used since Queen Mary's coronation in 1689, and it is unlikely that it will ever be used again.

SCEPTRES AND RODS

There are two kinds of sceptre. To distinguish between them we should look carefully at the top, for there is either a cross or a dove, each with its own significance. At a coronation service, the sovereign is invested with both sceptre with cross and sceptre with dove. A queen consort is also invested with both sceptres.

The Sovereign's Sceptre with Cross

It is the ultimate symbol of royal authority. When it is given to the sovereign in the coronation service, it is presented with the words: 'Receive the Royal Sceptre, the ensign of kingly power and justice.' It is held in the sovereign's right hand. The golden sovereign's sceptre with cross is the most magnificent of all the sceptres and the present sceptre with cross is set with the gigantic Star of Africa – the largest part of the Cullinan diamond, which is believed to be the biggest and most perfect diamond in the world.

The Sovereign's Sceptre with Dove

This is also called the 'Rod of Equity and Mercy'. The white enamelled dove, perched on a cross at the top is the symbol of the holy ghost. The sovereign holds this sceptre in the left hand, to symbolise the spiritual role of the monarchy.

The Queen Consort's Sceptre with Cross

The was first used by Mary of Modena, consort of James II, in 1685, and has been delivered into the right hand of every consort queen at all subsequent coronations since.

The Queen Consort's Ivory Rod with Dove

Like the queen consort's sceptre with cross, this was first made for Mary of Modena. It is held in the consort's left hand. It is easily recognisable because it is made of ivory instead of gold, and the white enamelled dove at the top has its wings closed.

Queen Mary II's Sceptre with Dove

This sceptre was made for Mary II, joint-sovereign with William III, for their coronation in 1689, and it has never been used since then. It can be recognised by the spreading wings of the dove, and the fact that it is smaller than the sovereign's sceptre with dove.

St Edward's Staff

Made by Sir Robert Vyner in 1661, this 56-inch staff is carried by a peer of the realm immediately before the sovereign in the procession to Westminster Abbey. It is made of gold, with a steel foot, and is surmounted by a golden ball and cross. The original staff, which was destroyed by the Puritans, was much venerated as it contained what was believed to be a relic of the Cross. Such a relic would have added greatly to the solemnity of the occasion.

SWORDS

There are five swords in the regalia, all of which are used in the coronation service: the Sword of State; the Jewelled State Sword; the Sword Spiritual; the Sword Temporal; and *Curtana*. By far the most important and magnificent sword is the Jewelled State Sword, specially made for the hugely ostentatious coronation of George IV in 1821. It is almost certainly the most costly sword in the world. At the time it was made it cost £6,000, but nowadays just one emerald in the hilt has been valued at over £3,000. During the reign of Queen Victoria this sword was lost, and only accidentally discovered some time later, placed in an old box that looked like a gun-case. The Jewelled State Sword, which is only used at coronations, is brought to the sovereign with the words: 'With this sword do justice, stop the growth of iniquity, protect the Holy Church of God, help and defend widows and orphans.'

The other, earlier Sword of State was purchased in 1677 or 1678 and is used on other occasions as well as at coronations. It is a long, two-handed sword, 32 in long. It is carried in procession by a peer of the realm with its point upwards. During the coronation service, because of its weight, its place is taken by the lighter Jewelled State Sword.

Two of the other three swords, the Sword Spiritual and the Sword Temporal, represent spiritual justice and temporal justice. The Sword Spiritual is a seventeenth-century copy of one of three similar swords sent by Pope Clement VII to Henry VIII when he conferred upon him the title of Defender of the Faith. It has an obtuse point, to show that sentences in the ecclesiastical courts do not have the sharpness of death. In contrast, the Sword Temporal has a meaningfully-sharp, pointed end.

Finally, *Curtana*, with about 6 in of its blade purposely broken off, is known as the 'Sword of Mercy', because, being blunt, it is the emblem of clemency. *Curtana* derives from the Latin word *curtus*, meaning 'short'. It is also named after the sword of an eighth century warrior, Ogier the Dane, who according to legend was just about to kill the Emperor Charlemagne's son in revenge for the murder of his own son, when he suddenly heard a voice from heaven, calling upon him to be merciful. Ogier's sword was called *Courtain* or 'short sword'.

SPURS

The Golden Spurs of St George

Made for Charles II in 1661, they are emblems of knighthood and chivalry, and as such are symbols of military eminence. In former times, the sovereign had spurs buckled on, but now the custom is merely to touch the monarch's heels with them.

RINGS

The Sovereign's Ring

Made for William IV in 1831, it is the symbol of the monarch's union with the people, and has been called the Wedding Ring of England. It has a sapphire background, upon which is laid a St George's cross of rubies, and the whole is surrounded with diamonds. Formerly, a new ring was made for each new king or queen, and then remained in the personal possession of the sovereign. However, the present Sovereign's Ring has been used for every coronation since 1831, except for that of Queen Victoria.

The Queen Consort's Ring

Made in 1831, for Queen Adelaide, it consists of a large, plain ruby, surrounded by diamonds, and the shank is set with rubies. It has been worn by all queen consorts since 1831.

Queen Victoria's Ring

This ring, specially made for Queen Victoria, was so small that the Archbishop of Canterbury had the greatest difficulty in forcing it on her finger. It caused her a great deal of pain, and after the coronation she could hardly get it off again. It is a smaller version of the Sovereign's Ring. Engraved inside the shank is 'Queen Victoria's Coronation Ring 1838'.

BRACELETS

Also known as armills, bracelets were an ancient emblem of royalty – so old an emblem that the Bible tells of how, when Saul, King of Israel, was slain, his crown and bracelet were brought to King David. In former times in England, bracelets were used at coronations, but the last time the older armills were worn was by the nine-year-old King Edward VI, in 1547. These were destroyed by the Parliamentarians, and a new pair were made for King Charles II in 1661. They are known as the 'bracelets of sincerity and wisdom' – but neither Charles nor any of his successors seem to have worn them.

The custom of wearing armills was revived in 1953 by Queen Elizabeth II, and the pair of bracelets that she wore at her coronation, and can be seen among the regalia today, were a present to her from the Commonwealth. The inscription on these armills is a testament to how the Commonwealth has changed during her reign:

Presented for the Coronation of Her Majesty Queen Elizabeth II by the Governments of the United Kingdom, Canada, Australia, New Zealand, South Africa, Pakistan, Ceylon and Southern Rhodesia.

THE AMPULLA

Shaped as a beautiful golden eagle with outstretched wings, the ampulla stands on an ornate pedestal. It is just over 8 in high and weighs 21 oz. It was made for the coronation of Charles II in 1661, to replace the ampulla destroyed by the Parliamentarians.

Although the present ampulla was the work of Sir Robert Vyner, the court jeweller, it is believed that only the wings and the pedestal were newly-made at that time, and that the eagle's body and head date back to the late fourteenth century, making it one of the oldest items used at a coronation. The head unscrews to allow the oil to be put in, but when the archbishop uses it to anoint the sovereign, the oil is poured out of its beak into the silver-gilt anointing spoon, into which the archbishop dips his fingers for the solemn act of anointing.

THE ANOINTING SPOON

This spoon is by far the oldest item used at a coronation. It is believed to date from the twelfth century and may even have been used at the coronation of King John in 1199. It was probably made for John's brother, Richard the Lionheart, or even his father, Henry II. It is certainly more than 800 years old.

Luckily, when items of the old regalia were being sold and broken up, this anointing spoon was bought by a royalist, Clement Kynnersley, a courtier of Charles I, who returned it to Charles II at the time of the Restoration.

The long stem is beautifully chased and is set with four freshwater pearls, added for the coronation of Charles II. It is silver-gilt, and over the centuries it has been regilded, and possibly partly refashioned.

4
THE HONOURS OF SCOTLAND

The Scottish crown, sceptre and Sword of State are known as the Honours of Scotland. They comprise regalia older than those of England, and are now on permanent public view in Edinburgh Castle. There are fewer items than in the English regalia: principally, a crown, sword, sceptre and ring. The present Scottish crown dates from the early sixteenth century, and is a replacement of an earlier crown; the sceptre was a gift from Pope Alexander VI in 1494, but shortly afterwards it was remodelled and lengthened; the Scottish Sword of State was a gift from Pope Julius II in 1507; and the Stuart Ring was formerly in the possession of Mary, Queen of Scots. A full and detailed description of all these would take too much space here, but the extraordinary story of what happened to them after the execution of King Charles I in 1649 deserves to be told.

The shock felt in Scotland following the execution of Charles I was enormous. The regalia immediately assumed an immense symbolic importance: they were seen to be memorials of a proud and independent past; emblems of a martyred king; and symbols of hope – however slight – of a future greatness to be regained. More urgently, the regalia was immediately seen to be at risk, especially as it became known that Cromwell was systematically destroying everything he could find of the English regalia. When news came that Cromwell was sending an army to Edinburgh expressly, among other purposes, to find Scotland's Crown Jewels, the alarm over their safety was paramount.

Cromwell's threat became even greater when he defeated a Scottish army at the Battle of Dunbar in 1650 and seemed likely to move on towards Edinburgh. In haste, the 'Honours of Scotland' were taken and hidden elsewhere, probably in Stirling Castle, for the coronation of Charles II, who had already been proclaimed king of Scotland by the Scottish Parliament. The Scottish coronation of Charles II took place, on 1 January

1651, at Scone. It was to be the last time the Honours of Scotland were used and the last time a king of Scotland was crowned. Immediately after this coronation, the Honours of Scotland were taken north to Dunnottar Castle for even safer keeping. However, Cromwell was determined to find them, and by September 1651 his army had surrounded Dunottar Castle, and beseiged it for eight long winter months.

However, the crown, sword and sceptre were smuggled out of the castle under the very noses of the English soldiers. A local minister's wife, Christian Granger, and her two servants, gained permission to enter the castle to visit the beseiged governor's wife, and with great daring they managed to hide the Honours under their clothes and in bundles of flax as they left. When they got back to their home in Kinneff, four miles away, the Honours were hidden, first in a bed in the minister's manse, and then more securely buried under flag-stones in his church.

After the restoration of the monarchy in 1660 the Scottish regalia was once more put on open view, and was used symbolically in the Scottish Parliament to signify the presence of royal authority. As each law was passed, the sceptre was used to touch the parchment – thus giving it the royal assent. However, the independence of a Scottish Parliament came to an end in 1707 when England and Scotland were formally joined in the Act of Union. The very ratification of this act demanded the final use of the sceptre. The Lord Chancellor touched the Articles of Union with it, and with that symbolic gesture, independent Scotland came to an end.

By now, the Honours of Scotland were beginning to acquire a powerful mystique in Scottish eyes. What was more, they became potentially dangerous. They were likely to provide a focal point for unrest, and could easily act as a rallying-point for any possible Scottish rebellion against English rule. However, if they were taken to London, it would be contrary to the Act of Union itself, which positively stipulated that they should remain in Scotland 'in all times coming, notwithstanding the Union'.

If they were kept anywhere in Scotland, however, there was a possibility that they would be used again, possibly to crown an illegal 'Jacobite' king, and of course they could never be destroyed; even Cromwell had never managed to do that.

The solution was drastic. In 1707 they were put in a locked oak chest; shut in the Crown Room of Edinburgh Castle; and the door was permanently sealed with solid blocks of stone. For the next eighty-seven years the room was left blocked up, but in 1794 the castle's lieutenant-governor, Major Drummond, felt he needed to open it up, trying to locate some lost parliamentary records – and sure enough, when he got inside the dust-laden room there was the ancient chest, just as it had been left. Natural curiosity made Drummond give the chest a shake, but whatever he did, no sound came from it. Of course, he had no authority to open it up. He had the doorway walled up again, and was left, puzzling whether or not the chest was the right one – or whether it really did contain the Honours.

Almost a quarter of a century elapsed. In 1818, Sir Walter Scott, the great authority on Scottish lore and legend, was foremost in begging the prince regent to give permission for the chest to be opened once more, if only to make sure that the Honours were still inside. Luckily, the prince was greatly in favour of the project, so in the summer of 1818 Scott and a number of officers of state gathered for the solemn task of wrenching the chest open. To everyone's relief, the Honours lay there, exactly where they had been placed 111 years before. The joy was intense; the Royal Standard was hoisted on the castle's tower; and the people of Scotland cheered to realise that their heritage was being restored.

In 1822, the year after his coronation, the prince – now King George IV – visited Scotland as the first reigning British monarch to do so since Charles II was crowned at Scone in 1651. He was presented with the Honours in the Palace of Holyrood and he symbolically touched them, signifying once again that he accepted the kingship of the nation. After the ceremony, a vast crowd of people assembled to watch as the Honours of Scotland were taken back once more to be put on view in the Crown Room of Edinburgh Castle.

The emotion surrounding the rediscovery of Scotland's regalia at that time can hardly be imagined today, but a story told by Frances Ann Kemble in her autobiography *Record of a Girlhood* may possibly give us some hint of the depth of Scottish feeling.

Sir Walter Scott told me that . . . he received a most urgent entreaty from an old lady of the Maxwell family to be permitted to see it. She was nearly ninety years old and feared she might not live till the Crown Jewels of Scotland were permitted to be become objects of public exhibition, and pressed Sir Walter Scott with importunate prayers to allow her to see them before she died.

Sir Walter's good sense and good nature alike induced him to take upon himself to grant the poor lady's petition, and he conducted her into the presence of these relics of her country's independent sovereignty, when he said, tottering hastily forward from his support, she fell on her knees before the crown, and clasping and wringing her wrinkled hands, wailed over it as a mother over her dead child.

His description of the scene was infinitely pathetic and it must have appealed to all his own poetical and imaginative sympathy with the former glories of his native land.

However, the Honours of Scotland were hidden and buried a *second* time. On 12 May 1941, four years to the day of the coronation of George VI and his Scottish-born consort, Elizabeth, the Honours of Scotland were buried once again, to avoid capture by a possible German attack. The place chosen was the ruins of the David's Tower. Some of the regalia was buried in an old latrine-closet, and some was hidden in a wall.

Only four people had access to knowledge of the secret locations: the king, the Secretary of State for Scotland, the King's and Lords' Treasurer's Remembrancer, and the Governor General of Canada. Each of these received a sealed envelope containing the secret of their whereabouts. Had it been necessary to transfer the seat of government to Canada during the Second World War, the Governor General of Canada would know where the Honours were hidden. Needless to say, such extreme precautions proved unnecessary.

After the Second World War the Honours were placed on view in Edinburgh Castle. They were used again in 1953. Just three weeks after her coronation in Westminster Abbey, Elizabeth II came to Scotland with the Duke of Edinburgh and attended a National Service of Thanksgiving in the High Kirk of St Giles,

Edinburgh. She received the Honours – the Sceptre of Scotland, the Sword of State and the Crown of Scotland – as they were ceremonially handed to her, and then at the end of the service, she walked down the nave, preceded by the Honours.

Since 1996 the Honours of Scotland have been displayed in Edinburgh Castle together with Scotland's other great historical treasure: the legendary Stone of Scone – they are all poignant reminders of Scotland's rich and troubled past.

HOW COLONEL BLOOD STOLE THE CROWN JEWELS FROM THE TOWER OF LONDON

Thomas Blood was an Irishman, living in London in the time of Charles II. He came from a good, respectable family in Ireland, and he had even been a magistrate at the early age of twenty-two; his grandfather had been an MP for Ennis. During the Commonwealth he had joined the Parliamentarian army and had risen to the rank of colonel; however, at the time of the Restoration he found himself in a state of poverty – his property had been confiscated, and he felt himself to be deeply wronged. With this burning sense of being a victim of injustice he had turned to a life of astonishing criminal adventure. One dark night in 1670, for example, he captured his enemy the Duke of Ormonde and almost succeeded in hanging him from the public gallows at Tyburn. The duke only just managed to escape with his life, wriggling free at the last moment. Shortly after this, in 1671, Thomas Blood came up with an even more extraordinary scheme – a plot which would not only vent his anger against king and country, but also restore his fortune: he would steal the crown jewels.

In those days the Crown Jewels – only ten years old, since they had been remade for the coronation of Charles II – were kept in the part of the Tower of London known as the 'Martin Tower'. They were in the care of an old man named Talbot Edwards, who lived in the Martin Tower with his wife, his unmarried daughter and a few servants. The crown, orb and sceptre and the other articles of the regalia were placed in a recess in one of the stone walls, protected by an iron grill which was hinged to swing outwards. The Edwards family lived in apartments above the room where the jewels were kept. It must be remembered that in those days the tourist industry as we know it simply did not exist. Visitors to the Tower of London were rare, and although Talbot

Edwards was permitted to show the crown jewels to anyone who might call and ask to see them, there would be many days or even weeks without any visitors at all.

However, one day in April 1671 Talbot Edwards did receive two visitors. It was Colonel Blood dressed as a clergyman and a woman who played the part of his wife. The pair were shown up into the room where the jewels were kept, and duly showed a polite interest. They were on the point of leaving when Blood's 'wife' pretended to be taken ill. Talbot Edwards, gentle old man that he was, was filled with concern and invited them both to go upstairs where the poor lady could lie down. Mrs Edwards fetched some cordial to revive her. After a little while Blood's 'wife' professed that she was feeling better, and they left, expressing much gratitude to Mr and Mrs Edwards for the kindness they had shown. A few days later, Blood called again, this time with half a dozen pairs of gloves as a thank you present to Mrs Edwards, and once more expressed his gratitude. Clearly a friendship was being set up, and over the following days the 'Reverend' Thomas Blood and his wife made a number of further visits.

So apparently friendly did the two couples become that it wasn't long before Blood actually proposed that it might be a good idea if the Edwards's daughter were to be married to a young nephew of his, who was quite well off and who would be pleased to marry an honest young woman such as Miss Edwards. It provides an interesting insight into the way some marriages were arranged at that time, especially when we learn that old Talbot Edwards fell for the idea almost immediately.

Accordingly, it was arranged that Blood and his 'wife' would bring the 'nephew' along for them all to meet one another. Edwards should have smelled a rat when it was arranged that Blood and his 'nephew' were to arrive at seven o'clock in the morning, and furthermore that two friends would be coming along with them too, to see the crown jewels.

Thus it was that, early on the morning of 9 May, Colonel Blood arrived at the Martin Tower with three companions, all secretly armed with rapier blades, daggers and pistols. They also had a large wooden mallet, and a metal file – items for which they had very special uses. Old Talbot Edwards met them eagerly, and his daughter, watching from an upstairs window, had got up early in a state of great expectancy to meet her future husband.

One of the men remained outside as a look-out, on the pretext that he would wait for Blood's wife to arrive. Meanwhile Talbot took Blood and the other two men up into the room where the crown jewels were kept. And no sooner were they in there than they gagged the old jewel-house keeper and threw a cloth over his head. They told him they were going to take the crown, orb and sceptre, and that they would kill him if he resisted.

Poor old Talbot yelled and shouted so much that they hit him with their mallet to keep him quiet. And when Talbot persisted in shouting, they knocked him out completely, whereupon they set to work to take the three items they had come for. Blood hid the State Crown under his cloak; another of them, Parrett, stuffed the orb down the front of his breeches; and the third villain, Hunt, was busy filing the sceptre in two, so that he could get it into his bag more easily.

By now, the whole episode had taken on an element of tragic farce. Miss Edwards was in raptures as she looked down at the look-out man, thinking he was the man of her dreams. Talbot had regained consciousness, but for the time being was scared into keeping quiet. Everything so far seemed to have gone completely according to plan.

However, just as always happens in the best thrillers, an extraordinary coincidence then occurred. Quite unexpectedly, coming home from army leave in Flanders, Talbot Edwards's son and a friend of his, a Captain Beckman, suddenly arrived at the front door of the Martin Tower. Pushing past the look-out man, they quickly dashed upstairs to find Blood hammering down the top of the crown with his mallet, trying to squash it flat; Parrett trying to do up his trousers over the orb; and a third stranger with a file, desperately sawing away at the sceptre.

Naturally, Blood and his companions were completely taken aback. They all fled, leaving the sceptre behind, but taking the crown and orb with them. Some jewels, including the Black Prince's Ruby, had fallen out of the crown as a result of the hammering, but Blood quickly scooped them up and put them in his pocket. As soon as they left the room, old Talbot Edwards regained courage enough to roar out 'Murder! Treason!' while his daughter rushed downstairs to cry out that the crown was being stolen.

Fortunately, by then young Mr Edwards and Captain Beckman

realised what was happening and quickly charged after Blood and Parrett, who by then had managed to get as far as the Byward Tower, where a sentry was on duty, guarding the drawbridge leading to the other side of the moat.† This sentry, armed only with a halberd (a long-shafted, axe-like weapon), ordered them to halt, but Blood was desperate and knocked him down, firing a pistol at him at close range. By now the thieves were on the drawbridge itself, running towards the gate on the other side. Another sentry was there, who was supposed to be guarding the final exit, but he had seen what had happened to his colleague, and so 'tactfully stepped aside' to let Blood and his companions reach freedom without challenge. Later, rumour had it that this sentry had been bribed.

Horses were waiting for the conspirators by the riverside, but just as Blood was getting into the stirrups Captain Beckman caught up with him and began struggling to wrest the crown from him. Blood's response was to fire his second pistol straight at Beckman's head. Luckily, Beckman saw what was happening, and ducked the bullet. By now others were on the scene, and after a violent struggle both Blood and Parrett were overpowered. Precious stones from the crown, loosened as they had been by the hammering they had received, were scattered on the ground, but fortunately everything was eventually recovered. Hunt, the third conspirator, had managed to gallop off, but soon fell off his horse when he hit his head against a pole sticking out from a passing waggon. He too was captured, and all three robbers were immediately clapped in the securest dungeons of the Tower.

However, the sequel to all this is perhaps the strangest part of the entire episode. . . .

One would naturally expect the severest penalties to have been imposed on Colonel Blood and his accomplices. In previous centuries to be hanged, drawn and quartered would have been

---

† The moat surrounding the Tower of London was drained of water in the 1840s, and the drawbridge is now replaced by a permanent bridge. The Byward Tower, where Blood fired at the sentry, is situated at the south-west corner of the Tower of London, where present-day tourists make their entrance; and the Martin Tower, where Talbot Edwards lived and looked after the jewels, is situated at the opposite, far north-east, corner. Thus Colonel Blood and his companions had the maximum distance to cover as they tried to make their escape.

the mildest punishment they could have hoped for. However, when the story of Colonel Blood's ingenious attempt to steal the crown jewels was told to Charles II, the Merry Monarch simply roared with laughter and ordered that Blood should be brought before him: he would deal with Blood himself. No one knows what Blood said to the king, or indeed what Charles said to Blood, but the upshot of it was that, instead of being executed, Blood was given a post among the bodyguard of His Majesty and a salary of £500 a year for life. The king's eccentric manner of dealing with this traitor is a comment on his relaxed stye of rule. No other English monarch, surely, would have reacted in such a way. Gossip-mongers of the day even spread the astonishing rumour that the king himself, being short of ready money, was behind the whole affair, and that he had conspired with Blood to steal his own State Crown.

How likely this is can be left to our imaginations. At all events, after this attempted robbery guards have always been provided for the protection of the regalia; and no further attempt has ever been made to steal the crown jewels. As a happy end to the story, it is recorded that Miss Edwards, the keeper's daughter, married the gallant Captain Beckman shortly afterwards.

THE MARTIN TOWER TODAY

The scene of Colonel Blood's bold attempt to steal the Crown Jewels – the Martin Tower – can be visited today, and it contains a permanent exhibition entitled *Crowns and Diamonds: the making of the Crown Jewels*.

This exhibition traces the development of the English royal crowns and there are several 'crown cases' on display – i.e. crowns which have been used by various monarchs, but which are now empty and without their jewels.

Of particular interest is the case of the crown used by George IV at his spectacular coronation in 1821. He chose not to use St Edward's Crown, but instead had this sumptuous new crown made, with 204 borrowed pearls and 12,314 borrowed diamonds. Alas for poor Prinny, despite his pleas, he had to give all these jewels back, and so the case now on view in the Martin Tower has never been used since.

Appendix A:
Genealogical Chart of the English Monarchy

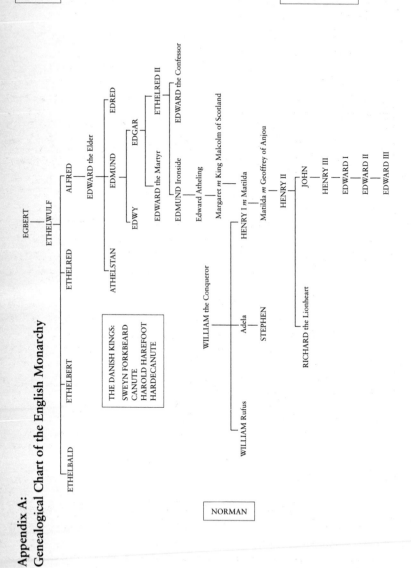

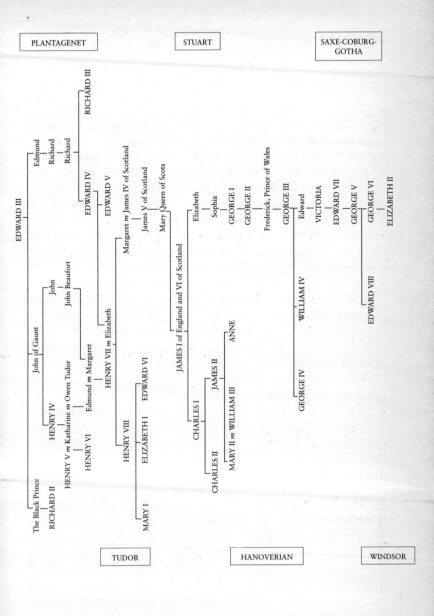

PLANTAGENET

STUART

SAXE-COBURG-GOTHA

TUDOR

HANOVERIAN

WINDSOR

EDWARD III

The Black Prince
RICHARD II

John of Gaunt
John
John Beaufort

Edmund
Richard
Richard

HENRY IV
HENRY V m Katharine m Owen Tudor
HENRY VI

Edmund m Margaret
HENRY VII m Elizabeth

EDWARD IV
EDWARD V
RICHARD III

HENRY VIII
MARY I
ELIZABETH I
EDWARD VI

Margaret m James IV of Scotland
James V of Scotland
Mary Queen of Scots

JAMES I of England and VI of Scotland

CHARLES I
CHARLES II
JAMES II
MARY II m WILLIAM III
ANNE

Elizabeth
Sophia
GEORGE I
GEORGE II
Frederick, Prince of Wales
GEORGE III
GEORGE IV
WILLIAM IV
Edward
VICTORIA

EDWARD VII
GEORGE V
EDWARD VIII
GEORGE VI
ELIZABETH II

APPENDIX B
THE ORDER OF THE CORONATION SERVICE

Queen Elizabeth's coronation service follows the pattern of the service laid down by Dunstan in the tenth century, but inevitably there have always been variations of detail; and of course it is now conducted entirely in English, whereas for many centuries it was spoken in Latin. Witness to this is a uniquely precious book belonging to Westminster Abbey known as the *Liber Regalis*, or Royal Book, drawn up in the fourteenth century by the Abbot of Westminster, Nicholas Littlington, probably for the coronation of Richard II, and setting out the order of service for a coronation. From Henry IV to Elizabeth I this book was used by the sovereigns themselves at their coronations.

Westminster Abbey was rebuilt by Henry III in the thirteenth century specifically to carry on the tradition of holding coronation services there. Henry wanted it to outshine Rheims Cathedral where the French kings were crowned. In particular, Henry's rebuilt abbey provided a very large area in the centre, where a 'theatre' or raised dais could be constructed, upon which the throne may be placed.

Before a coronation begins, the uncrowned sovereign enters the abbey wearing the crimson velvet robes of a peer. The entry is accompanied by sounds of fanfares and great music. The words of Psalm 122, *I was Glad when they said unto me, Let us go into the house of the Lord* have been sung at every coronation since 1626, and since 1902 the musical setting by Hubert Parry has always been used. Written into that music are trumpets and welcoming shouts of the Scholars of Westminster School, who have the privilege of exclaiming the traditional greeting, '*VIVAT!*' When Queen Elizabeth II was crowned, the boys shouted '*VIVAT REGINA ELIZABETHA*' – 'Long live Queen Elizabeth!' These shouts of acclamation, known as *Laudes*, or 'Praises', were introduced into the service by William the Conqueror for his queen's coronation in Winchester.

The sovereign having arrived, there now follow five distinct parts in the lengthy service: The Recognition, The Oath, The Anointing, The Investiture, and finally The Homage.

The Recognition

This is when the queen was formally presented to everyone in the abbey. She turned to each of the four sides of the theatre, and at each the archbishop repeated the words:

> Sirs, I here present unto you Queen Elizabeth, your undoubted Queen. Wherefore all you who are come this day to do your homage and service. Are you willing to do the same?

At each repetition, everyone replied 'God Save Queen Elizabeth.'

The Oath

The wording of the oath has given much concern over the centuries, and it needs to be revised at almost every coronation. It reflects the sovereign's position with regard to the Church, to Parliament, and to the countries of the Commonwealth. At the time of each and every coronation the political situation will have changed since that of the previous one. It is of historic interest that the oath taken by Queen Elizabeth is already partly out of date. After any long reign it is only natural that things will have changed. The oath was administered thus:

> Will you solemnly promise and swear to govern the Peoples of the United Kingdom, of Great Britain and Northern Ireland, Canada, Australia, New Zealand, the Union of South Africa, Pakistan and Ceylon, and of your Possessions and the Territories to any of them belonging or pertaining, according to their respective laws and customs?
> (Queen): I solemnly promise to do so.

The oath continued, as the queen promised to uphold the laws of the land and the Established Church. Then, all these promises were signed on the Coronation Roll, which is kept afterwards at the Public Record Office. Should any monarch show signs of failing to keep these promises, this document, in theory at least, could be brought out as a reminder.

After this, a copy of the Bible was presented to the queen, to signify where inspiration may be drawn from. At Elizabeth II's coronation, it was the Moderator of the General Assembly of the Church of Scotland who presented the Bible, using these words:

> Here is Wisdom; this is the royal Law; these are the lively Oracles of God.

The time had now come to the most important part of all – the anointing. However, before this, the archbishop began the communion service, because the Coronation Service is, as it were, a service *within* a service. The Communion Service followed with epistle, gospel and creed. Then, as a preliminary to the actual moment of anointing, the choir sang *Veni Creator Spiritus* (*Come, Holy Ghost*), and at last came Handel's great anthem, *Zadok the Priest*.

The Anointing

This is the sacred act which Dunstan brought so significantly into the coronation of King Edgar. The queen took off her crimson robe, her diadem and the Collar of the Garter as a symbol of humility. Then, as was printed in the Order of Service

> . . . being uncovered, shall go before the Altar, supported and attended as before. The Queen shall sit down in King Edward's Chair . . . wherein she is to be anointed. Four Knights of the Garter shall hold over her a rich pall of silk, or cloth of gold: the Dean of Westminster, taking the Ampulla and Spoon from off the Altar, shall hold them ready, pouring some of the holy Oil into the Spoon, and with it the Archbishop shall anoint the Queen in the form of a cross:

> On the palms of both the hands, saying,
> >   Be thy Hands anointed with holy Oil.
> On the breast, saying,
> >   Be thy Breast anointed with holy Oil.

On the crown of the head, saying,
Be thy Head anointed with holy Oil; as kings, priests, and
prophets were anointed. And as Solomon was anointed king
by Zadok the priest and Nathan the prophet, so be thou
anointed, blessed, and consecrated Queen over the Peoples,
whom the Lord thy God hath given thee to rule and govern,
In the Name of the Father, and of the Son, and of the Holy
Ghost. Amen.

After the anointing, the queen went to a faldstool placed in
front of St Edward's Chair, where she knelt for blessing by the
archbishop, and then with assistance she dressed herself first in
the plain white sleeveless linen *Colobium Sindonis*, which looks
something like a choirboy's surplice, and over this she put on the
shimmering, golden, sleeved *Supertunica* and also a Girdle cloth
of gold. Then, having been anointed and blessed, and wearing
these magnificent robes, she was ready to receive all the various
emblems of office. So inevitably the next stage was the
Investiture of all these symbolic objects.

The Investiture

Solemnly, one by one, the queen was presented with various
emblems. Each of them is an outward and visible sign of an
intangible quality or virtue.

The first items to be presented were the spurs, symbolising
knighthood and chivalry. (The queen touched these. They are no
longer buckled on, as they used to be in earlier times. The
practice of actually wearing them was dispensed with at the
coronation of Queen Anne, whose legs were gouty.)

Then she was presented with the Jewelled Sword, symbol of
justice. (She handed this back; it is placed on the altar; it is
then 'redeemed' – i.e. 'bought back' – for the sum of 100s.
This curious custom dates back to medieval times when
anyone entering a church was expected to give up his sword
while he was there, and then he was expected to pay up to get
it back. At the coronation service a peer redeems it on behalf
of the sovereign, and then carries it before the sovereign for
the rest of the ceremony.)

Next she was invested with the armills, which are 'Bracelets of sincerity and wisdom'. Fourthly came the magnificent *Pallium Regale*, or *Imperial Mantle* made of cloth of gold for George IV in 1821. Assistants helped the queen to put this over the *Colobium Sindonis* and *Supertunica*, which she was already wearing. Finally she put on the Stole, and when the queen had been robed with these heavy royal vestments, the archbishop continued:

> Receive this Imperial Robe, and the Lord your God endue you with knowledge and wisdom, with majesty and with power from on high: the Lord clothe you with the robe of righteousness, and with the garments of salvation.

The queen was presented with the orb:

> Receive this Orb set under the Cross, and remember that the whole world is subject to the Power and Empire of Christ our Redeemer.

(The queen held the orb only briefly at this stage of the service, and then handed it back, for it to be laid on the altar. Thus her hands were free to receive the ring and the sceptres.) The 'Ring of kingly dignity' was placed on the fourth finger of the queen's right hand. The first of the two sceptres was presented, the sceptre with the cross:

> Receive the Royal Sceptre, the ensign of kingly power and justice.

The second of the two sceptres, the rod with the dove:

> Receive the Rod of Equity and Mercy. Be so merciful that you be not too remiss; so execute justice that you forget not mercy. Punish the wicked, protect and cherish the just, and lead your people in the way wherein they should go.

And finally, the great climax came – the moment which everyone had been waiting for – the 'putting on of the crown'. This moment is of such importance that it is always accompanied by all kinds of 'special effects'. It is worth setting down the actual words of the coronation service, as printed for Queen Elizabeth's coronation:

Then the Queen still sitting in King Edward's Chair, the Archbishop, assisted with other Bishops, shall come from the Altar: the Dean of Westminster shall bring the Crown, and the Archbishop taking it of him shall reverently put it upon the Queen's head. At the sight whereof the people, with loud and repeated shouts, shall cry,

GOD SAVE THE QUEEN

The Princes and Princesses, the Peers and Peeresses shall put on their coronets and caps, and the Kings of Arms their Crowns; and the trumpets shall sound, and by a signal given, the great guns at the Tower shall be shot off.

The acclamation ceasing, the Archbishop shall go on, and say:

God crown you with a crown of glory and righteousness, that having a right faith and manifold fruit of good works, you may obtain the crown of an everlasting kingdom by the gift of him whose kingdom endureth for ever.

The crowning took place while the queen was seated in King Edward's Chair, which was directly in front of the altar, and some distance from the throne, which is on top of the steps of the 'theatre'. The next stage in proceedings was the most difficult of all for the queen – the moment she was worried about and the part which she practised with great care. It involved moving from St Edward's Chair, and going up the steps to the elevated throne, balancing the heavy crown of St Edward on her head; wearing long, trailing robes; and carrying a sceptre in each hand. Much help was needed to arrange the train. Once the queen had reached the throne successfully, she was 'lifted up into it by the Archbishops and Bishops, and other Peers of the Kingdom; and (was) enthroned, or placed therein . . .'.

The Homage

All that remained now was for her subjects to acknowledge her and offer their allegiance.

This part of the service, consists of a public demonstration of loyalty as, one by one, the senior peers come to the newly-crowned monarch to kiss her hand. The Archbishop of Canterbury, as head of the church, leads this homage, and then, in strict order of precedence, the peers of the realm come up and pay their respects. In earlier times, it was expedient that possible trouble-makers should make a public show of loyalty, as it was treasonable to be absent.

At the coronation of Queen Elizabeth II, it was the Duke of Edinburgh who followed the Archbishop of Canterbury to offer his allegiance. The order of service enjoined that 'placing his hands between the Queen's shall pronounce the words of Homage, saying:

> I, Philip, Duke of Edinburgh, do become your liege man of life and limb, and of earthly worship; and faith and truth I will bear unto you, to live and die, against all manner of folks. So help me God.
>
> And arising he shall touch the Crown upon her Majesty's head and kiss her Majesty's left cheek.

As the other dukes, earls, and peers came up in turn, the choir provided background music of Homage Anthems. Then this part of the service concluded with the congregation shouting their acclamations again:

GOD SAVE QUEEN ELIZABETH
LONG LIVE QUEEN ELIZABETH
MAY THE QUEEN LIVE FOR EVER

This ended the Coronation Service. The Communion Service, which had been interrupted after the Creed, was now resumed. The queen then went into St Edward's Chapel to change into yet another robe, the robe of *purple* velvet, and to exchange the heavy St Edward's Crown – which she never wore again – for the lighter Imperial Crown of State.

The final movement in this elaborate and lengthy ritual came with the outgoing procession, the Recess, with the queen wearing the State Crown and 'bearing in her right hand the sceptre and in her left hand the orb'. The queen's arrival and departure from the abbey provided yet another spectacular sight, as it has been the tradition, since the coronation of George IV in 1821, to use the enormous gilded State Coach. This had been intended for George III's coronation, but it was not completed in time. It is 24 ft long, 8 ft 3 in wide, and 12 ft high; it weighs four tons and eight horses are needed to pull it. This huge coach is very rarely used, but it can be seen displayed on permanent exhibition at the Royal Mews, behind Buckingham Palace. George VI described his ride in it, in 1937, as 'one of the most uncomfortable rides I have ever had in my life'. The suspension was improved for Queen Elizabeth's coronation, sixteen years later.

No mere description or film footage can do justice either to the coronation ceremony itself or to all the vast amount of preparation required. Over the years, each coronation has had its problems, and the circumstances surrounding the arrival of one monarch are always bound up with the memories of his or her predecessor.

However, despite forty-one coronations their essence lies in the abiding tradition of royal continuity. Kings and queens may come and go, but the crown itself remains: a permanent and enduring symbol of our heritage.

BIBLIOGRAPHY

Armytage, P., C.V.O., *By the Clock of St. James's*, John Murray, London, 1927

Benson, A.C. and Viscount Esher (eds), *The Letters of Queen Victoria*, John Murray, London, 1908

Browning, N.L., *The Psychic World of Peter Hurkos*, Frederick Muller, London, 1972

Burnett, C.J. and Tabraham, C.J., *The Honours of Scotland*, Historic Scotland, Edinburgh, 1993

Campbell, U., *Robes of the Realm*, Michael O'Mara Books, London, 1989

Carpenter, E. (ed.), *A House of Kings*, John Baker, 1966

Compton, P., *Harold the King*, Robert Hale, London, 1961

Dibble, J., *C. Hubert H. Parry, His Life and Music*, Clarendon Press, Oxford, 1992

Duff, D., *Alexandra, Princess and Queen*, William Collins & Sons, London, 1980

Earle, P., *Henry V*, George Weidenfeld and Nicolson, London, 1972

Farmer, D.H., *The Oxford Book of Saints*, Oxford University Press, Oxford, 1978

Fraser, A., *King James*, Book Club Associates, 1974

— —, *The Six Wives of Henry VIII*, Weidenfeld & Nicolson, London, 1992

Garrett, R., *Royal Travel*, Blandford Press, London, 1982

Judd, D., *Edward the Seventh*, Futura Publications, 1975

Lander, J.R., *The Wars of the Roses*, Sutton Publishing, Stroud, 1990

Legg, L.G.W. (ed.), *English Coronation Records*, Archibald Constable, London, 1901

Lindsay, P., *Crowned King of England*, Ivor Nicholson & Watson, London, 1937

Longford, E. (ed.), *The Oxford Book of Royal Anecdotes*, Oxford University Press, Oxford, 1991

Huizinga, J., *The Waning of the Middle Ages*, Edward Arnold, London, 1924

Magnus, P., *King Edward the Seventh*, John Murray, London, 1964

Middlemas, K., *The Life and Times of Edward VII*, Weidenfeld & Nicolson, London, 1972

Moore, J.N., *Edward Elgar, Letters of a Lifetime*, Clarendon Press, Oxford, 1990

Mundy, S., *Elgar, His Life and Times*, Midas Books, 1980

Ollard, S.L. and Crosse, G., *A Dictionary of English Church History*, A.R. Mowbray, 1912

Panter, H., *King Edgar, His Coronation in Bath*, Morgan Books, 1971

Perkins, J., *The Coronation Book*, Sir Isaac Pitman & Sons, 1911

——, *Westminster Abbey, the Empire's Crown*, Duckworth, 1937

Prestwich, M. *Edward I*, Methuen, London, 1988

Ross, C., *Edward IV*, Eyre Methuen, London, 1974

Rowse, A.L., *An Elizabethan Garland*, Macmillan, 1953

Saunders, H. St George, *Westminster Hall*, Michael Joseph, 1951

Schramm, P.E. (Trans. L.G. Wickham Legg), *A History of the English Coronation*, Oxford University Press, 1937

Sinclair-Stevenson, C., *Blood Royal, The Illustrious House of Hanover*, Jonathan Cape, 1979

Sitwell, Major General H.D.W., *The Crown Jewels and other Regalia in the Tower of London*, Dropmore Press, 1953

Stanley, A., *Historical Memorials of Westminster Abbey*, John Murray, 1867

Strickland, A., *Lives of the Queens of England*, G. Bell & Sons, 1911

Tierney, N., *William Walton, His Life and Music*, Robert Hale, 1984

Tull, G.F., *Henry the Sixth*, Winchester Press, 1973

Van der Kiste, J., *Queen Victoria's Children*, Sutton, Stroud, 1986.

Weir, A., *Lancaster and York, The Wars of the Roses*, Jonathan Cape, 1995

Younghusband, Major General Sir G., *The Jewel House*, Herbert Jenkins, *c.* 1920

INDEX